Mastering Social Media Mining with Python

Acquire and analyze data from all corners of the social web with Python

Marco Bonzanini

BIRMINGHAM - MUMBAI

Mastering Social Media Mining with Python

Copyright © 2016 Packt Publishing

All rights reserved. No part of this book may be reproduced, stored in a retrieval system, or transmitted in any form or by any means, without the prior written permission of the publisher, except in the case of brief quotations embedded in critical articles or reviews.

Every effort has been made in the preparation of this book to ensure the accuracy of the information presented. However, the information contained in this book is sold without warranty, either express or implied. Neither the author, nor Packt Publishing, and its dealers and distributors will be held liable for any damages caused or alleged to be caused directly or indirectly by this book.

Packt Publishing has endeavored to provide trademark information about all of the companies and products mentioned in this book by the appropriate use of capitals. However, Packt Publishing cannot guarantee the accuracy of this information.

First published: July 2016

Production reference: 1260716

Published by Packt Publishing Ltd.
Livery Place
35 Livery Street
Birmingham
B3 2PB, UK.
ISBN 978-1-78355-201-6

www.packtpub.com

Credits

Author

Marco Bonzanini

Reviewer

Weiai Wayne Xu

Commissioning Editor

Pramila Balan

Acquisition Editor

Sonali Vernekar

Content Development Editor

Siddhesh Salvi

Technical Editor

Pranil Pathare

Copy Editor

Vibha Shukla

Project Coordinator

Nidhi Joshi

Proofreader

Safis Editing

Indexer

Mariammal Chettiyar

Graphics

Jason Monteiro

Disha Haria

Production Coordinator

Arvindkumar Gupta

About the Author

Marco Bonzanini is a data scientist based in London, United Kingdom. He holds a PhD in information retrieval from Queen Mary University of London. He specializes in text analytics and search applications, and over the years, he has enjoyed working on a variety of information management and data science problems.

He maintains a personal blog at `http://marcobonzanini.com`, where he discusses different technical topics, mainly around Python, text analytics, and data science.

When not working on Python projects, he likes to engage with the community at PyData conferences and meet-ups, and he also enjoys brewing homemade beer.

This book is the outcome of a long journey that goes beyond the mere content preparation. Many people have contributed in different ways to shape the final result. Firstly, I would like to thank the team at Packt Publishing, particularly Sonali Vernekar and Siddhesh Salvi, for giving me the opportunity to work on this book and for being so helpful throughout the whole process. I would also like to thank Dr. Weiai "Wayne" Xu for reviewing the content of this book and suggesting many improvements. Many colleagues and friends, through casual conversations, deep discussions, and previous projects, strengthened the quality of the material presented in this book. Special mentions go to Dr. Miguel Martinez-Alvarez, Marco Campana, and Stefano Campana. I'm also happy to be part of the PyData London community, a group of smart people who regularly meet to talk about Python and data science, offering a stimulating environment. Last but not least, a distinct special mention goes to Daniela, who has encouraged me during the whole journey, sharing her thoughts, suggesting improvements, and providing a relaxing environment to go back to after work.

About the Reviewer

Weiai Wayne Xu is an assistant professor in the department of communication at University of Massachusetts – Amherst and is affiliated with the University's Computational Social Science Institute. Previously, Xu worked as a network science scholar at the Network Science Institute of Northeastern University in Boston. His research on online communities, word-of-mouth, and social capital have appeared in various peer-reviewed journals. Xu also assisted four national grant projects in the area of strategic communication and public opinion. Aside from his professional appointment, he is a co-founder of a data lab called CuriosityBits Collective (http://www.curiositybits.org/).

www.PacktPub.com

eBooks, discount offers, and more

Did you know that Packt offers eBook versions of every book published, with PDF and ePub files available? You can upgrade to the eBook version at www.PacktPub.com and as a print book customer, you are entitled to a discount on the eBook copy. Get in touch with us at customercare@packtpub.com for more details.

At www.PacktPub.com, you can also read a collection of free technical articles, sign up for a range of free newsletters and receive exclusive discounts and offers on Packt books and eBooks.

https://www2.packtpub.com/books/subscription/packtlib

Do you need instant solutions to your IT questions? PacktLib is Packt's online digital book library. Here, you can search, access, and read Packt's entire library of books.

Why subscribe?

- Fully searchable across every book published by Packt
- Copy and paste, print, and bookmark content
- On demand and accessible via a web browser

Table of Contents

Preface

In the past few years, the popularity of social media has grown dramatically, with more and more users sharing all kinds of information through different platforms. Companies use social media platforms to promote their brands, professionals maintain a public profile online and use social media for networking, and regular users discuss about any topic. More users also means more data waiting to be mined.

You, the reader of this book, are likely to be a developer, engineer, analyst, researcher, or student who wants to apply data mining techniques to social media data. As a data mining practitioner (or practitioner-to-be), there is no lack of opportunities and challenges from this point of view.

Mastering Social Media Mining with Python will give you the basic tools you need to take advantage of this wealth of data. This book will start a journey through the main tools for data analysis in Python, providing the information you need to get started with applications such as NLP, machine learning, social network analysis, and data visualization. A step-by-step guide through the most popular social media platforms, including Twitter, Facebook, Google+, Stack Overflow, Blogger, YouTube and more, will allow you to understand how to access data from these networks, and how to perform different types of analysis in order to extract useful insight from the raw data.

There are three main aspects being touched in the book, as listed in the following list:

- Social media APIs: Each platform provides access to their data in different ways. Understanding how to interact with them can answer the questions: *how do we get the data?* and also *what kind of data can we get?* This is important because, without access to the data, there would be no data analysis to carry out. Each chapter focuses on different social media platforms and provides details on how to interact with the relevant API.
- Data mining techniques: Just getting the data out of an API doesn't provide much value to us. The next step is answering the question: *what can we do with the data?* Each chapter provides the concepts you need to appreciate the kind of analysis that you can carry out with the data, and why it provides value. In terms of theory, the choice is to simply scratch the surface of what is needed, without digging too much into details that belong to academic textbooks. The purpose is to provide practical examples that can get you easily started.

- Python tools for data science: Once we understand what we can do with the data, the last question is: *how do we do it?* Python has established itself as one of the main languages for data science. Its easy-to-understand syntax and semantics, together with its rich ecosystem for scientific computing, provide a gentle learning curve for beginners and all the sharp tools required by experts at the same time. The book introduces the main Python libraries used in the world of scientific computing, such as NumPy, pandas, NetworkX, scikit-learn, NLTK, and many more. Practical examples will take the form of short scripts that you can use (and possibly extend) to perform different and interesting types of analysis over the social media data that you have accessed.

If exploring the area where these three main topics meet is something of interest, this book is for you.

What this book covers

Chapter 1, *Social Media, Social Data, and Python*, introduces the main concepts of data mining applied to social media using Python. By walking the reader through a brief overview on machine learning, NLP, social network analysis, and data visualization, this chapter discusses the main Python tools for data science and provides some help to set up the Python environment.

Chapter 2, *#MiningTwitter – Hashtags, Topics, and Time Series*, opens the practical discussion on data mining using the Twitter data. After setting up a Twitter app to interact with the Twitter API, the chapter explains how to get data through the streaming API and how to perform some frequentist analysis on hashtags and text. The chapter also discusses some time series analysis to understand the distribution of tweets over time.

Chapter 3, *Users, Followers, and Communities on Twitter*, continues the discussion on Twitter mining, focusing the attention on users and interactions between users. This chapter shows how to mine the connections and conversations between the users. Interesting applications explained in the chapter include user clustering (segmentation) and how to measure influence and user engagement.

Chapter 4, *Posts, Pages, and User Interactions on Facebook*, focuses on Facebook and the Facebook Graph API. After understanding how to interact with the Graph API, including aspects of security and privacy, examples of how to mine posts from a user's profile and Facebook pages are provided. The concepts of time series analysis and user engagement are applied to user interactions such as comments, Likes, and Reactions.

Chapter 5, *Topic Analysis on Google+*, covers the social network by Google. After understanding how to access the Google centralized platform, examples of how to search content and users on Google+ are discussed. This chapter also shows how to embed data coming from the Google API into a custom web application that is built using the Python microframework, Flask.

Chapter 6, *Questions and Answers on Stack Exchange*, explains the topic of question answering and uses the Stack Exchange network as paramount example. The reader has the opportunity to learn how to search for users and content on the different sites of this network, most notably Stack Overflow. By using their data dumps for online processing, this chapter introduces supervised machine learning methods applied to text classification and shows how to embed machine learning model into a real-time application.

Chapter 7, *Blogs, RSS, Wikipedia, and Natural Language Processing*, teaches text analytics. The Web is full of opportunities in terms of text mining, and this chapter shows how to interact with several data sources such as the WordPress.com API, Blogger API, RSS feeds, and Wikipedia API. Using textual data, the basic notions of NLP briefly mentioned throughout the book are formalized and expanded. The reader is then walked through the process of information extraction with custom examples on how to extract references of entities from free text.

Chapter 8, *Mining All the Data!*, reminds us of the many opportunities, in terms of data mining, that are available out there beyond the most common social networks. Examples of how to mine data from YouTube, GitHub, and Yelp are provided, along with a discussion on how to build your own API client, in case a particular platform doesn't provide one.

Chapter 9, *Linked Data and the Semantic Web*, provides an overview on the Semantic Web and related technologies. This chapter discusses the topics of Linked Data, microformats, and RDF, and offers examples on how to mine semantic information from DBpedia and Wikipedia.

What you need for this book

The code examples provided in this book assume that you are running a recent version of Python on either Linux, macOS, or Windows. The code has been tested on Python 3.4.* and Python 3.5.*. Older versions (Python 3.3.* or Python 2.*) are not explicitly supported.

Chapter 1, *Social Media, Social Data, and Python*, provides some instructions to set up a local development environment and introduces a brief list of tools that are going to be used throughout the book. We're going to take advantage of some of the essential Python libraries for scientific computing (for example, NumPy, pandas, and matplotlib), machine learning (for example, scikit-learn), NLP (for example, NLTK), and social network analysis (for example, NetworkX).

Who this book is for

This book is for intermediate Python developers who want to engage with the use of public APIs to collect data from social media platforms and perform statistical analysis in order to produce useful insights from the data. The book assumes a basic understanding of Python standard library and provides practical examples to guide you towards the creation of your data analysis project based on social data.

Conventions

In this book, you will find a number of text styles that distinguish between different kinds of information. Here are some examples of these styles and an explanation of their meaning.

Code words in text, database table names, folder names, filenames, file extensions, pathnames, dummy URLs, user input, and Twitter handles are shown as follows: "Moreover, the genre attribute is here presented as a list, with a variable number of values."

A block of code is set as follows:

```
from timeit import timeit
import numpy as np

if __name__ == '__main__':
    setup_sum = 'data = list(range(10000))'
    setup_np = 'import numpy as np;'
    setup_np += 'data_np = np.array(list(range(10000)))'
```

When we wish to draw your attention to a particular part of a code block, the relevant lines or items are set in bold:

```
Type your question, or type "exit" to quit.
> What's up with Gandalf and Frodo lately? They haven't been in the Shire
for a while...
Question: What's up with Gandalf and Frodo lately? They haven't been in the
Shire for a while...
Predicted labels: plot-explanation, the-lord-of-the-rings
```

Any command-line input or output is written as follows:

```
$ pip install --upgrade [package name]
```

New terms and important words are shown in bold. Words that you see on the screen, for example, in menus or dialog boxes, appear in the text like this: "On the **Keys and Access Tokens** configuration page, the developer can find the API key and secret, as well as the access token and access token secret."

Warnings or important notes appear in a box like this.

Tips and tricks appear like this.

Reader feedback

Feedback from our readers is always welcome. Let us know what you think about this book-what you liked or disliked. Reader feedback is important for us as it helps us develop titles that you will really get the most out of. To send us general feedback, simply e-mail feedback@packtpub.com, and mention the book's title in the subject of your message. If there is a topic that you have expertise in and you are interested in either writing or contributing to a book, see our author guide at www.packtpub.com/authors.

Customer support

Now that you are the proud owner of a Packt book, we have a number of things to help you to get the most from your purchase.

Downloading the example code

You can download the example code files for this book from your account at http://www.packtpub.com. If you purchased this book elsewhere, you can visit http://www.packtpub.com/support and register to have the files e-mailed directly to you.

You can download the code files by following these steps:

1. Log in or register to our website using your e-mail address and password.
2. Hover the mouse pointer on the SUPPORT tab at the top.
3. Click on Code Downloads & Errata.
4. Enter the name of the book in the Search box.
5. Select the book for which you're looking to download the code files.
6. Choose from the drop-down menu where you purchased this book from.
7. Click on Code Download.

Once the file is downloaded, please make sure that you unzip or extract the folder using the latest version of:

- WinRAR / 7-Zip for Windows
- Zipeg / iZip / UnRarX for Mac
- 7-Zip / PeaZip for Linux

The code bundle for the book is also hosted on GitHub at `https://github.com/bonzanini/Book-SocialMediaMiningPython`. We also have other code bundles from our rich catalog of books and videos available at `https://github.com/PacktPublishing/`. Check them out!

Downloading the color images of this book

We also provide you with a PDF file that has color images of the screenshots/diagrams used in this book. The color images will help you better understand the changes in the output. You can download this file from `https://www.packtpub.com/sites/default/files/downloads/MasteringSocialMediaMiningWithPython_ColorImages.pdf`.

Errata

Although we have taken every care to ensure the accuracy of our content, mistakes do happen. If you find a mistake in one of our books-maybe a mistake in the text or the code-we would be grateful if you could report this to us. By doing so, you can save other readers from frustration and help us improve subsequent versions of this book. If you find any errata, please report them by visiting `http://www.packtpub.com/submit-errata`, selecting your book, clicking on the Errata Submission Form link, and entering the details of your errata. Once your errata are verified, your submission will be accepted and the errata will be uploaded to our website or added to any list of existing errata under the Errata section of that title.

To view the previously submitted errata, go to `https://www.packtpub.com/books/content/support` and enter the name of the book in the search field. The required information will appear under the Errata section.

Piracy

Piracy of copyrighted material on the Internet is an ongoing problem across all media. At Packt, we take the protection of our copyright and licenses very seriously. If you come across any illegal copies of our works in any form on the Internet, please provide us with the location address or website name immediately so that we can pursue a remedy.

Please contact us at copyright@packtpub.com with a link to the suspected pirated material.

We appreciate your help in protecting our authors and our ability to bring you valuable content.

Questions

If you have a problem with any aspect of this book, you can contact us at questions@packtpub.com, and we will do our best to address the problem.

1

Social Media, Social Data, and Python

This book is about applying *data mining* techniques to *social media* using *Python*. The three highlighted keywords in the previous sentence help us define the intended audience of this book: any developer, engineer, analyst, researcher, or student who is interested in exploring the area where the three topics meet.

In this chapter, we will cover the following topics:

- Social media and social data
- The overall process of data mining from social media
- Setting up the Python development environment
- Python tools for data science
- Processing data in Python

Getting started

In the second quarter of 2015, Facebook reported nearly 1.5 billion monthly active users. In 2013, Twitter had reported a volume of 500+ million tweets per day. On a smaller scale, but certainly of interest for the readers of this book, in 2015, Stack Overflow announced that more than 10 million programming questions had been asked on their platform since the website has opened.

These numbers are just the tip of the iceberg when describing how the popularity of social media has grown exponentially with more users sharing more and more information through different platforms. This wealth of data provides unique opportunities for data mining practitioners. The purpose of this book is to guide the reader through the use of social media APIs to collect data that can be analyzed with Python tools in order to produce interesting insights on how users interact on social media.

This chapter lays the ground for an initial discussion on challenges and opportunities in social media mining and introduces some Python tools that will be used in the following chapters.

Social media – challenges and opportunities

In traditional media, users are typically just consumers. Information flows in one direction: from the publisher to the users. Social media breaks this model, allowing every user to be a consumer and publisher at the same time. Many academic publications have been written on this topic with the purpose of defining what the term *social media* really means (for example, *Users of the world, unite! The challenges and opportunities of Social Media, Andreas M. Kaplan* and *Michael Haenlein, 2010*). The aspects that are most commonly shared across different social media platforms are as follows:

- Internet-based applications
- User-generated content
- Networking

Social media are Internet-based applications. It is clear that the advances in Internet and mobile technologies have promoted the expansion of social media. Through your mobile, you can, in fact, immediately connect to a social media platform, publish your content, or catch up with the latest news.

Social media platforms are driven by user-generated content. As opposed to the traditional media model, every user is a potential publisher. More importantly, any user can interact with every other user by sharing content, commenting, or expressing positive appraisal via the *like* button (sometimes referred to as upvote, or thumbs up).

Social media is about networking. As described, social media is about the users interacting with other users. Being connected is the central concept for most social media platform, and the content you consume via your *news feed* or *timeline* is driven by your connections.

With these main features being central across several platforms, social media is used for a variety of purposes:

- Staying in touch with friends and family (for example, via Facebook)
- Microblogging and catching up with the latest news (for example, via Twitter)
- Staying in touch with your professional network (for example, via LinkedIn)
- Sharing multimedia content (for example, via Instagram, YouTube, Vimeo, and Flickr)
- Finding answers to your questions (for example, via Stack Overflow, Stack Exchange, and Quora)
- Finding and organizing items of interest (for example, via Pinterest)

This book aims to answer one central question: how to extract useful knowledge from the data coming from the social media? Taking one step back, we need to define what is *knowledge* and what is *useful*.

Traditional definitions of knowledge come from information science. The concept of knowledge is usually pictured as part of a pyramid, sometimes referred to as **knowledge hierarchy**, which has data as its foundation, information as the middle layer, and knowledge at the top. This knowledge hierarchy is represented in the following diagram:

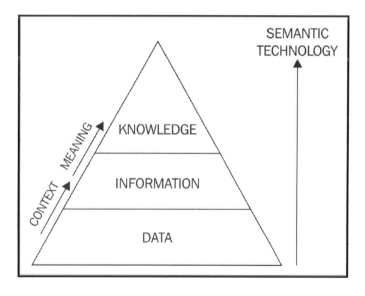

Figure 1.1: From raw data to semantic knowledge

Climbing the pyramid means refining knowledge from raw data. The journey from raw data to distilled knowledge goes through the integration of context and meaning. As we climb up the pyramid, the technology we build gains a deeper understanding of the original data, and more importantly, of the users who generate such data. In other words, it becomes more useful.

In this context, useful knowledge means *actionable* knowledge, that is, knowledge that enables a decision maker to implement a business strategy. As a reader of this book, you'll understand the key principles to extract value from social data. Understanding how users interact through social media platforms is one of the key aspects in this journey.

The following sections lay down some of the challenges and opportunities of mining data from social media platforms.

Opportunities

The key opportunity of developing data mining systems is to *extract useful insights* from data. The aim of the process is to answer interesting (and sometimes difficult) questions using data mining techniques to enrich our knowledge about a particular domain. For example, an online retail store can apply data mining to understand how their customers shop. Through this analysis, they are able to recommend products to their customers, depending on their shopping habits (for example, users who buy item A, also buy item B). This, in general, will lead to a better customer experience and satisfaction, which in return can produce better sales.

Many organizations in different domains can apply data mining techniques to improve their business. Some examples include the following:

- Banking:
    - Identifying loyal customers to offer them exclusive promotions
    - Recognizing patterns of fraudulent transaction to reduce costs
- Medicine:
    - Understanding patient behavior to forecast surgery visits
    - Supporting doctors in identifying successful treatments depending on the patient's history

- Retail:
    - Understanding shopping patterns to improve customer experience
    - Improving the effectiveness of marketing campaigns with better targeting
    - Analyzing real-time traffic data to find the quickest route for food delivery

So how does it translate to the realm of social media? The core of the matter consists of how the users share their data through social media platforms. Organizations are not limited to analyze the data they directly collect anymore, and they have access to much more data.

The solution for this data collection happens through well-engineered language-agnostic APIs. A common practice among social media platforms is, in fact, to offer a Web API to developers who want to integrate their applications with particular social media functionalities.

Application Programming Interface

An **Application Programming Interface (API)** is a set of procedure definitions and protocols that describe the behavior of a software component, such as a library or remote service, in terms of its allowed operations, inputs, and outputs. When using a third-party API, developers don't need to worry about the internals of the component, but only about how they can use it.

With the term Web API, we refer to a web service that exposes a number of URIs to the public, possibly behind an authentication layer, to access the data. A common architectural approach for designing this kind of APIs is called **Representational State Transfer (REST)**. An API that implements the REST architecture is called **RESTful API**. We still prefer the generic term Web API, as many of the existing API do not strictly follow the REST principles. For the purpose of this book, a deep understanding of the REST architecture is not required.

Challenges

Some of the challenges of social media mining are inherited from the broader field of data mining.

When dealing with social data, we're often dealing with **big data**. To understand the meaning of big data and the challenges it entails, we can go back to the traditional definition (*3D Data Management: Controlling Data Volume, Velocity and Variety, Doug Laney, 2001*) that is also known as *the three Vs of big data*: volume, variety, and velocity. Over the years, this definition has also been expanded by adding more Vs, most notably value, as providing value to an organization is one the main purposes of exploiting big data. Regarding the original three Vs, *volume* means dealing with data that spans over more than one machine. This, of course, requires a different infrastructure from small data processing (for example, in-memory). Moreover, volume is also associated with *velocity* in the sense that data is growing so fast that the concept of *big* becomes a moving target. Finally, *variety* concerns how data is present in different formats and structures, often incompatible between them and with different semantics. Data from social media can check all the three Vs.

The rise of big data has pushed the development of new approaches to database technologies towards a family of systems called NoSQL. The term is an umbrella for multiple database paradigms that share the common trait of moving away from traditional relational data, promoting dynamic schema design. While this book is not about database technologies, from this field, we can still appreciate the need for dealing with a mixture of well-structured, unstructured, and semi-structured data. The phrase *structured data* refers to information that is well organized and typically presented in a tabular form. For this reason, the connection with relational databases is immediate. The following table shows an example of structured data that represents books sold by a bookshop:

Title	Genre	Price
1984	Political fiction	12
War and Peace	War novel	10

This kind of data is structured as each represented item has a precise organization, specifically, three attributes called title, genre, and price.

The opposite of structured data is unstructured data, which is information without a predefined data model, or simply not organized according to a predefined data model. Unstructured data is typically in the form of textual data, for example, e-mails, documents, social media posts, and so on. Techniques presented throughout this book can be used to extract patterns in unstructured data to provide some structure.

Between structured and unstructured data, we can find semi-structured data. In this case, the structure is either flexible or not fully predefined. It is sometimes also referred to as a self-describing structure. A typical example of data format that is semi-structured is JSON. As the name suggests, JSON borrows its notation from the programming language JavaScript. This data format has become extremely popular due to its wide use as a way to exchange data between client and server in a web application. The following snippet shows an example of the JSON representation that extends the previous book data:

```
[
  {
    "title": "1984",
    "price": 12,
    "author": "George Orwell",
    "genre": ["Political fiction", "Social science fiction"]
  },
  {
    "title": "War and Peace",
    "price": 10,
    "genre": ["Historical", Romance", "War novel"]
  }
]
```

What we can observe from this example is that the first book has the `author` attribute, whereas, this attribute is not present in the second book. Moreover, the `genre` attribute is here presented as a list, with a variable number of values. Both these aspects are usually avoided in a well-structured (relational) data format, but are perfectly fine in JSON and more in general when dealing with semi-structured data.

The discussion on structured and unstructured data translates into handling different data formats and approaching data integrity in different ways. The phrase **data integrity** is used to capture the combination of challenges coming from the presence of dirty, inconsistent, or incomplete data.

The case of inconsistent and incomplete data is very common when analyzing user-generated content, and it calls for attention, especially with data from social media. It is very rare to observe users who share their data methodically, almost in a formal fashion. On the contrary, social media often consists of informal environments, with some contradictions. For example, if a user wants to complain about a product on the company's Facebook page, the user first needs to *like* the page itself, which is quite the opposite of being upset with a company due to the poor quality of their product. Understanding how users interact on social media platforms is crucial to design a good analysis.

Developing data mining applications also requires us to consider issues related to **data access**, particularly when company policies translate into the lack of data to analyze. In other words, data is not always openly available. The previous paragraph discussed how in social media mining, this is a little less of an issue compared to other corporate environments, as most social media platforms offer well-engineered language-agnostic APIs that allow us to access the data we need. The availability of such data is, of course, still dependent on how users share their data and how they grant us access. For example, Facebook users can decide the level of detail that can be shown in their public profile and the details that can be shown only to their friends. Profile information, such as birthday, current location, and work history (as well as many more), can all be individually flagged as private or public. Similarly, when we try to access such data through the Facebook API, the users who sign up to our application have the opportunity to grant us access only to a limited subset of the data we are asking for.

One last general challenge of data mining lies in understanding the data mining process itself and being able to explain it. In other words, coming up with the right question before we start analyzing the data is not always straightforward. More often than not, **research and development (R&D)** processes are driven by exploratory analysis, in the sense that in order to understand how to tackle the problem, we first need to start tampering with it. A related concept in statistics is described by the phrase *correlation does not imply causation*. Many statistical tests can be used to establish correlation between two variables, that is, two events occurring together, but this is not sufficient to establish a cause-effect relationship in either direction. Funny examples of bizarre correlations can be found all over the Web. A popular case was published in the New England Journal of Medicine, one of the most reputable medical journals, showing an interesting correlation between the amount of chocolate consumed per capita per country versus the number of Nobel prices awarded (*Chocolate Consumption, Cognitive Function, and Nobel Laureates, Franz H. Messerli, 2012*).

When performing an exploratory analysis, it is important to keep in mind that correlation (two events occurring together) is a bidirectional relationship, while causation (event A has caused event B) is a unidirectional one. Does chocolate make you smarter or do smart people like chocolate more than an average person? Do the two events occur together just by a random chance? Is there a third, yet unseen, variable that plays some role in the correlation? Simply observing a correlation is not sufficient to describe causality, but it is often an interesting starting point to ask important questions about the data we are observing.

The following section generalizes the way our application interacts with a social media API and performs the desired analysis.

Social media mining techniques

This section briefly discusses the overall process for building a social media mining application, before digging into the details in the next chapters.

The process can be summarized in the following steps:

1. Authentication
2. Data collection
3. Data cleaning and pre-processing
4. Modeling and analysis
5. Result presentation

Figure 1.2 shows an overview of the process:

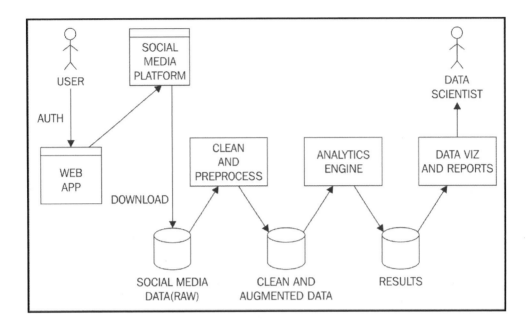

Figure 1.2: The overall process of social media mining

The authentication step is typically performed using the industry standard called **Open Authorization (OAuth)**. The process is *three legged*, meaning that it involves three actors: a user, consumer (our application), and resource provider (the social media platform). The steps in the process are as follows:

1. The user agrees with the consumer to grant access to the social media platform.
2. As the user doesn't give their social media password directly to the consumer, the consumer has an initial exchange with the resource provider to generate a token and a secret. These are used to sign each request and prevent forgery.
3. The user is then redirected with the token to the resource provider, which will ask to confirm authorizing the consumer to access the user's data.
4. Depending on the nature of the social media platform, it will also ask to confirm whether the consumer can perform any action on the user's behalf, for example, post an update, share a link, and so on.
5. The resource provider issues a valid token for the consumer.
6. The token can then go back to the user confirming the access.

Figure 1.3 shows the OAuth process with references to each of the steps described earlier. The aspect to remember is that the exchange of credentials (username/password) only happens between the user and the resource provider through the steps **3** and **4**. All other exchanges are driven by tokens:

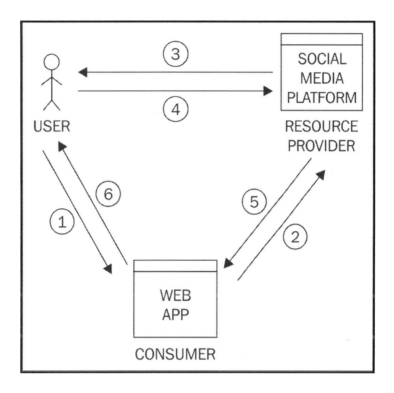

Figure 1.3: The OAuth process

From the user's perspective, this apparently complex process happens when the user is visiting our web app and hits the **Login with Facebook** (or Twitter, Google+, and so on) button. Then the user has to confirm that they are granting privileges to our app, and everything for them happens behind the scenes.

From a developer's perspective, the nice part is that the Python ecosystem has already well-established libraries for most social media platforms, which come with an implementation of the authentication process. As a developer, once you have registered your application with the target service, the platform will provide the necessary authorization tokens for your app. *Figure 1.4* shows a screenshot of a custom Twitter app called **Intro to Text Mining**. On the **Keys and Access Tokens** configuration page, the developer can find the API key and secret, as well as the access token and access token secret. We'll discuss the details of the authorization for each social media platform in the relevant chapters:

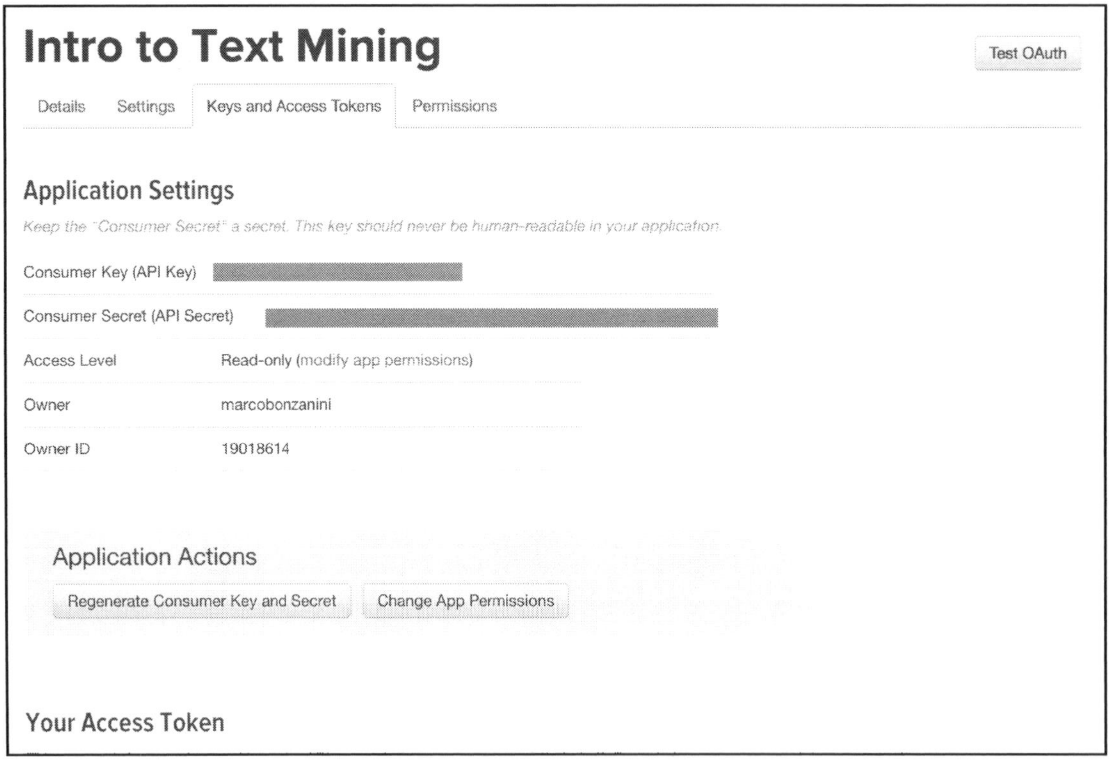

Intro to Text Mining

Test OAuth

Details   Settings   Keys and Access Tokens   Permissions

Application Settings

Keep the "Consumer Secret" a secret. This key should never be human-readable in your application.

Consumer Key (API Key)

Consumer Secret (API Secret)

Access Level   Read-only (modify app permissions)

Owner   marcobonzanini

Owner ID   19018614

Application Actions

Regenerate Consumer Key and Secret   Change App Permissions

Your Access Token

Figure 1.4: Configuration page for a Twitter app called Intro to Text Mining. The page contains all the authorization tokens for the developers to use in their app.

The data collection, cleaning, and pre-processing steps are also dependent on the social media platform we are dealing with. In particular, the data collection step is tied to the initial authorization as we can only download data that we have been granted access to. Cleaning and pre-processing, on the other hand, are functional to the type of data modeling and analysis that we decide to employ to produce insights on the data.

Back to *Figure 1.2*, the modeling and analysis is performed by the component labeled **ANALYTICS ENGINE**. Typical data processing tasks that we'll encounter throughout this book are text mining and graph mining.

Text mining (also referred to as text analytics) is the process of deriving structured information from unstructured textual data. Text mining is applicable to most social media platforms, as the users are allowed to publish content in the form of posts or comments.

Some examples of text mining applications include the following:

- **Document classification**: This is the task of assigning a document to one or more categories
- **Document clustering**: This is the task of grouping documents into subsets (called clusters) that are coherent and distinct from one another (for example, by topic or sub-topic)
- **Document summarization**: This is the task of creating a shortened version of the document in order to reduce the information overload to the user, while still retaining the most important aspects described in the original source
- **Entity extraction**: This is the task of locating and classifying entity references from a text into some desired categories such as persons, locations, or organizations
- **Sentiment analysis**: This is the task of identifying and categorizing sentiments and opinions expressed in a text in order to understand the attitude towards a particular product, topic, service, and so on

Not all these applications are tailored for social media, but the growing amount of textual data available through these platforms makes social media a natural playground for text mining.

Graph mining is also focused on the structure of the data. Graphs are a simple-to-understand, yet powerful, data structure that is generic enough to be applied to many different data representations. In graphs, there are two main components to consider: nodes, which represent entities or objects, and edges, which represent relationships or connections between nodes. In the context of social media, the obvious use of a graph is to represent the social relationships of our users. More in general, in social sciences, the graph structure used to represent social relationship is also referred to as social network.

In terms of using such data structure within social media, we can naturally represent users as nodes, and their relationships (such as *friends of* or *followers*) as edges. In this way, information such as *friends of friends who like Python* becomes easily accessible just by traversing the graph (that is, walking from one node to the other by following the edges). Graph theory and graph mining offer more options to discover deeper insights that are not as clearly visible as the previous example.

After a high-level discussion on social media mining, the following section will introduce some of the useful Python tools that are commonly used in data mining projects.

Python tools for data science

Until now, we've been using the term data mining when referring to problems and techniques that we're going to apply throughout this book. The title of this section, in fact, mentions the term *data science*. The use of this term has exploded in the recent years, especially in business environments, while many academics and journalists have also criticized its use as a buzzword. Meanwhile, other academic institutions started offering courses on data science, and many books and articles have been published on the subject. Rather than having a strong opinion on where we should draw the border between different disciplines, we limit ourselves to observe how, nowadays, there is a general interest in multiple fields, including data science, data mining, data analysis, statistics, machine learning, artificial intelligence, data visualization, and more. The topics we're discussing are interdisciplinary by their own nature, and they all borrow from each other from time to time. These is certainly an amazing time to be working in any of these fields, with a lot of interest from the public and a constant buzz with new advances in interesting projects.

The purpose of this section is to introduce Python as a tool for data science, and to describe part of the Python ecosystem that we're going to use in the next chapters.

Python is one of the most interesting languages for data analytics projects. The following are some of the reasons that make it fit for purpose:

- Declarative and intuitive syntax
- Rich ecosystem for data processing
- Efficiency

Python has a shallow learning curve due to its elegant syntax. Being a dynamic and interpreted language, it facilitates rapid development and interactive exploration. The ecosystem for data processing is partially described in the following sections, which will introduce the main packages we'll use in this book.

In terms of efficiency, interpreted and high-level languages are not famous for being furiously fast. Tools such as NumPy achieve efficiency by hooking to low-level libraries under the hood, and exposing a friendly Python interface. Moreover, many projects employ the use of **Cython**, a superset of Python that enriches the language by allowing, among other features, to define strong variable types and compile into C. Many other projects in the Python world are in the process of tackling efficiency issues with the overall goal of making pure Python implementations faster. In this book, we won't dig into Cython or any of these promising projects, but we'll make use of NumPy (especially through other libraries that employ NumPy) for data analysis.

Python development environment setup

When this book was started, Python 3.5 had just been released and received some attention for some its latest features, such as improved support for asynchronous programming and semantic definition of type hints. In terms of usage, Python 3.5 is probably not widely used yet, but it represents the current line of development of the language.

 The examples in this book are compatible with Python 3, particularly with versions 3.4+ and 3.5+.

In the never-ending discussion about choosing between Python 2 and Python 3, one of the points to keep in mind is that the support for Python 2 will be dismissed in a few years (at the time of writing, the sunset date is 2020). New features are not developed in Python 2, as this branch is only for bug fixes. On the other hand, many libraries are still developed for Python 2 first, and then the support for Python 3 is added later. For this reason, from time to time, there could be a minor hiccup in terms of compatibility of some library, which is usually resolved by the community quite quickly. In general, if there is no strong reason against this choice, the preference should go to Python 3, especially for new green-field projects.

pip and virtualenv

In order to keep the development environment clean, and ease the transition from prototype to production, the suggestion is to use virtualenv to manage a virtual environment and install dependencies. virtualenv is a tool for creating and managing isolated Python environments. By using an isolated virtual environment, developers avoid polluting the global Python environment with libraries that could be incompatible with each other. The tools allow us to maintain multiple projects that require different configurations and easily switch from one to the other. Moreover, the virtual environment can be installed in a local folder that is accessible to users without administrative privileges.

To install virtualenv in the global Python environment in order to make it available to all users, we can use pip from a terminal (Linux/Unix) or command prompt (Windows):

```
$ [sudo] pip install virtualenv
```

The sudo command might be necessary on Linux/Unix or macOS if our current user doesn't have administrator privileges on the system.

If a package is already installed, it can be upgraded to the latest version:

```
$ pip install --upgrade [package name]
```

Since Python 3.4, the pip tool is shipped with Python. Previous versions require a separate installation of pip as explained on the project page (htt ps://github.com/pypa/pip). The tool can also be used to upgrade itself to the latest version:
```
$ pip install --upgrade pip
```

Once virtualenv is globally available, for each project, we can define a separate Python environment where dependencies are installed in isolation, without tampering with the global environment. In this way, tracking the required dependencies of a single project is extremely easy.

In order to set up a virtual environment, follow these steps:

```
$ mkdir my_new_project # creat new project folder
$ cd my_new_project # enter project folder
$ virtualenv my_env # setup custom virtual environment
```

This will create a `my_env` subfolder, which is also the name of the virtual environment we're creating, in the current directory. Inside this subfolder, we have all the necessary tools to create the isolated Python environment, including the Python binaries and the standard library. In order to activate the environment, we can type the following command:

```
$ source my_env/bin/activate
```

Once the environment is active, the following will be visible on the prompt:

```
(my_env)$
```

Python packages can be installed for this particular environment using `pip`:

```
(my_env)$ pip install [package-name]
```

All the new Python libraries installed with `pip` when the environment is active will be installed into `my_env/lib/python{VERSION}/site-packages`. Notice that being a local folder, we won't need administrative access to perform this command.

When we want to deactivate the virtual environment, we can simply type the following command:

```
$ deactivate
```

The process described earlier should work for the official Python distributions that are shipped (or available for download) with your operating system.

Conda, Anaconda, and Miniconda

There is also one more option to consider, called **conda** (http://conda.pydata.org/), which is gaining some traction in the scientific community as it makes the dependency management quite easy. Conda is an open source package manager and environment manager for installing multiple versions of software packages (and related dependencies), which makes it easy to switch from one version to the other. It supports Linux, macOS, and Windows, and while it was initially created for Python, it can be used to package and distribute any software.

There are mainly two distributions that ship with conda: the batteries-included version, Anaconda, which comes with approximately 100 packages for scientific computing already installed, and the lightweight version, Miniconda, which simply comes with Python and the conda installer, without external libraries.

If you're new to Python, have some time for the bigger download and disk space to spare, and don't want to install all the packages manually, you can get started with Anaconda. For Windows and macOS, Anaconda is available with either a graphical or command-line installer. *Figure 1.5* shows a screen capture of the installationprocedure on a macOS. For Linux, only the command-line installer is available. In all cases, it's possible to choose between Python 2 and Python 3. If you prefer to have full control of your system, Miniconda will probably be your favorite option:

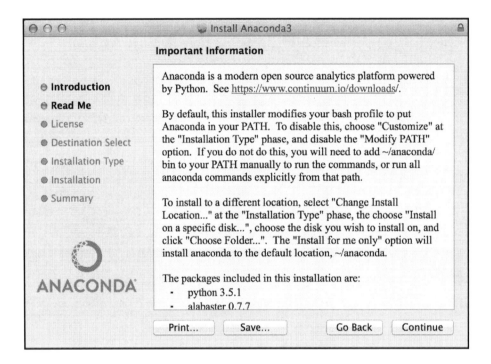

Figure 1.5: Screen capture of the Anaconda installation

Once you've installed your version of conda, in order to create a new conda environment, you can use the following command:

```
$ conda create --name my_env python=3.4 # or favorite version
```

The environment can be activated with the following command:

```
$ conda activate my_env
```

Similar to what happens with `virtualenv`, the environment name will be visible in the prompt:

```
(my_env) $
```

New packages can be installed for this environment with the following command:

```
$ conda install [package-name]
```

Finally, you can deactivate an environment by typing the following command:

```
$ conda deactivate
```

Another nice feature of conda is the ability to install packages from pip as well, so if a particular library is not available via `conda install`, or it's not been updated to the latest version we need, we can always fall back to the traditional Python package manager while using a conda environment.

If not specified otherwise, by default, conda will look up for packages on `https://anaconda.org`, while `pip` makes use of the **Python Package Index (PyPI** in short, also known as **CheeseShop)** at `https://pypi.python.org/pypi`. Both installers can also be instructed to install packages from the local filesystem or private repository.

The following section will use `pip` to install the required packages, but you can easily switch to conda if you prefer to use this alternative.

Efficient data analysis

This section introduces two of the foundational packages for scientific Python: NumPy and **pandas**.

NumPy (Numerical Python) offers fast and efficient processing or array-like data structures. For numerical data, storing and manipulating data with the Python built-ins (for example, lists or dictionaries) is much slower than using a NumPy array. Moreover, NumPy arrays are often used by other libraries as containers for input and output of different algorithms that require vectorized operations.

To install NumPy with `pip`/`virtualenv`, use the following command:

```
$ pip install numpy
```

When using the batteries-included Anaconda distribution, developers will find both NumPy and pandas preinstalled, so the preceding installation step is not necessary.

The core datastructure of this library is the multi-dimensional array called `ndarray`.

The following snippet, run from the interactive interpreter, showcases the creation of a simple array with NumPy:

```
>>> import numpy as np
>>> data = [1, 2, 3] # a list of int
>>> my_arr = np.array(data)
>>> my_arr
array([1, 2, 3])
>>> my_arr.shape
(3,)
>>> my_arr.dtype
dtype('int64')
>>> my_arr.ndim
1
```

The example shows that our data are represented by a one-dimensional array (the `ndim` attribute) with three elements as we expect. The data type of the array is `int64` as all our inputs are integers.

We can observe the speed of the NumPy array by profiling a simple operation, such as the sum of a list, using the `timeit` module:

```
# Chap01/demo_numpy.py
from timeit import timeit
import numpy as np

if __name__ == '__main__':
    setup_sum = 'data = list(range(10000))'
    setup_np = 'import numpy as np;'
    setup_np += 'data_np = np.array(list(range(10000)))'
    run_sum = 'result = sum(data)'
    run_np = 'result = np.sum(data_np)'

    time_sum = timeit(run_sum, setup=setup_sum, number=10000)
    time_np = timeit(run_np, setup=setup_np, number=10000)

    print("Time for built-in sum(): {}".format(time_sum))
    print("Time for np.sum(): {}".format(time_np))
```

The `timeit` module takes a piece of code as the first parameter and runs it a number of times, producing the time required for the run as output. In order to focus on the specific piece of code that we're analyzing, the initial data setup and the required imports are moved to the `setup` parameter that will be run only once and will not be included in the profiling. The last parameter, `number`, limits the number of iterations to 10,000 instead of the default, which is 1 million. The output you observe should look as follows:

```
Time for built-in sum(): 0.9970562970265746
Time for np.sum(): 0.07551316602621228
```

The built-in `sum()` function is more than 10 times slower than the NumPy `sum()` function. For more complex pieces of code, we can easily observe differences of a greater order of magnitude.

Naming conventions

The Python community has converged on some *de-facto* standards to import some popular libraries. NumPy and pandas are two well-known examples, as they are usually imported with an alias, for example:
`import numpy as np`
In this way, NumPy functionalities can be accessed with `np.function_name()` as illustrated in the preceding examples. Similarly, the pandas library is aliased to `pd`. In principle, importing the whole library namespace with `from numpy import *` is considered bad practice because it pollutes the current namespace.

Some of the characteristics of a NumPy array that we want to keep in mind are detailed as follows:

- The size of a NumPy array is fixed at creation, unlike, for example, Python lists that can be changed dynamically, so operations that change the size of the array are really creating a new one and deleting the original.
- The data type for each element of the array must be the same (with the exception of having arrays of objects, hence potentially of different memory sizes).
- NumPy promotes the use of operations with vectors, producing a more compact and readable code.

The second library introduced in this section is pandas. It is built on top of NumPy, so it also provides fast computation, and it offers convenient data structures, called **Series** and **DataFrame**, which allow us to perform data manipulation in a flexible and concise way.

Some of the nice features of pandas include the following:

- Fast and efficient objects for data manipulation
- Tools to read and write data between different formats such as CSV, text files, MS Excel spreadsheets, or SQL data structures
- Intelligent handling of missing data and related data alignment
- Label-based slicing and dicing of large datasets
- SQL-like data aggregations and data transformation
- Support for time series functionalities
- Integrated plotting functionalities

We can install pandas from the CheeseShop with the usual procedure:

```
$ pip install pandas
```

Let's consider the following example, run from the Python interactive interpreter, using a small made-up toy example of user data:

```
>>> import pandas as pd
>>> data = {'user_id': [1, 2, 3, 4], 'age': [25, 35, 31, 19]}
>>> frame = pd.DataFrame(data, columns=['user_id', 'age'])
>>> frame.head()
   user_id  age
0        1   25
1        2   35
2        3   31
3        4   19
```

The initial data layout is based on a dictionary, where the keys are attributes of the users (a user ID and age represented as number of years). The values in the dictionary are lists, and for each user, the corresponding attributes are aligned depending on the position. Once we create the DataFrame with these data, the alignment of the data becomes immediately clear. The head() function prints the data in a tabular form, truncating to the first ten lines if the data is bigger than that.

We can now augment the DataFrame by adding one more column:

```
>>> frame['over_thirty'] = frame['age'] > 30
>>> frame.head()
   user_id  age over_thirty
0        1   25       False
1        2   35        True
2        3   31        True
3        4   19       False
```

Using pandas declarative syntax, we don't need to iterate through the whole column in order to access its data, but we can apply a SQL-like operation as shown in the preceding example. This operation has used the existing data to create a column of Booleans. We can also augment the DataFrame by adding new data:

```
>>> frame['likes_python'] = pd.Series([True, False, True, True],
index=frame.index)
>>> frame.head()
   user_id  age over_thirty likes_python
0        1   25       False         True
1        2   35        True        False
2        3   31        True         True
3        4   19       False         True
```

We can observe some basic descriptive statistics using the describe() method:

```
>>> frame.describe()
          user_id   age over_thirty likes_python
count    4.000000   4.0           4            4
mean     2.500000  27.5         0.5         0.75
std      1.290994   7.0     0.57735          0.5
min      1.000000  19.0       False        False
25%      1.750000  23.5           0         0.75
50%      2.500000  28.0         0.5            1
75%      3.250000  32.0           1            1
max      4.000000  35.0        True         True
```

So, for example, 50% of our users are over 30, and 75% of them like Python.

Downloading the example code

Detailed steps to download the code bundle are mentioned in the Preface of this book. Please have a look.

The code bundle for the book is also hosted on GitHub at https://githu b.com/bonzanini/Book-SocialMediaMiningPython. We also have other code bundles from our rich catalog of books and videos available at https://github.com/PacktPublishing/. Check them out!

Machine learning

Machine learning is the discipline that studies and develops algorithms to learn from, and make predictions on, data. It is strongly related to data mining, and sometimes, the names of the two fields are used interchangeably. A common distinction between the two fields is roughly given as follows: machine learning focuses on predictions based on known properties of the data, while data mining focuses on discovery based on unknown properties of the data. Both fields borrow algorithms and techniques from their counterpart. One of the goals of this book is to be practical, so we acknowledge that academically the two fields, despite the big overlap, often have distinct goals and assumptions, but we will not worry too much about it.

Some examples of machine learning applications include the following:

- Deciding whether an incoming e-mail is spam or not
- Choosing the topic of a news article from a list of known subjects such as sport, finance, or politics
- Analyzing bank transactions to identify fraud attempts
- Deciding, from the *apple* query, whether a user is interested in fruit or in computers

Some of the most popular methodologies can be categorized into supervised and unsupervised learning approaches, described in the following section. This is an over simplification that doesn't describe the whole breadth and depth of the machine learning field, but it's a good starting point to appreciate some of its technicalities.

Supervised learning approaches can be employed to solve problems such as classification, in which the data comes with the additional attributes that we want to predict, for example, the label of a class. In this case, the classifier can associate each input object with the desired output. By inferring from the features of the input objects, the classifier can then predict the desired label for the new unseen inputs. Common techniques include **Naive Bayes (NB)**, **Support Vector Machine (SVM)** and models that belong to the **Neural Networks (NN)** family, such as perceptrons or multi-layer perceptrons.

The sample inputs used by the learning algorithm to build the mathematical model are called **training data**, while the unseen inputs that we want to obtain a prediction on are called **test data**. Inputs of a machine learning algorithm are typically in the form of a vector with each element of the vector representing a *feature* of the input. For supervised learning approaches, the desired output to assign to each of the unseen inputs is typically called **label** or **target**.

Unsupervised learning approaches are instead applied to problems in which the data come without a corresponding output value. A typical example of this kind of problems is clustering. In this case, an algorithm tries to find hidden structures in the data in order to group similar items into clusters. Another application consists of identifying items that don't appear to belong to a particular group (for example, outlier detection). An example of a common clustering algorithm is k-means.

The main Python package for machine learning is **scikit-learn**. It's an open source collection of machine learning algorithms that includes tools to access and preprocess data, evaluate the output of an algorithm, and visualize the results.

You can install scikit-learn with the common procedure via the CheeseShop:

```
$ pip install scikit-learn
```

Without digging into the details of the techniques, we will now walkthrough an application of scikit-learn to solve a clustering problem.

As we don't have social data yet, we can employ one of the datasets that is shipped together with scikit-learn.

The data that we're using is called the Fisher's Iris dataset, also referred to as Iris flower dataset. It was introduced in the 1930s by Ronald Fisher and it's today one of the classic datasets: given its small size, it's often used in the literature for toy examples. The dataset contains 50 samples from each of the three species of Iris, and for each sample four features are reported: the length and width of petals and sepals.

The dataset is commonly used as a showcase example for classification as the data comes with the correct labels for each sample, while its application for clustering is less common, mainly because there are just two well-visible clusters with a rather obvious separation. Given its small size and simple structure, it makes the case for a gentle introduction to data analysis with scikit-learn. If you want to run the example, including the data visualization part, you need to install also the **matplotlib** library with `pip install matplotlib`. More details on data visualization with Python are discussed later in this chapter.

Let's take a look at the following sample code:

```python
# Chap01/demo_sklearn.py
from sklearn import datasets
from sklearn.cluster import KMeans
import matplotlib.pyplot as plt

if __name__ == '__main__':
    # Load the data
    iris = datasets.load_iris()
```

```
X = iris.data
petal_length = X[:, 2]
petal_width = X[:, 3]
true_labels = iris.target
# Apply KMeans clustering
estimator = KMeans(n_clusters=3)
estimator.fit(X)
predicted_labels = estimator.labels_
# Color scheme definition: red, yellow and blue
color_scheme = ['r', 'y', 'b']
# Markers definition: circle, "x" and "plus"
marker_list = ['o', 'x', '+']
# Assign colors/markers to the predicted labels
colors_predicted_labels = [color_scheme[lab] for lab in
                           predicted_labels]
markers_predicted = [marker_list[lab] for lab in
                     predicted_labels]
# Assign colors/markers to the true labels
colors_true_labels = [color_scheme[lab] for lab in true_labels]
markers_true = [marker_list[lab] for lab in true_labels]
# Plot and save the two scatter plots
for x, y, c, m in zip(petal_width,
                      petal_length,
                      colors_predicted_labels,
                      markers_predicted):
  plt.scatter(x, y, c=c, marker=m)
plt.savefig('iris_clusters.png')
for x, y, c, m in zip(petal_width,
                      petal_length,
                      colors_true_labels,
                      markers_true):
  plt.scatter(x, y, c=c, marker=m)
plt.savefig('iris_true_labels.png')

print(iris.target_names)
```

Firstly, we will load the dataset into the `iris` variable, which is an object containing both the data and information about the data. In particular, `iris.data` contains the data itself, in the form of a NumPy array or arrays, while `iris.target` contains a numeric label that represent the class a sample belongs to. In each sample vector, the four values represent, respectively, sepal length in cm, sepal width in cm, petal length in cm, and petal width in cm. Using the slicing notation for the NumPy array, we extract the third and fourth element of each sample into `petal_length` and `petal_width`, respectively. These will be used to plot the samples in a two-dimensional representation, even though the vectors have four dimensions.

The clustering process consists in two lines of code: one to create an instance of the KMeans algorithm and the second to fit() the data to the model. The simplicity of this interface is one of the characteristics of scikit-learn, which in most cases, allows you to apply a learning algorithms with just a few lines of code. For the application of the k-means algorithm, we choose the number of clusters to be three, as this is given by the data. Keep in mind that knowing the appropriate number of clusters in advance is not something that usually happens. Determining the correct (or the most interesting) number of clusters is a challenge in itself, distinct from the application of a clustering algorithm *per se*. As the purpose of this example is to briefly introduce scikit-learn and the simplicity of its interface, we take this shortcut. Normally, more effort is put into preparing the data in a format that is understood by scikit-learn.

The second half of the example serves the purpose of visualizing the data using matplotlib. Firstly, we will define a color scheme to visually differentiate the three clusters, using red, yellow, and blue defined in the color_scheme list. Secondly, we will exploit the fact that both the real labels and cluster associations for each sample are given as integers, starting from 0, so they can be used as indexes to match one of the colors.

Notice that while the numbers for the real labels are associated to the particular meaning of the labels, that is, a class name; the cluster numbers are simply used to clarify that a given sample belongs to a cluster, but there is no information on the meaning of the cluster. Specifically, the three classes for the real labels are setosa, versicolor, and virginica, respectively-the three species of Iris represented in the dataset.

The last lines of the example produce two scatterplots of the data, one for the real labels and another for the cluster association, using the petal length and width as two dimensions. The two plots are represented in *Figure 1.6*. The position of the items in the two plots is, of course, the same, but what we can observe is how the algorithm has split the three groups. In particular, the cluster at the bottom left is clearly separated by the other two, and the algorithm can easily identify it without doubt. Instead, the other two clusters are more difficult to distinguish as some of the elements overlap, so the algorithm makes some mistakes in this context.

Once again, it's worth mentioning that here we can spot the mistakes because we know the real class of each sample. The algorithm has simply created an association based on the features given to it as input:

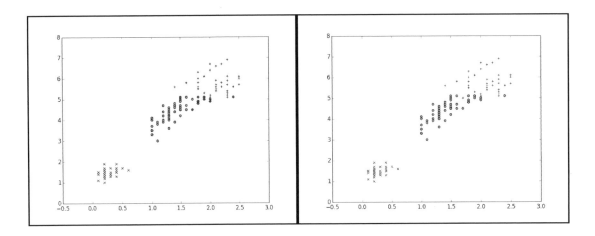

Figure 1.6: A 2-D representation of the Iris data, colored according to the real labels (left) and clustering results (right)

Natural language processing

Natural language processing (**NLP**) is the discipline related to the study of methods and techniques for automatic analysis, understanding, and generation of natural language, that is, the language as written or spoken naturally by humans.

Academically, it's been an active field of study for many decades, as its early days are generally attributed to Alan Turing, one of the fathers of computer science, who proposed a test to evaluate machine intelligence in 1950. The concept is fairly straightforward: if a human judge is having a written conversation with two agents-a human and a machine-can the machine fool the judge into thinking it's not a machine? If this happens, the machine passes the test and shows signs of *intelligence*.

The test is nowadays known as the Turing Test, and after being common knowledge only in computer science circles for a long time, it's been recently brought to a wider audience by pop media. The movie *The Imitation Game* (*2014*), for example, is loosely based on the biography of Alan Turing, and its title is a clear reference to the test itself. Another movie that mentions the Turing Test is *Ex Machina* (*2015*), with a stronger emphasis on the development of an artificial intelligence that can lie and fool humans for its own benefits. In this movie, the Turing Test is played between a human judge and the human-looking robot, Ava, with direct verbal interaction. Without spoiling the end of the movie for those who haven't watched it, the story develops with the artificial intelligence showing to be much smarter, in a shady and artful way, than the human. Interestingly, the futuristic robot was trained using search engine logs, to understand and mimic how humans ask questions.

This little detour between past and hypothetical future of artificial intelligence is to highlight how mastering human language will be central for development of an advanced **artificial intelligence (AI)**. Despite all the recent improvements, we're not quite there yet, and NLP is still a hot topic at the moment.

In the contest of social media, the obvious opportunity for us is that there's a huge amount of natural language waiting to be mined. The amount of textual data available via social media is continuously increasing, and for many questions, the answer has probably been already written; but transforming raw text into information is not an easy task. Conversations happen on social media all the time, users ask technical questions on web forums and find answers and customers describe their experiences with a particular product through comments or reviews on social media. Knowing the topics of these conversations, finding the most expert users who answer these questions, and understanding the opinion of the customers who write these reviews, are all tasks that can be achieved with a fair level of accuracy by means of NLP.

Moving on to Python, one of the most popular packages for NLP is **Natural Language Toolkit (NLTK)**. The toolkit provides a friendly interface for many of the common NLP tasks, as well as lexical resources and linguistic data.

Some of the tasks that we can easily perform with the NLTK include the following:

- Tokenization of words and sentences, that is, the process of breaking a stream of text down to individual tokens
- Tagging words for part-of-speech, that is, assigning words to categories according to their syntactic function, such as nouns, adjectives, verbs, and so on
- Identifying named entities, for example, identifying and classifying references of persons, locations, organizations, and so on
- Applying machine learning techniques (for example, classification) to text
- In general, extracting information from raw text

The installation of NLTK follows the common procedure via the CheeseShop:

```
$ pip install nltk
```

A difference between NLTK and many other packages is that this framework also comes with linguistic resources (that is, data) for specific tasks. Given their size, such data is not included in the default installation, but has to be downloaded separately.

The installation procedure is fully documented at `http://www.nltk.org/data.html` and it's strongly recommended that you read this official guide for all the details.

In short, from a Python interpreter, you can type the following code:

```
>>> import nltk
>>> nltk.download()
```

If you are in a desktop environment, this will open a new window that allows you to browse the available data. If a desktop environment is not available, you'll see a textual interface in the terminal. You can select individual packages to download, or even download all the data (that will take approximately 2.2 GB of disk space).

The downloader will try to save the file at a central location (`C:\nltk_data` on Windows and `/usr/share/nltk_data` on Unix and Mac) if you are working from an administrator account, or at your home folder (for example, `~/nltk_data`) if you are a regular user. You can also choose a custom folder, but in this case, NLTK will look for the `$NLTK_DATA` environment variable to know where to find its data, so you'll need to set it accordingly.

If disk space is not a problem, installing all the data is probably the most convenient option, as you do it once and you can forget about it. On the other hand, downloading everything doesn't give you a clear understanding of what resources are needed. If you prefer to have full control on what you install, you can download the packages you need one by one. In this case, from time to time during your NLTK development, you'll find a little bump on the road in the form of `LookupError`, meaning that a resource you're trying to use is missing and you have to download it.

For example, after a fresh NLTK installation, if we try to tokenize some text from the Python interpreter, we can type the following code:

```
>>> from nltk import word_tokenize
>>> word_tokenize('Some sample text')
Traceback (most recent call last):
  # some long traceback here
LookupError:
**********************************************************************
  Resource 'tokenizers/punkt/PY3/english.pickle' not found.
```

```
Please use the NLTK Downloader to obtain the resource:  >>>
nltk.download()
Searched in:
  - '/Users/marcob/nltk_data'
  - '/usr/share/nltk_data'
  - '/usr/local/share/nltk_data'
  - '/usr/lib/nltk_data'
  - '/usr/local/lib/nltk_data'
  - ''
**********************************************************************
```

This error tells us that the `punkt` resource, responsible for the tokenization, is not found in any of the conventional folders, so we'll have to go back to the NLTK downloader and solve the issue by getting this package.

Assuming that we now have a fully working NLTK installation, we can go back to the previous example and discuss tokenization with a few more details.

In the context of NLP, tokenization (also called segmentation) is the process of breaking a piece of text into smaller units called tokens or segments. While tokens can be interpreted in many different ways, typically we are interested in words and sentences. A simple example using `word_tokenize()` is as follows:

```
>>> from nltk import word_tokenize
>>> text = "The quick brown fox jumped over the lazy dog"
>>> words = word_tokenize(text)
>>> print(words)
# ['The', 'quick', 'brown', 'fox', 'jumped', 'over', 'the', 'lazy', 'dog']
```

The output of `word_tokenize()` is a list of strings, with each string representing a word. The word boundaries in this example are given by white spaces. In a similar fashion, `sent_tokenize()` returns a list of strings, with each string representing a sentence, bounded by punctuation. An example that involves both functions:

```
>>> from nltk import word_tokenize, sent_tokenize
>>> text = "The quick brown fox jumped! Where? Over the lazy dog."
>>> sentences = sent_tokenize(text)
>>> print(sentences)
#['The quick brown fox jumped!', 'Where?', 'Over the lazy dog.']
>>> for sentence in sentences:
...     words = word_tokenize(sentence)
...     print(words)
# ['The', 'quick', 'brown', 'fox', 'jumped', '!']
# ['Where', '?']
# ['Over', 'the', 'lazy', 'dog', '.']
```

As you can see, the punctuation symbols are considered tokens on their own, and as such, are included in the output of `word_tokenize()`. This opens for a question that we haven't really asked so far: how do we define a token? The `word_tokenize()` function implements an algorithm designed for standard English. As the focus of this book is on data from social media, it's fair to investigate whether the rules for standard English also apply in our context. Let's consider a fictitious example for Twitter data:

```
>>> tweet = '@marcobonzanini: an example! :D http://example.com #NLP'
>>> print(word_tokenize(tweet))
# ['@', 'marcobonzanini', ':', 'an', 'example', '!', ':', 'D', 'http', ':',
'//example.com', '#', 'NLP']
```

The sample tweet introduces some peculiarities that break the standard tokenization:

- Usernames are prefixed with an @ symbol, so @marcobonzanini is split into two tokens with @ being recognized as punctuation
- Emoticons such as :D are common slang on chats, text messages, and of course, social media, but they're not officially part of standard English, hence the split
- URLs are frequently used to share articles or pictures, but once again, they're not part of standard English, so they are broken down into components
- Hash-tags such as #NLP are strings prefixed by # and are used to define the topic of the post, so that other users can easily search for a topic or follow the conversation

The previous example shows that an apparently straightforward problem such as tokenization can hide many tricky edge cases that will require something smarter than the initial intuition to be solved. Fortunately, NLTK offers the following off-the-shelf solution:

```
>>> from nltk.tokenize import TweetTokenizer
>>> tokenizer = TwitterTokenizer()
>>> tweet = '@marcobonzanini: an example! :D http://example.com #NLP'
>>> print(tokenizer.tokenize(tweet))
# ['@marcobonzanini', ':', 'an', 'example', '!', ':D',
'http://example.com', '#NLP']
```

The previous examples should provide the taste of NLTK's simple interface. We will be using this framework on different occasions throughout the book.

With increasing interest in NLP applications, the Python-for-NLP ecosystem has grown dramatically in recent years, with a whole lot of interesting projects getting more and more attention. In particular, **Gensim**, dubbed *topic modeling for humans,* is an open-source library that focuses on semantic analysis. Gensim shares with NLTK the tendency to offer an easy-to-use interface, hence the *for humans* part of the tagline. Another aspect that pushed its popularity is efficiency, as the library is highly optimized for speed, has options for distributed computing, and can process large datasets without the need to hold all the data in memory.

The simple installation of Gensim follows the usual procedure:

```
$ pip install gensim
```

The main dependencies are NumPy and SciPy, although if you want to take advantage of the distributed computing capabilities of Gensim, you'll also need to install **PYthon Remote Objects (Pyro4)**:

```
$ pip install Pyro4
```

In order to showcase Gensim's simple interface, we can take a look at the text summarization module:

```python
# Chap01/demo_gensim.py
from gensim.summarization import summarize
import sys

fname = sys.argv[1]

with open(fname, 'r') as f:
  content = f.read()
  summary = summarize(content, split=True)
  for i, sentence in enumerate(summary):
    print("%d) %s" % (i+1, sentence))
```

The demo_gensim.py script takes one command-line parameter, which is the name of a text file to summarize. In order to test the script, I took a piece of text from the Wikipedia page about The Lord of the Rings, the paragraph with the plot of the first volume, The Fellowship of the Ring, in particular. The script can be invoked with the following command:

```
$ python demo_gensim.py lord_of_the_rings.txt
```

This produces the following output:

```
1) They nearly encounter the NazgÃ»l while still in the Shire, but shake
off pursuit by cutting through the Old Forest, where they are aided by the
enigmatic Tom Bombadil, who alone is unaffected by the Ring's corrupting
influence.
2) Aragorn leads the hobbits toward the Elven refuge of Rivendell, while
Frodo gradually succumbs to the wound.
3) The Council of Elrond reveals much significant history about Sauron and
the Ring, as well as the news that Sauron has corrupted Gandalf's fellow
wizard, Saruman.
4) Frodo volunteers to take on this daunting task, and a "Fellowship of the
Ring" is formed to aid him: Sam, Merry, Pippin, Aragorn, Gandalf, Gimli the
Dwarf, Legolas the Elf, and the Man Boromir, son of the Ruling Steward
Denethor of the realm of Gondor.
```

The `summarize()` function in Gensim implements the classic TextRank algorithm. The algorithm ranks sentences according to their importance and selects the most peculiar ones to produce the output summary. It's worth noting that this approach is an *extractive summarization* technique, meaning that the output only contains sentences selected from the input as they are, that is, there is no text transformation, rephrasing, and so on. The output size is approximately 25% of the original text. This can be controlled with the optional `ratio` argument for a proportional size, or `word_count` for a fixed number of words. In both cases, the output will only contain full sentences, that is, sentences will not be broken down to respect the desired output size.

Social network analysis

Network theory, part of the graph theory, is the study of graphs as a representation of relationships between discrete objects. Its application to social media takes the form of **Social network analysis (SNA)**, which is a strategy to investigate social structures such as friendships or acquaintances.

NetworkX is one of the main Python libraries for the creation, manipulation, and study of complex network structures. It provides data structures for graphs, as well as many well-known standard graph algorithms.

For the installation from the CheeseShop, we follow the usual procedure:

```
$ pip install networkx
```

The following example shows how to create a simple graph with a few nodes, representing users, and a few edges between nodes, representing social relationships between users:

```python
# Chap01/demo_networkx.py
import networkx as nx
from datetime import datetime

if __name__ == '__main__':
    g = nx.Graph()
    g.add_node("John", {'name': 'John', 'age': 25})
    g.add_node("Peter", {'name': 'Peter', 'age': 35})
    g.add_node("Mary", {'name': 'Mary', 'age': 31})
    g.add_node("Lucy", {'name': 'Lucy', 'age': 19})

    g.add_edge("John", "Mary", {'since': datetime.today()})
    g.add_edge("John", "Peter", {'since': datetime(1990, 7, 30)})
    g.add_edge("Mary", "Lucy", {'since': datetime(2010, 8, 10)})

    print(g.nodes())
    print(g.edges())
print(g.has_edge("Lucy", "Mary"))
# ['John', 'Peter', 'Mary', 'Lucy']
# [('John', 'Peter'), ('John', 'Mary'), ('Mary', 'Lucy')]
# True
```

Both nodes and edges can carry additional attributes in the form of a Python dictionary, which help in describing the semantics of the network.

The `Graph` class is used to represent an undirected graph, meaning that the direction of the edges is not considered. This is clear from the use of the `has_edge()` function, which checks whether an edge between Lucy and Mary exists. The edge was inserted between Mary and Lucy, but the function shows that the direction is ignored. Further edges between the same nodes will also be ignored, that is, only one edge per node pair is considered. Self-loops are allowed by the `Graph` class, although in our example, they are not needed.

Other types of graphs supported by NetworkX are `DiGraph` for directed graphs (the direction of the nodes matters) and their counterparts for multiple (parallel) edges between nodes, `MultiGraph` and `MultiDiGraph`, respectively.

Data visualization

Data visualization (or data viz) is a cross-field discipline that deals with the visual representation of data. Visual representations are powerful tools that offer the opportunity of understanding complex data and are efficient ways to present and communicate the results of a data analysis process in general. Through data visualizations, people can see aspects of the data that are not immediately clear. After all, if a picture is worth a thousand words, a good data visualization allows the reader to absorb complex concepts with the help of a simple picture. For example, data visualization can be used by data scientists during the exploratory data analysis steps in order to understand the data. Moreover, data scientists can also use data visualization to communicate with nonexperts and explain them what is interesting about the data.

Python offers a number of tools for data visualization, for example, the matplotlib library briefly used in the *Machine learning* section of this chapter. To install the library, use the following command:

```
$ pip install matplotlib
```

Matplotlib produces publication quality figures in a variety of formats. The philosophy behind this library is that a developer should be able to create simple plots with a small number of lines of code. Matplotlib plots can be saved into different file formats, for example, **Portable Network Graphics (PNG)** or **Portable Document Format (PDF)**.

Let's consider a simple example that plots some two-dimensional data:

```
# Chap01/demo_matplotlib.py
import matplotlib.pyplot as plt
import numpy as np

if __name__ == '__main__':
  # plot y = x^2 with red dots
  x = np.array([1, 2, 3, 4, 5])
  y = x * x
  plt.plot(x, y, 'ro')
  plt.axis([0, 6, 0, 30])
  plt.savefig('demo_plot.png')
```

The output of this code is shown in the following diagram:

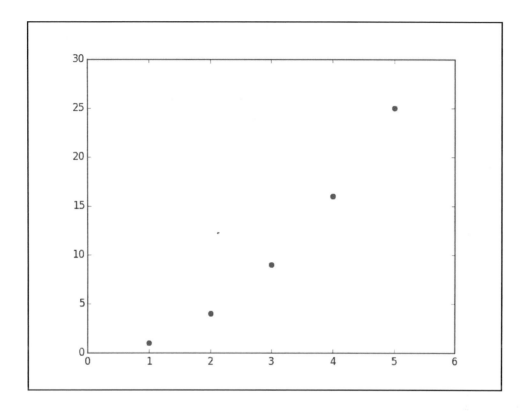

Figure 1.7: A plot created with matplotlib

Aliasing `pyploy` to `plt` is a common naming convention, as discussed earlier, also for other packages. The `plot()` function takes two sequence-like parameters containing the coordinates for x and y, respectively. In this example, these coordinates are created as the NumPy array, but they could be Python lists. The `axis()` function defines the visible range for the axis. As we're plotting the numbers 1 to 5 squared, our range is 0-6 for x axis and 0-30 for y axis. Finally, the `savefig()` function produces an image file with the output visualized in *Figure 1.7*, guessing the image format from the file extension.

Matplotlib produces excellent images for publication, but sometimes there's a need for some interactivity to allow the user to explore the data by zooming into the details of a visualization dynamically. This kind of interactivity is more in the realm of other programming languages, for example, JavaScript (especially through the popular **D3.js** library at `https://d3js.org`), that allow building interactive web-based data visualizations. While this is not the central topic of this book, it is worth mentioning that Python doesn't fall short in this domain, thanks to the tools that translate Python objects into the Vega grammar, a declarative format based on JSON that allows creating interactive visualizations.

A particularly interesting situation where Python and JavaScript can cooperate well is the case of geographical data. Most social media platforms are accessible through mobile devices. This offers the opportunity of tracking the user's location to also include the geographical aspect of data analysis. A common data format used to encode and exchange a variety of geographical data structures (such as points or polygons) is GeoJSON (`http://geojson.org`). As the name suggests, this format is JSON-based grammar.

A popular JavaScript library for plotting interactive maps is Leaflet (`http://leafletjs.com`). The bridge between JavaScript and Python is provided by **folium**, a Python library that makes it easy to visualize geographical data, handled with Python via, for example, GeoJSON, over a Leaflet.js map.

It's also worth mentioning that third-party services such as Plotly (`https://plot.ly`) offer support for the automatic generation of data visualization, off-loading the burden of creating interactive components of their services. Specifically, Plotly offers ample support for creating bespoke data visualizations using their Python client (`https://plot.ly/python`). The graphs are hosted online by Plotly and linked to a user account (free for public hosting, while private graphs have paid plans).

Processing data in Python

After introducing some the most important Python packages for data analytics, we take a small step back to describe some of the tools of interest to load and manipulate data from different formats with Python.

Most social media APIs provide data in JSON or XML. Python comes well equipped, from this point of view, with packages to support these formats that are part of the standard library.

For convenience, we will focus on JSON as this format can be mapped nicely into Python dictionaries and it's easier to read and understand. The interface of the JSON library is pretty straightforward, you can either load or dump data, from and to JSON to Python dictionaries.

Let's consider the following snippet:

```
# Chap01/demo_json.py
import json

if __name__ == '__main__':
  user_json = '{"user_id": "1", "name": "Marco"}'
  user_data = json.loads(user_json)
  print(user_data['name'])
  # Marco

  user_data['likes'] = ['Python', 'Data Mining']
  user_json = json.dumps(user_data, indent=4)
  print(user_json)
  # {
  #     "user_id": "1",
  #     "name": "Marco",
  #     "likes": [
  #         "Python",
  #         "Data Mining"
  #     ]
  # }
```

The json.loads() and json.dumps() functions manage the conversion from JSON strings to Python dictionaries and back. There are also two counterparts, json.load() and json.dump(), which operate with file pointers, in case you want to load or save JSON data from/to files.

The json.dumps() function also takes a second parameter, indent, to specify the number of characters of the indentation, which is useful for pretty printing.

When manually analyzing more complex JSON files, it's probably convenient to use an external JSON viewer that performs pretty printing within the browser, allowing the users to collapse and expand the structure as they wish.

There are several free tools for this, some of them are web-based services, such as JSON Viewer (http://jsonviewer.stack.hu). The user simply needs to paste a piece of JSON, or pass a URL that serves a piece of JSON, and the viewer will load it and display it in a user-friendly format.

The following image shows how the JSON document from the previous example is shown in JSON Viewer:

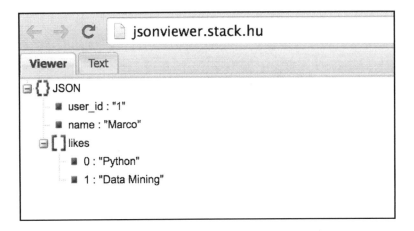

Figure 1.8: An example of pretty-printed JSON on JSON Viewer

As we can see in *Figure 1.8*, the `likes` field is a list, that can be collapsed to hide its element and ease the visualization. While this example is minimal, this feature becomes extremely handy to inspect complex documents with several nested layers.

 When using a web-based service or browser extension, loading large JSON documents for pretty printing can clog up your browser and slow your system down.

Building complex data pipelines

As soon as the data tools that we're building grow into something a bigger than a simple script, it's useful to split data pre-processing tasks into small units, in order to map all the steps and dependencies of the data pipeline.

With the term *data pipeline*, we intend a sequence of data processing operations, which cleans, augments, and manipulates the original data, transforming it into something digestible by the analytics engine. Any non-trivial data analytics project will require a data pipeline that is composed of a number of steps.

In the prototyping phase, it is common to split these steps into different scripts, which are then run individually, for example:

```
$ python download_some_data.py
$ python clean_some_data.py
$ python augment_some_data.py
```

Each script in this example produces the output for the following script, so there are dependencies between the different steps. We can refactor data processing scripts into a large script that does everything, and then run it in one go:

```
$ python do_everything.py
```

The content of such script might look similar to the following code:

```
if __name__ == '__main__':
    download_some_data()
    clean_some_data()
    augment_some_data()
```

Each of the preceding functions will contain the main logic of the initial individual scripts. The problem with this approach is that errors can occur in the data pipeline, so we should also include a lot of boilerplate code with `try` and `except` to have control over the exceptions that might occur. Moreover, parameterizing this kind of code might feel a little clumsy.

In general, when moving from prototyping to something more stable, it's worth thinking about the use of a data orchestrator, also called workflow manager. A good example of this kind of tool in Python is given by Luigi, an open source project introduced by Spotify. The advantages of using a data orchestrator such as Luigi include the following:

- Task templates: Each data task is defined as a class with a few methods that define how the task runs, its dependencies, and its output

Dependency graph: Visual tools assist the data engineer to visualize and understand the dependencies between tasks Recovery from intermediate failure: If the data pipeline fails halfway through the tasks, it's possible to restart it from the last consistent state

- Integration with command-line interface, as well as system job schedulers such as cron job
- Customizable error reporting

We won't dig into all the features of Luigi, as a detailed discussion would go beyond the scope of this book, but the readers are encouraged to take a look at this tool and use it to produce a more elegant, reproducible, and easily maintainable and expandable data pipeline.

Summary

This chapter introduced the different aspects of a multifaceted topic such as data mining applied to social media using Python. We have gone through some of the challenges and opportunities that make this topic interesting to study and valuable to businesses that want to gather meaningful insights from social media data.

After introducing the topic, we also discussed the overall process of social media mining, including aspects such as authentication with OAuth. We also analyzed the details of the Python tools that should be part of the data toolbox of any data mining practitioner. Depending on the social media platform we're analyzing, and the type of insights that we are concerned about, Python offers robust and well-established packages for machine learning, NLP, and SNA.

We recommend that you set up a Python development environment with `virtualenv` as described in *pip and virtualenv* section of this chapter, as this allows us to keep the global development environment clean.

The next chapter will focus on Twitter, particularly discussing on how to get access to Twitter data via the Twitter API and how to dice and slice such data in order to produce interesting information.

2
#MiningTwitter – Hashtags, Topics, and Time Series

This chapter is about data mining on Twitter. The topics covered in this chapter include the following:

- Interacting with the Twitter API using Tweepy
- Twitter data – the anatomy of a tweet
- Tokenization and frequency analysis
- Hashtags and user mentions in tweets
- Time series analysis

Getting started

Twitter is one of the most well-known online social networks that enjoy extreme popularity in the recent years. The service they provide is referred to as *microblogging*, which is a variant of blogging where the pieces of content are extremely short-in the case of Twitter, there is a limitation of 140 characters like an SMS for each *tweet*. Different from other social media platforms, such as Facebook, the Twitter network is not bidirectional, meaning that the connections don't have to be mutual: you can follow users who don't follow you back, and the other way round.

Traditional media is adopting social media as a way to reach a wider audience, and most celebrities have a Twitter account to keep in touch with their fans. Users discuss happening events in real time, including celebrations, TV shows, sport events, political elections, and so on.

Twitter is also responsible for popularizing the use of the term hashtag as a way to group conversations and allow users to follow a particular topic. A hashtag is a single keyword prefixed by a # symbol, for example, #halloween (used to show pictures of Halloween costumes) or #WaterOnMars (which was trending after NASA announced that they found evidence of water on Mars).

Given the variety of uses, Twitter is a potential gold mine for data miners, so let's get started.

The Twitter API

Twitter offers a series of APIs to provide programmatic access to Twitter data, including reading tweets, accessing user profiles, and posting content on behalf of a user.

In order to set up our project to access Twitter data, there are two preliminary steps, as follows:

- Registering our application
- Choosing a Twitter API client

The registration step will take a few minutes. Assuming that we are already logged in to our Twitter account, all we need to do is point our browser to the Application Management page at http://apps.twitter.com and create the new app.

Once the app is registered, under the **Keys and Access Tokens** tab, we can find the information we need to authenticate our application. The **Consumer Key** and **Consumer Secret** (also called **API Key** and **API Secret**, respectively) are a setting of your application. The **Access Token** and **Access Token Secret** are instead a setting for your user account. Your application can potentially ask for access to several users through their access token. The **Access Level** of these settings defines what the application can do while interacting with Twitter on behalf of a user: read-only is the more conservative option, as the application will not be allowed to publish anything or interact with other users via direct messaging.

Rate limits

The Twitter API limits access to applications. These limits are set on a per-user basis, or to be more precise, on a per-access-token basis. This means that when an application uses the application-only authentication, the rate limits are considered globally for the entire application; while with the per-user authentication approach, the application can enhance the global number of requests to the API.

It's important to familiarize yourself with the concept of rate limit, described in the official documentation (https://dev.twitter.com/rest/public/rate-limiting). It's also important to consider that different APIs have different rate limits (https://dev.twitter.com/rest/public/rate-limits).

The implications of hitting the API limits is that Twitter will return an error message rather than the data we're asking for. Moreover, if we continue performing more requests to the API, the time required to obtain regular access again will increase as Twitter could flag us as potential abusers. When many API requests are needed by our application, we need a way to avoid this. In Python, the `time` module, part of the standard library, allows us to include arbitrary suspensions of the code execution, using the `time.sleep()` function. For example, a pseudo-code is as follows:

```
# Assume first_request() and second_request() are defined.
# They are meant to perform an API request.
import time

first_request()
time.sleep(10)
second_request()
```

In this case, the second request will be executed 10 seconds (as specified by the `sleep()` argument) after the first one.

Search versus Stream

Twitter provides more than a single API. In fact, it will be explained in the following section that there is more than one way to access Twitter data. To keep things simple, we can categorize our options into two classes: REST APIs and Streaming API:

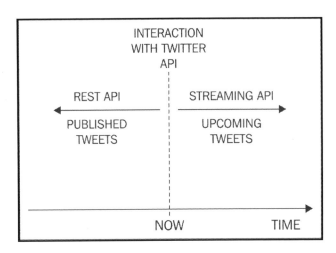

Figure 2.1: The time dimension of searching versus streaming

The difference, summarized in *Figure 2.1*, is fairly simple: all the REST APIs only allow you to go back in time. When interacting with Twitter via a REST API, we can search for existing tweets in fact, that is, tweets that have already been published and made available for search. Often these APIs limit the amount of tweets you can retrieve, not just in terms of rate limits as discussed in the previous section, but also in terms of time span. In fact, it's usually possible to go back in time up to approximately one week, meaning that older tweets are not retrievable. A second aspect to consider about the REST API is that these are usually a best effort, but they are not guaranteed to provide all the tweets published on Twitter, as some tweets could be unavailable to search or simply indexed with a small delay.

On the other hand, the Streaming API looks into the future. Once we open a connection, we can keep it open and go forward in time. By keeping the HTTP connection open, we can retrieve all the tweets that match our filter criteria, as they are published.

The Streaming API is, generally speaking, the preferred way of downloading a huge amount of tweets, as the interaction with the platform is limited to keeping one of the connections open. On the downside, collecting tweets in this way can be more time consuming, as we need to wait for the tweets to be published before we can collect them.

To summarize, the REST APIs are useful when we want to search for tweets authored by a specific user or we want to access our own timeline, while the Streaming API is useful when we want to filter a particular keyword and download a massive amount of tweets about it (for example, live events).

Collecting data from Twitter

In order to interact with the Twitter APIs, we need a Python client that implements the different calls to the API itself. There are several options as we can see from the official documentation (`https://dev.twitter.com/overview/api/twitter-libraries`). None of them are officially maintained by Twitter and they are backed by the open source community. While there are several options to choose from, some of them almost equivalent, so we will choose to use **Tweepy** here as it offers a wider support for different features and is actively maintained.

The library can be installed via `pip`:

```
$ pip install tweepy==3.3.0
```

Python 3 compatibility

We're specifically installing version 3.3 of Tweepy, because of an issue with the latest version of Tweepy and Python 3, which prevents running the examples in our Python 3.4 environment. The issue was still unresolved at the time of writing, but it's likely to be fixed soon.

The first part of the interaction with the Twitter API involves setting up the authentication as discussed in the previous section. After registering your application, at this point, you should have a consumer key, consumer secret, access token, and access token secret.

In order to promote the separation of concerns between application logic and configuration, we're storing the credentials in environment variables. Why not just hard-code these values as Python variables? There are a few reasons for this, well summarized in The Twelve-Factor App manifesto (`http://12factor.net/config`). Using the environment to store configuration details is language- and OS-agnostic. Changing configuration between different deployments (for example, using personal credentials for local tests and a company account for production) doesn't require any change in the code base. Moreover, environment variables don't get accidentally checked into your source control system for everyone to see.

In Unix environments, such as Linux or macOS, if your shell is Bash, you can set the environment variables as follows:

```
$ export TWITTER_CONSUMER_KEY="your-consumer-key"
```

In a Windows environment, you can set the variables from the command line as follows:

```
$ set TWITTER_CONSUMER_KEY="your-consumer-key"
```

The command should be repeated for all the four variables we need.

Once the environment is set up, we will wrap the Tweepy calls to create the Twitter client into two functions: one that reads the environment variables and performs the authentication, and the other that creates the API object needed to interface with Twitter:

```python
# Chap02-03/twitter_client.py
import os
import sys
from tweepy import API
from tweepy import OAuthHandler

def get_twitter_auth():
  """Setup Twitter authentication.

  Return: tweepy.OAuthHandler object
  """
  try:
    consumer_key = os.environ['TWITTER_CONSUMER_KEY']
    consumer_secret = os.environ['TWITTER_CONSUMER_SECRET']
    access_token = os.environ['TWITTER_ACCESS_TOKEN']
    access_secret = os.environ['TWITTER_ACCESS_SECRET']
  except KeyError:
    sys.stderr.write("TWITTER_* environment variables not set\n")
    sys.exit(1)
  auth = OAuthHandler(consumer_key, consumer_secret)
  auth.set_access_token(access_token, access_secret)
  return auth

def get_twitter_client():
  """Setup Twitter API client.

  Return: tweepy.API object
  """
  auth = get_twitter_auth()
  client = API(auth)
  return client
```

The `get_twitter_auth()` function is responsible for the authentication. The `try/except` block shows how to read the environment variables. The `os` module contains a dictionary called `os.environ`, which can be accessed by a key, just like a regular dictionary. If one of the `TWITTER_*` environment variables is missing, trying to access the key will raise a `KeyError` exception, which we will capture in order to show an error message and exit the application.

This function is called by `get_twitter_client()`, which is used to create an instance of `tweepy.API`, used for many different types of interaction with Twitter. The reason for breaking the logic down into two separate functions is that the authentication code can also be reused for the Streaming API, as we'll discuss in the following sections.

Getting tweets from the timeline

Once the client authentication is in place, we can start using it to download the tweets.

Let's first consider a simple scenario: how to get the first ten tweets of your own home timeline:

```
from tweepy import Cursor
from twitter_client import get_twitter_client

if __name__ == '__main__':
  client = get_twitter_client()

  for status in Cursor(client.home_timeline).items(10):
    # Process a single status
    print(status.text)
```

As a Twitter user, your home timeline is the screen that you see when you log in to Twitter. It contains a sequence of tweets from the accounts you've chosen to follow, with the most recent and interesting tweets at the top.

The preceding snippet shows how to use `tweepy.Cursor` to loop through the first ten items of your home timeline. Firstly, we need to import `Cursor` and the `get_twitter_client` function that was previously defined. In the main block, we will then use this function to create the client, which provides access to the Twitter API. In particular, the `home_timeline` attribute is what we need to access our own home timeline, and this will be the argument to pass to `Cursor`.

`tweepy.Cursor` is an *iterable* object, meaning that it provides an easy-to-use interface to perform iteration and pagination over different objects. In the previous example, it provides a minimal abstraction that allows the developer to loop through the object itself, without worrying about how the requests to the Twitter API are made.

Iterables

An iterable in Python is an object capable of returning its members, one at a time. Iterables include built-in data types such as lists or dictionaries, as well as objects of any class that implements the __iter__() or __getitem__() method.

The `status` variable used in the iteration represents an instance of `tweepy.Status`, which is a model used by Tweepy to wrap statuses (that is, tweets). In the preceding snippet, we're just using its text, but this object has a number of attributes. These are all described in *The structure of a tweet* section.

Rather than just printing the text on screen, we would like to store the tweets we retrieve from the API so that we can perform some analysis later.

We will refactor the previous snippet to get tweets from our own home timeline so that we can store the JSON information on a file:

```
# Chap02-03/twitter_get_home_timeline.py
import json
from tweepy import Cursor
from twitter_client import get_twitter_client

if __name__ == '__main__':
  client = get_twitter_client()

  with open('home_timeline.jsonl', 'w') as f:
    for page in Cursor(client.home_timeline, count=200).pages(4):
      for status in page:
        f.write(json.dumps(status._json)+"\n")
```

Running this code will generate a `home_timeline.jsonl` file within a few moments.

The JSON Lines format

The file in the preceding example has a `.jsonl` extension rather than just `.json`. In fact, this file is in the **JSON Lines** format (`http://jsonlines.org/`), meaning that each line of the file is a valid JSON document. Trying to load the entire content of this file with, for example, `json.loads()` will raise `ValueError` as the entire content is not a valid JSON document. Rather, if we're using functions that expect valid JSON documents, we need to process one line at a time.

The JSON Lines format is particularly well suited for large-scale processing: many big data frameworks allow the developers to easily split the input file into chunks that can be processed in parallel by different workers.

In this code, we're iterating through four pages, containing 200 tweets, each as declared in the `count` argument of the cursor. The reason for this is a limitation given by Twitter: we can only retrieve up to the most recent 800 tweets from our home timeline.

If we retrieve tweets from a specific user timeline, that is, using the `user_timeline` method rather than `home_timeline`, this limit is increased to 3,200.

Let's consider the following script to get a specific user timeline:

```
# Chap02-03/twitter_get_user_timeline.py
import sys
import json
from tweepy import Cursor
from twitter_client import get_twitter_client

if __name__ == '__main__':
  user = sys.argv[1]
  client = get_twitter_client()

  fname = "user_timeline_{}.jsonl".format(user)

  with open(fname, 'w') as f:
    for page in Cursor(client.user_timeline, screen_name=user,
                       count=200).pages(16):
      for status in page:
        f.write(json.dumps(status._json)+"\n")
```

To run the script, we need to provide one command-line argument for the user's screen name. For example, to retrieve my whole timeline (well below the 3,200-tweets limit at the moment), we will use the following command:

```
$ python twitter_get_user_timeline.py marcobonzanini
```

As the traffic from my timeline is relatively low, we can retrieve a higher number of tweets from the Packt Publishing account, @PacktPub:

```
$ python twitter_get_user_timeline.py PacktPub
```

In a similar way to what we have seen with the home timeline, the script will create a .jsonl file with a single JSON document on each line. The size of the file when we hit the 3,200 limit is approximatively 10 Mb.

Conceptually, the code to get a user timeline is very similar to the one that retrieves the home timeline. The only difference is in the single command-line argument used to specify the Twitter handle of the user we're interested in.

Up to this point, the only attribute of a single tweet that we have used through the Tweepy interface is _json, which has been used to store the original JSON response. The following section discusses the details of the structure of a tweet, before moving on to other ways to get data from Twitter.

The structure of a tweet

A tweet is a complex object. The following table provides a list of all its attributes and a brief description of their meaning. In particular, the content of the API response for the particular tweet is fully contained in the _json attribute, which is loaded into a Python dictionary:

Attribute Name	Description
_json	This is a dictionary with the JSON response of the status
author	This is the tweepy.models.User instance of the tweet author
contributors	This is a list of contributors, if the feature is enabled
coordinates	This is the dictionary of coordinates in the GeoJSON format
created_at	This is the datetime.datetime instance of the tweet-creation time

entities	This is a dictionary of URLs, hashtags, and mentions in the tweets
favorite_count	This is the number of times the tweet has been favorited
favorited	This flags whether the authenticated user has favorited the tweet
geo	These are the coordinates (deprecated, use `coordinates` instead)
id	This is the unique ID of the tweets as big integer
id_str	This is the unique ID of the tweet as string
in_reply_to_screen_name	This is the username of the status the tweet is replying to
in_reply_to_status_id	This is the status ID of the status the tweet is replying to, as big integer
in_reply_to_status_id_str	This is the status ID of the status the tweet is replying to, as string
in_reply_to_user_id	This is the user ID of the status the tweet is replying to, as big integer
in_reply_to_user_id_str	This is the user ID of the status the tweet is replying to, as string
is_quote_status	This flags whether the tweet is a quote (that is, contains another tweet)
lang	This is the string with the language code of the tweet
place	This is the `tweepy.models.Place` instance of the place attached to the tweet
possibly_sensitive	This flags whether the tweet contains URL with possibly sensitive material
retweet_count	This is the number of times the status has been retweeted
retweeted	This flags whether the status is a retweet
source	This is the string describing the tool used to post the status
text	This is the string with the content of the status
truncated	This flags whether the status was truncated (for example, retweet exceeding 140 chars)

user	This is the `tweepy.models.User` instance of the tweet author (deprecated, use `author` instead)

The attributes that hold an ID (for example, user ID or tweet ID) have a counterpart where the same value is repeated as a string. This is necessary because some programming languages (most notably JavaScript) cannot support numbers with more than 53 bits, while Twitter uses 64-bit numbers. To avoid numerical problems, Twitter recommends the use of the `*_str` attributes.

We can see that not all the attributes are translated into a Python built-in type such as strings or Booleans. In fact, some complex objects such as the user profile are included completely within the API response, and Tweepy takes care of translating these objects into the appropriate model.

The following example showcases a sample tweet by Packt Publishing in the original JSON format as given by the API and as accessible via the `_json` attribute (several fields have been omitted for brevity).

Firstly, the creation date in the expected format, is as follows:

```
{
  "created_at": "Fri Oct 30 05:26:05 +0000 2015",
```

The `entities` attribute is a dictionary that contains different lists of labeled entities. For example, the `hashtags` element shows that the `#Python` hashtag was present in the given tweet. Similarly, we have photos, URLs, and user mentions:

```
"entities": {
  "hashtags": [
    {
      "indices": [
        72,
        79
      ],
      "text": "Python"
    }
  ],
  "media": [
    {
      "display_url": "pic.twitter.com/muZlMreJNk",
      "id": 659964467430735872,
      "id_str": "659964467430735872",
      "indices": [
        80,
```

```
        103
    ],
    "type": "photo",
    "url": "https://t.co/muZlMreJNk"
  }
],
"symbols": [],
"urls": [
  {
    "indices": [
      48,
      71
    ],
    "url": "https://t.co/NaBNan3iVt"
  }
],
"user_mentions": [
  {
    "id": 80589255,
    "id_str": "80589255",
    "indices": [
      33,
      47
    ],
    "name": "Open Source Way",
    "screen_name": "opensourceway"
  }
]
},
```

The following attributes are well described in the previous table and shouldn't require much information to be understood. We can notice that the geographical information for this tweet is missing. We can also compare the previous information about the entities with the actual tweet stored in the `text` attribute:

```
"favorite_count": 4,
"favorited": false,
"geo": null,
"id": 659964467539779584,
"id_str": "659964467539779584",
"lang": "en",
"retweet_count": 1,
"retweeted": false,
"text": "Top 3 open source Python IDEs by @opensourceway
  https://t.co/NaBNan3iVt #Python https://t.co/muZlMreJNk",
```

The `user` attribute is a dictionary that represents the user who sent the tweet, in this case, `@PacktPub`. As previously mentioned, this is a complex object with all the user-related information embedded in the tweet:

```
"user": {
  "created_at": "Mon Dec 01 13:16:47 +0000 2008",
  "description": "Providing books, eBooks, video tutorials, and
    articles for IT developers, administrators, and users.",
  "entities": {
    "description": {
      "urls": []
    },
    "url": {
      "urls": [
        {
          "display_url": "PacktPub.com",
          "expanded_url": "http://www.PacktPub.com",
          "indices": [
            0,
            22
          ],
          "url": "http://t.co/vEPCgOu235"
        }
      ]
    }
  },
  "favourites_count": 548,
  "followers_count": 10090,
  "following": true,
  "friends_count": 3578,
  "id": 17778401,
  "id_str": "17778401",
  "lang": "en",
  "location": "Birmingham, UK",
  "name": "Packt Publishing",
  "screen_name": "PacktPub",
  "statuses_count": 10561,
  "time_zone": "London",
  "url": "http://t.co/vEPCgOu235",
  "utc_offset": 0,
  "verified": false
}
}
```

This example shows two interesting aspects to consider when analyzing tweets, as follows:

- The entities are already labeled
- The user profile is fully embedded

The first point means that entity analysis is simplified as we do not need to explicitly search for entities such as hashtags, user mentions, embedded URLs, or media, because these are all provided by the Twitter API together with their offset within the text (the attribute called `indices`).

The second point means that we do not need to store user profile information somewhere else and then join/merge the data via a foreign key, for example. The user profile is, in fact, redundantly replicated within each tweet.

Working with denormalized data

The approach of embedding redundant data is related to the concept of denormalization. While normalization is considered a good practice in relational database design, denormalization finds its role in large-scale processing and databases that belong to the wide NoSQL family. The rationale behind this approach is that the additional disk space required to redundantly store the user profile only has a marginal cost, while the gain (in terms of performances) obtained by removing the need for a join/merge operation is substantial.

Using the Streaming API

The Streaming API is one of the favorite ways of getting a massive amount of data without exceeding the rate limits. We have already discussed how this API differs from the other REST APIs, in particular, the Search API, and how we might need to rethink the way our application interacts with the user.

Before digging into the details, it is worth looking at the documentation of the Streaming API to understand its peculiarities (`https://dev.twitter.com/streaming/overview`).

In this section, we'll implement a custom stream listener by extending the default `StreamListener` class offered by Tweepy:

```
# Chap02-03/twitter_streaming.py
import sys
import string
import time
from tweepy import Stream
from tweepy.streaming import StreamListener
```

```
from twitter_client import get_twitter_auth

class CustomListener(StreamListener):
    """Custom StreamListener for streaming Twitter data."""

    def __init__(self, fname):
        safe_fname = format_filename(fname)
        self.outfile = "stream_%s.jsonl" % safe_fname

    def on_data(self, data):
        try:
            with open(self.outfile, 'a') as f:
                f.write(data)
                return True
        except BaseException as e:
            sys.stderr.write("Error on_data: {}\n".format(e))
            time.sleep(5)
        return True

    def on_error(self, status):
        if status == 420:
            sys.stderr.write("Rate limit exceeded\n")
            return False
        else:
            sys.stderr.write("Error {}\n".format(status))
            return True

def format_filename(fname):
    """Convert fname into a safe string for a file name.

    Return: string
    """
    return ''.join(convert_valid(one_char) for one_char in fname)

def convert_valid(one_char):
    """Convert a character into '_' if "invalid".

    Return: string
    """
    valid_chars = "-_.%s%s" % (string.ascii_letters, string.digits)
    if one_char in valid_chars:
        return one_char
    else:
        return '_'

if __name__ == '__main__':
    query = sys.argv[1:] # list of CLI arguments
    query_fname = ' '.join(query) # string
```

```
auth = get_twitter_auth()
twitter_stream = Stream(auth, CustomListener(query_fname))
twitter_stream.filter(track=query, async=True)
```

The core of the streaming logic is implemented in the CustomListener class, which extends StreamListener and overrides two methods: on_data() and on_error(). These are handlers that are triggered when data is coming through and an error is given by the API.

The return type for both these methods is a Boolean: True to continue the streaming and False to stop the execution. For this reason, it's important to return False only on fatal errors, so the application can continue downloading data. In this way, we can avoid killing the application if a temporary error occurs, such as a network hiccup on our side, or an HTTP 503 error from Twitter, which means that the service is temporarily unavailable (but likely to be back shortly).

The on_error() method in particular will deal with explicit errors from Twitter. For a complete list of status codes from the Twitter API, we can check the documentation (https://dev.twitter.com/overview/api/response-codes). Our implementation of the on_error() method will stop the execution only if there's error 420, meaning that we have been rate limited by the Twitter API. The more we exceed the rate limit, the more we need to wait before we can use the service again. Therefore, for this reason, it's better to stop downloading and investigating the problem. Every other error will simply be printed on the stderr interface. This is, in general, better than just using print(), so we can redirect the error output to a specific file if needed. Even better, we could use the logging module to build a proper log-handling mechanism, but this is beyond the scope of this chapter.

The on_data() method is called when data is coming through. This function simply stores the data as it is received in a .jsonl file. Each line of this file will then contain a single tweet, in the JSON format. Once the data is written, we will return True to continue the execution. If anything goes wrong in this process, we will catch any exception, print a message on stderr, put the application to sleep for five seconds, and then continue the execution by returning True again. The short sleep, in case of exception, is simply to prevent an occasional network hiccup that causes the application to get stuck.

The CustomListener class uses a helper to sanitize the query and use it for the filename. The format_filename() function, in fact, goes through the given string, one character at a time, and uses the convert_valid() function to convert invalid characters into underscores. In this context, the valid characters are the three symbols-dash, underscore, and dot (-, _, and .)-ASCII letters, and digits.

When we run the `twitter_streaming.py` script, we have to provide arguments from the command line. These arguments, separated by a white space, will be the keywords used by the listener to download tweets.

To provide an example, I've run the script to capture tweets about the final match of the 2015 Rugby World Cup played between New Zealand and Australia (`https://en.wikipe dia.org/wiki/2015_Rugby_World_Cup`). The fans following the event on Twitter were mostly using the `#RWC2015` (used throughout the competition) and `#RWCFinal` (used to follow the conversation about the final day) hashtags. I've used these two hashtags together with the term `rugby` as search keywords for stream listener:

```
$ python twitter_streaming.py \#RWC2015 \#RWCFinal rugby
```

The backslashes before the hash symbols, `#`, are needed to escape this character because the shell uses the hash to represent the beginning of a comment. Escaping the character ensures that the string is passed correctly to the script.

The kickoff of the event was set for 4 p.m. **Greenwich Mean Time (GMT)** on the 31st of October, 2015. Running the script for three hours between 3 p.m. and 6 p.m. has produced nearly 800 MB of data, with more than 200,000 tweets in total. The buzz on Twitter has continued for a while after the event, but the amount of data collected during this time frame is enough to perform some interesting analysis.

Analyzing tweets – entity analysis

This section is all about analyzing entities in tweets. We're going to perform some frequency analysis using the data collected in the previous section. Slicing and dicing this data will allow users to produce some interesting statistics that can be used to get some insights on the data and answer some questions.

Analyzing entities such as hashtags is interesting as these annotations are an explicit way for the author to label the topic of the tweet.

We start with the analysis of the tweets by Packt Publishing. As Packt Publishing supports and promotes open source software, we are interested in finding what kind of technologies are mentioned often by Packt Publishing.

The following script extracts the hashtags from a user timeline, producing a list of the most common ones:

```
# Chap02-03/twitter_hashtag_frequency.py
import sys
from collections import Counter
import json

def get_hashtags(tweet):
  entities = tweet.get('entities', {})
  hashtags = entities.get('hashtags', [])
  return [tag['text'].lower() for tag in hashtags]

if __name__ == '__main__':
  fname = sys.argv[1]
  with open(fname, 'r') as f:
    hashtags = Counter()
    for line in f:
      tweet = json.loads(line)
      hashtags_in_tweet = get_hashtags(tweet)
      hashtags.update(hashtags_in_tweet)
    for tag, count in hashtags.most_common(20):
      print("{}: {}".format(tag, count))
```

This code can be run with the following command:

```
$ python twitter_hashtag_frequency.py user_timeline_PacktPub.jsonl
```

Here, `user_timeline_PacktPub.jsonl` is the JSON Lines file that we previously collected.

This script takes the name of a `.jsonl` file as argument from the command line and reads its content, one line at a time. As each line contains a JSON document, it loads the document into the `tweet` variable and uses the `get_hashtags()` helper function to extract a list of hashtags. These type of entities are stored in the `hashtags` variable, which is declared as `collections.Counter`, a special type of dictionary that is used to count hashable objects- in our case, strings. The counter holds the strings as keys of the dictionary and their respective frequency as values.

Being a subclass of `dict`, the `Counter` object per se is an unordered collection. The `most_common()` method is responsible for ordering the keys depending on their values (most frequent first) and returning a list of `(key, value)` tuples.

The `get_hashtags()` helper function is responsible for retrieving a list of hashtags from the tweet. The whole tweet, loaded into a dictionary, is given as the only argument of this function. If entities are present in the tweet, the dictionary will have an `entities` key. Since this is optional, we can't access `tweet['entities']` directly as this could raise `KeyError`, so we will use the `get()` function instead, specifying an empty dictionary as default value if the entities are not present. The second step consists of getting the hashtags from the entities. As `entities` is also a dictionary, and the `hashtags` key is also optional, we use the `get()` function again, but this time, we will specify an empty list as the default value if no hashtag is present. Finally, we will use a list comprehension to iterate through the hashtags in order to extract their text. The hashtags are normalized using `lower()` to force the text to be lowercase, so mentions such as `#Python` or `#PYTHON` will all be grouped into `#python`.

Running the script to analyze the PacktPub tweets produces the following output:

```
packt5dollar: 217
python: 138
skillup: 132
freelearning: 107
gamedev: 99
webdev: 96
angularjs: 83
bigdata: 73
javascript: 69
unity: 65
hadoop: 46
raspberrypi: 43
js: 37
pythonweek: 36
levelup: 35
r: 29
html5: 28
arduino: 27
node: 27
nationalcodingweek: 26
```

As we can see, there are references about events and promotions by PacktPub (such as `#packt5dollar`), but most hashtags mention a specific technology, with Python and JavaScript being the most tweeted.

The previous script gave an overview of the hashtags most frequently used by PacktPub, but we want to dig a little bit deeper. We can, in fact, produce more descriptive statistics that give us an overview of how hashtags are used by Packt Publishing:

```python
# Chap02-03/twitter_hashtag_stats.py
import sys
from collections import defaultdict
import json

def get_hashtags(tweet):
  entities = tweet.get('entities', {})
  hashtags = entities.get('hashtags', [])
  return [tag['text'].lower() for tag in hashtags]

def usage():
  print("Usage:")
  print("python {} <filename.jsonl>".format(sys.argv[0]))

if __name__ == '__main__':
  if len(sys.argv) != 2:
    usage()
    sys.exit(1)
  fname = sys.argv[1]
  with open(fname, 'r') as f:
    hashtag_count = defaultdict(int)
    for line in f:
      tweet = json.loads(line)
      hashtags_in_tweet = get_hashtags(tweet)
      n_of_hashtags = len(hashtags_in_tweet)
      hashtag_count[n_of_hashtags] += 1
    tweets_with_hashtags = sum([count for n_of_tags, count in
                                hashtag_count.items() if n_of_tags > 0])
    tweets_no_hashtags = hashtag_count[0]
    tweets_total = tweets_no_hashtags + tweets_with_hashtags
    tweets_with_hashtags_percent = "%.2f" % (tweets_with_hashtags
                                             / tweets_total * 100)
    tweets_no_hashtags_percent = "%.2f" % (tweets_no_hashtags /
                                           tweets_total * 100)
    print("{} tweets without hashtags
          ({}%)".format(tweets_no_hashtags,
          tweets_no_hashtags_percent))
    print("{} tweets with at least one hashtag
          ({}%)".format(tweets_with_hashtags,
          tweets_with_hashtags_percent))

    for tag_count, tweet_count in hashtag_count.items():
      if tag_count > 0:
        percent_total = "%.2f" % (tweet_count / tweets_total *
```

```
                                          100)
            percent_elite = "%.2f" % (tweet_count /
                                      tweets_with_hashtags * 100)
            print("{} tweets with {} hashtags ({}% total, {}%
                  elite)".format(tweet_count, tag_count,
                  percent_total, percent_elite))
```

We can run the preceding script with the following command:

```
$ python twitter_hashtag_stats.py user_timeline_PacktPub.jsonl
```

With the collected data, the previous command will produce the following output:

```
1373 tweets without hashtags (42.91%)
1827 tweets with at least one hashtag (57.09%)
1029 tweets with 1 hashtags (32.16% total, 56.32% elite)
585 tweets with 2 hashtags (18.28% total, 32.02% elite)
181 tweets with 3 hashtags (5.66% total, 9.91% elite)
29 tweets with 4 hashtags (0.91% total, 1.59% elite)
2 tweets with 5 hashtags (0.06% total, 0.11% elite)
1 tweets with 7 hashtags (0.03% total, 0.05% elite)
```

We can see that majority of the tweets by PacktPub have at least one hashtag, which confirms the importance of this type of entity in the way people communicate via Twitter.

On the other hand, the breakdown of the hashtag count shows that the number of hashtags per tweet is not large. Approximately 1% of tweets have four or more hashtags. For this breakdown, we will observe two different percentages: the first is calculated over the total number of tweets, while the second is calculated over the number of tweets with at least one tweet (called elite set).

In a similar fashion, we can observe user mentions, as follows:

```
# Chap02-03/twitter_mention_frequency.py
import sys
from collections import import Counter
import json

def get_mentions(tweet):
  entities = tweet.get('entities', {})
  hashtags = entities.get('user_mentions', [])
  return [tag['screen_name'] for tag in hashtags]

if __name__ == '__main__':
  fname = sys.argv[1]
  with open(fname, 'r') as f:
    users = Counter()
    for line in f:
```

```
    tweet = json.loads(line)
    mentions_in_tweet = get_mentions(tweet)
    users.update(mentions_in_tweet)
for user, count in users.most_common(20):
    print("{}: {}".format(user, count))
```

The script can be run with the following command:

```
$ python twitter_mention_frequency.py user_timeline_PacktPub.jsonl
```

This will produce the following output:

```
PacktPub: 145
De_Mote: 15
antoniogarcia78: 11
dptech23: 10
platinumshore: 10
packtauthors: 9
neo4j: 9
Raspberry_Pi: 9
LucasUnplugged: 9
ccaraus: 8
gregturn: 8
ayayalar: 7
rvprasadTweet: 7
triqui: 7
rukku: 7
gileadslostson: 7
gringer_t: 7
kript: 7
zaherg: 6
otisg: 6
```

Analyzing tweets – text analysis

The previous section analyzed the entity field of a tweet. This provides useful knowledge on the tweet, because these entities are explicitly curated by the author of the tweet. This section will focus on unstructured data instead, that is, the raw text of the tweet. We'll discuss aspects of text analytics such as text preprocessing and normalization and we'll perform some statistical analysis on the tweets. Before digging the details, we'll introduce some terminology.

Tokenization is one of the important steps in the preprocessing phase. Given a stream of text (such as a tweet status), tokenization is the process of breaking this text down into individual units called tokens. In the simplest form, these units are words, but we could also work on a more complex tokenization that deals with phrases, symbols, and so on.

Tokenization sounds like a trivial task, and it's been widely studied by the natural language processing community. Chapter 1, *Social Media, Social Data, and Python*, provided a brief introduction of this field, and mentioned how Twitter changes the rules of tokenization because the content of a tweet includes emoticons, hashtags, user mentions, URLs, and is quite different from standard English. For this reason, when using the **Natural Language Toolkit (NLTK)** library, we showcased the TweetTokenizer class as a tool to tokenize Twitter content. We'll make use of this tool again in this chapter.

Another preprocessing step that is worth considering is **stop word removal**. Stop words are words that, when taken in isolation, are not content-bearing. This category of words include articles, propositions, adverbs, and so on. Frequency analysis will show that these words are typically the most common in any dataset. While a list of stop words can be compiled automatically by analyzing the data (for example, by including words that are present in more than an arbitrary percentage of the documents, such as 95%), in general, it pays off to be more conservative and use only common English stop words. NLTK provides a list of common English stop words via the nltk.corpus.stopwords module.

Stop word removal can be extended to include symbols as well (such as punctuation) or domain-specific words. In our Twitter context, common stop words are the terms **RT** (short for Retweet) and **via**, often used to mention the author of the content being shared.

Finally, another important preprocessing step is normalization. This is an umbrella term that can consist of several types of processing. In general, normalization is used when we need to aggregate different terms in the same unit. The special case of normalization considered here is **case normalization**, where every term is lowercase so that strings with originally different casing will match (for example, 'python' == 'Python'.lower()). The advantage of performing case normalization is that the frequency of a given term will be automatically aggregated, rather than being dispersed into the different variations of the same term.

We will produce our first term frequency analysis with the following script:

```
# Chap02-03/twitter_term_frequency.py
import sys
import string
import json
from collections import Counter
from nltk.tokenize import TweetTokenizer
from nltk.corpus import stopwords
```

```
def process(text, tokenizer=TweetTokenizer(), stopwords=[]):
  """Process the text of a tweet:
  - Lowercase
  - Tokenize
  - Stopword removal
  - Digits removal

  Return: list of strings
  """
  text = text.lower()
  tokens = tokenizer.tokenize(text)
  return [tok for tok in tokens if tok not in stopwords and not
          tok.isdigit()]

if __name__ == '__main__':
  fname = sys.argv[1]
  tweet_tokenizer = TweetTokenizer()
  punct = list(string.punctuation)
  stopword_list = stopwords.words('english') + punct + ['rt',
                                                        'via', '...']

  tf = Counter()
  with open(fname, 'r') as f:
    for line in f:
      tweet = json.loads(line)
      tokens = process(text=tweet['text'],
              tokenizer=tweet_tokenizer,
              stopwords=stopword_list)
      tf.update(tokens)
    for tag, count in tf.most_common(20):
      print("{}: {}".format(tag, count))
```

The core of the preprocessing logic is implemented by the process() function. The function takes a string as input and returns a list of strings as output. All the preprocessing steps mentioned earlier, case normalization, tokenization, and stop words removal are implemented here in a few lines a code.

The function also takes two more optional arguments: a tokenizer, that is, an object that implements a tokenize() method and a list of stop words, so the stop word-removal process can be customized. When applying stop word removal, the function also removes numerical tokens (for example, '5' or '42') using the isdigit() function over a string.

The script takes a command-line argument for the .jsonl file to analyze. It initializes TweetTokenizer used for tokenization, and then defines a list of stop words. Such list is made up of common English stop words coming from NLTK, as well as punctuation symbols defined in string.punctuation. To complete the stop word list, we also include the 'rt', 'via', and '...' tokens (a single-character Unicode symbol for a horizontal ellipses).

The script can be run with the following command:

```
$ python twitter_term_frequency.py filename.jsonl
```

The output is as follows:

```
free: 477
get: 450
today: 437
ebook: 342
http://t.co/wrmxoton95: 295
-: 265
save: 259
ebooks: 236
us: 222
http://t.co/ocxvjqbbiw: 214
#packt5dollar: 211
new: 208
data: 199
@packtpub: 194
': 192
hi: 179
titles: 177
we'll: 160
find: 160
guides: 154
videos: 154
sorry: 150
books: 149
thanks: 148
know: 143
book: 141
we're: 140
#python: 137
grab: 136
#skillup: 133
```

As we can see, the output contains a mix of words, hashtags, user mentions, URLs, and Unicode symbols not captured by `string.punctuation`. Regarding the extra symbols, we could simply extend the list of stop words to capture this type of punctuation. Regarding hashtags and user mentions, this is exactly what we expect from `TweetTokenizer`, as all these tokens are valid. Maybe something that we didn't expect is the presence of tokens such as `we're` and `we'll`, because these are contracted forms of two separate tokens, rather than individual tokens on their own. If the contracted form is expanded, in both cases (*we are* and *we will*), all we have is a sequence of stop words because these contracted forms are usually pronouns and common verbs. A full list of English contractions is given on, for example, Wikipedia (https://en.wikipedia.org/wiki/Wikipedia%3aList_of_Engl ish_contractions).

One way to deal with this aspect of the English language is to normalize these contractions into their extended form. For example, the following function takes a list of tokens and returns a normalized list of tokens (to be more precise, a generator, as we're using the `yield` keyword):

```
def normalize_contractions(tokens):
  token_map = {
    "i'm": "i am",
    "you're": "you are",
    "it's": "it is",
    "we're": "we are",
    "we'll": "we will",
  }
  for tok in tokens:
    if tok in token_map.keys():
      for item in token_map[tok].split():
        yield item
    else:
      yield tok
```

Let's consider the following example from the interactive interpreter:

```
>>> tokens = tokens = ["we're", "trying", "something"]
>>> list(normalize_contractions(tokens))
['we', 'are', 'trying', 'something']
```

The main problem with this approach is the need to manually specify all the contractions we're dealing with. While the number of such contractions is limited, it would be a tedious job to translate everything into a dictionary. Moreover, there are some ambiguities that cannot be easily dealt with, for example, the case of *we'll* that we previously encountered: this contraction can be mapped into *we will* as well as *we shall*, and the list is, of course, longer.

A different approach consists of considering these tokens as stop words, because after normalization, all their components seem to be stop words.

The best course of action is probably dependent on your application, so the key question is what is going on after the preprocessing step formalized in the `process()` function. For the time being, we can also keep the preprocessing as it is, without explicitly dealing with contractions.

Yield and generators

The `normalize_contractions()` function uses the `yield` keyword instead of `return`. This keyword is used to produce a *generator*, which is an iterator that you can only iterate over once, as it doesn't store its items in the memory, but generates them on the fly. One of the advantages is to reduce memory consumption, so it's recommendable for iterations over big objects. The keyword also allows to generate multiple items within the same function call, while `return` would close the computation as soon as it's called (for example, the `for` loop in `normalize_contractions()` would run only over the first token).

To conclude this section, we will look into the analysis of term and entity frequencies from a different perspective.

Given the source code shown in `twitter_hashtag_frequency.py` and `twitter_term_frequency.py`, we can extend these scripts by implementing a simple plot rather than printing out the frequencies of the most common terms:

```
# Chap02-03/twitter_term_frequency_graph.py
y = [count for tag, count in tf.most_common(30)]
x = range(1, len(y)+1)

plt.bar(x, y)
plt.title("Term Frequencies")
plt.ylabel("Frequency")
plt.savefig('term_distribution.png')
```

The preceding snippet shows how to plot the term frequencies from
`twitter_term_frequency.py`; it's also easy to apply it for hashtag frequencies. After
running the script over the tweets by `@PacktPub`, you'll create the
`term_distribution.png` file that will look like *Figure 2.2*:

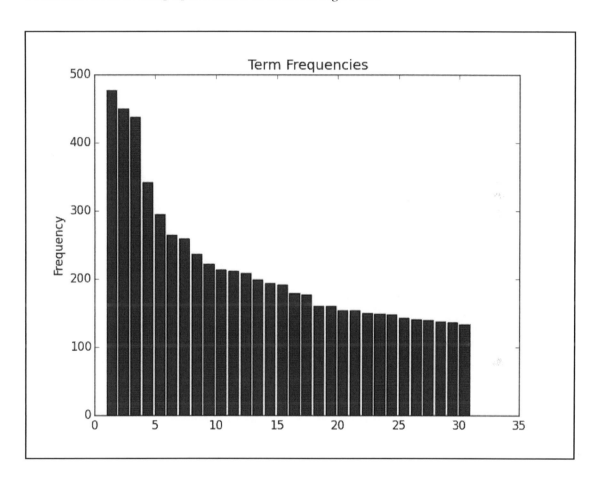

Figure 2.2: The frequency of terms in recent tweets by @PacktPub

The preceding figure doesn't report the terms per se, as the focus of this last analysis is
frequency distribution. As we can see from the figure, there are a few terms on the left with
very high frequency, for example, the most frequent term is twice more frequent than the
ones after position **10** or so. As we move towards the right-hand side of the figure, the curve
becomes less steep, meaning that the terms on the right share similar frequencies.

With little modification, if we rerun the same code using `most_common(1000)` (that is, the 1,000 most frequent terms), we can observe this phenomenon even clearer, as shown in *Figure 2.3*:

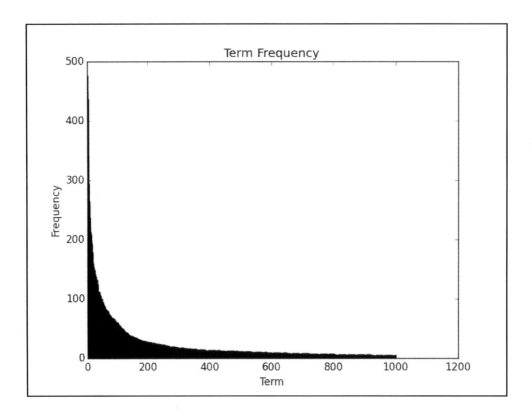

Figure 2.3: The frequency of the 1,000 most common terms in tweets by @PacktPub

The curve that we can observe in *Figure 2.3* represents an approximation of a **power law**(ht tps://en.wikipedia.org/wiki/Power_law). In statistics, a power law is a functional relationship between two quantities; in this case, the frequency of a term and its position within the ranking of terms by frequency. This type of distribution always shows a **long tail** (https://en.wikipedia.org/wiki/Long_tail), meaning that a small portion of frequent items dominate the distribution, while there is a large number of items with smaller frequencies. Another name for this phenomenon is the **80-20 rule** or **Pareto principle** (https://en.wikipedia.org/wiki/Pareto_principle), which states that roughly 80% of the effect comes from 20% of the cause (in our context, 20% of the unique terms account for 80% of all term occurrences).

A few decades ago, the American linguist George Zipf popularized what is nowadays known as the **Zipf's law** (`https://en.wikipedia.org/wiki/Zipf%27s_law`). This empirical law states that given a collection of documents, the frequency of any word is inversely proportional to its rank in the frequency table. In other words, the most frequent word will be seen twice as often as the second most frequent one, three times as often as the third most frequent one, and so on. In practice, this law describes a trend rather than the precise frequencies. Interestingly enough, Zipf's law can be generalized for many different natural languages, as well as many language-unrelated rankings studies in social sciences.

Analyzing tweets – time series analysis

The previous sections analyzed the content of tweets. In this section, we will discuss another interesting aspect of analyzing data from Twitter-the distribution of tweets over time.

Generally speaking, a time series is a sequence of data points that consists of successive observations over a given interval of time. As Twitter provides a `created_at` field with the precise timestamp of the tweet, we can rearrange tweets into temporal buckets so that we can examine how users react to real-time events. We are interested in observing how a population of users is tweeting, not just a single user, so the data gathered via the Streaming API is most suited for this type of analysis.

The analysis in this section uses the dataset from the 2015 Rugby World Cup Final. This is a nice example of how users react to real-time events such as sport events, concerts, political elections, and everything from major disasters to TV shows. Other applications of time series analysis of Twitter data is online reputation management. A company can, in fact, be interested in monitoring what the users (possibly customers) say about them on social media, and the dynamic nature of Twitter seems to be perfect to track reactions to, for example, news releases about products.

We'll take advantage of pandas capabilities to manipulate time series and again we'll use matplotlib for a visual interpretation of the series:

```
# Chap02-03/twitter_time_series.py
import sys
import json
from datetime import datetime
import matplotlib.pyplot as plt
import matplotlib.dates as mdates

import pandas as pd
import numpy as np
```

```
import pickle

if __name__ == '__main__':
  fname = sys.argv[1]

  with open(fname, 'r') as f:
    all_dates = []
    for line in f:
      tweet = json.loads(line)
      all_dates.append(tweet.get('created_at'))
    idx = pd.DatetimeIndex(all_dates)
    ones = np.ones(len(all_dates))
    # the actual series (at series of 1s for the moment)
    my_series = pd.Series(ones, index=idx)

    # Resampling / bucketing into 1-minute buckets
    per_minute = my_series.resample('1Min', how='sum').fillna(0)
    # Plotting the series
    fig, ax = plt.subplots()
    ax.grid(True)
    ax.set_title("Tweet Frequencies")
    hours = mdates.MinuteLocator(interval=20)
    date_formatter = mdates.DateFormatter('%H:%M')

    datemin = datetime(2015, 10, 31, 15, 0)
    datemax = datetime(2015, 10, 31, 18, 0)

    ax.xaxis.set_major_locator(hours)
    ax.xaxis.set_major_formatter(date_formatter)
    ax.set_xlim(datemin, datemax)
    max_freq = per_minute.max()
    ax.set_ylim(0, max_freq)
    ax.plot(per_minute.index, per_minute)

    plt.savefig('tweet_time_series.png')
```

The code can be run with the following command:

```
$ python twitter_time_series.py stream__RWC2015__RWCFinal_Rugby.jsonl
```

The script reads the `.jsonl` file given as the command-line argument, loading tweets one line at a time as discussed in the previous scripts. As we are interested only in the publication date of the tweets, we build a list, `all_dates`, which contains only the `created_at` attribute for each tweet.

The pandas series is indexed by the creation time, which is represented in the `idx` variable as `pd.DatetimeIndex` of the previously collected dates. The granularity of these dates goes down to the second. We then create `np.array` of 1s, using the `ones()` function, which will be used to aggregate the tweet frequencies.

Once the series is created, we use a technique called bucketing or resampling, which basically changes the way we index the series, in this case, grouping the tweets per minute. As we specify that we're resampling by `sum`, each bucket will contain the count of tweets published in that particular minute. The `fillna(0)` call appended at the end of the resampling is just a precaution in case a particular bucket doesn't have any tweet; in this case, the bucket will not be discarded, but will contain 0 as the frequency. This is unlikely to happen given the size of our dataset, but it's a real possibility for smaller data.

To clarify what happens with the resampling, we can observe the following example, obtained by printing `my_series.head()` and `per_minute.head()`:

```
# Before resampling
# my_series.head()
2015-10-31 15:11:32    1
2015-10-31 15:11:32    1
2015-10-31 15:11:32    1
2015-10-31 15:11:32    1
2015-10-31 15:11:32    1
dtype: float64
# After resampling
# per_minute.head()
2015-10-31 15:11:00    195
2015-10-31 15:12:00    476
2015-10-31 15:13:00    402
2015-10-31 15:14:00    355
2015-10-31 15:15:00    466
dtype: float64
```

The first column of the output contains the series index, which is the `datetime` object (the time precision is down to the seconds), while the second column is the value (frequency) associated to this index.

As there is a high number of tweets per second, the original series, `my_series`, shows the same index (`15:11:32` in the example) several times. Once the series has been resampled, the granularity of the series index is instead down to a minute.

The code that follows uses the matplotlib library to create a nice visualization of the time series. Matplotlib is, in general, more verbose than other data analysis libraries, but it's not complicated. The interesting part in this example is the use of `MinuteLocator` and `DateFormatter` to label correctly the time intervals on the *x* axis. In this case, an interval of 20 minutes is used.

The plot is saved in `tweet_time_series.png`, which we can observe in *Figure 2.4*:

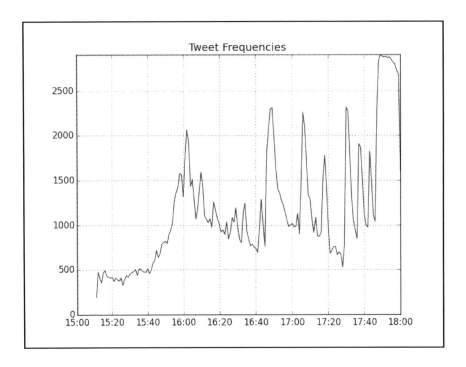

Figure 2.4: The frequency of tweets during the 2015 Rugby World Cup Final

The time zone of the timestamps in *Figure 2.4* is GMT, that is, UK time. The kickoff of the final was set at 4 p.m. As we can see, as we get closer to the kick-off time, there is an increase in user activity, with a peak coming shortly after the match started. Few peaks that exceed 2,000 tweets per minute are some of the topical moments of the match-first, New Zealand taking a large lead, and Australia getting close to a comeback (for the neutral fan, it was an entertaining match). The final huge spike is in line with the end of the match, award ceremony, and celebrations that continued for a while (even though the stream stopped at around 6 p.m.).

Summary

This chapter introduced some data mining applications using the Twitter data. We discussed how to register an application with the Twitter platform in order to get the credentials and interact with the Twitter APIs. We have considered different ways to download tweets, particularly using the REST endpoints to search for published tweets, and using the Streaming API to keep the connection open and collect upcoming tweets.

When observing the anatomy of a tweet, we found that a tweet is much more than 140 characters. In fact, it is a complex object with a lot of information in it.

The starting point of our analysis opened the discussion on frequency analysis based on entities. Our focus has been on hashtags, one of Twitter's peculiarities, widely adopted by users to track specific topics. We also discussed aspects of **natural language processing (NLP)** such as tokenization and normalization of tokens. As we have seen, the language on Twitter doesn't follow the conventions of standard English, with specific traits such as hashtags, user mentions, URLs, emoticons, and so on. On the other hand, we found that the language on Twitter follows a statistical rule called the Zipf's law, just like any other natural language corpus of a decent size.

To conclude our analysis, we took a look at the time series. It's extremely interesting to observe how users react to real-time events, and time series analysis can be a powerful tool to analyze large datasets.

The next chapter is also about Twitter, but the focus will be on the users. In particular, we want to understand the users that are connected to this social network.

3
Users, Followers, and Communities on Twitter

This chapter continues the discussion on mining Twitter data. After focusing on the analysis of tweets in the previous chapter, we will now shift our attention to the users, their connections, and their interactions.

In this chapter, we will discuss the following topics:

- How to download a list of friends and followers for a given user
- How to analyze connections between users, mutual friends, and so on
- How to measure influence and engagement on Twitter
- Clustering algorithms and how to cluster users using **scikit-learn**
- Network analysis and how to use it to mine conversations on Twitter
- How to create dynamic maps to visualize the location of tweets

Users, friends, and followers

One of the main differences between Twitter and other popular social networks is the way users can connect. Relationships on Twitter are, in fact, not necessarily bidirectional. A user can choose to subscribe to other users' tweets, becoming their follower, but the act of following might not be reciprocated. This is very different from what happens with other social networks such as Facebook and LinkedIn, where the relationship has to be confirmed by both parties before taking place.

Using the Twitter terminology, the two directions of the relationship (people I follow versus the people who follow me) have different names. The people I follow are referred to as *friends*, while the people who follow me are referred to as my *followers*. When the relationship is bidirectional, the user is commonly described as a *mutual friend*.

Back to the Twitter API

The Twitter API provides several endpoints to retrieve information about followers, friends, and user profiles in general. The choice of the specific endpoint will be dictated by the task we're trying to solve.

A quick look at the documentation (`https://dev.twitter.com/rest/public`) will highlight some of the interesting ones.

Starting from a single-user profile, the obvious endpoint to consider is `users/show`: given a screen name or user ID, the endpoint will retrieve the full profile for a user. This functionality is severely rate-limited, as only 180 requests are possible every 15 minutes, which means only 180 user profiles in the 15-minute window. Given this limitation, this endpoint should be used only if we need to retrieve a specific profile, and it's not suitable for batch downloads.

A list of followers for a given user can be retrieved using the `followers/list` endpoint (`https://dev.twitter.com/rest/reference/get/followers/list`), implemented in Tweepy with the `API.followers()` function. Similarly, the `friends/list` endpoint allows retrieving the list of friends for the given user, with the Tweepy implementation available as `API.friends()`. The main problem with these endpoints is the strict rate limit: only 15 requests in a 15-minute window, with each request providing up to 20 user profiles. This means retrieving up to 300 profiles every 15 minutes.

While this approach could be feasible for profiles with a very small number of followers and friends, it is not uncommon to have a profile with thousands of followers (for celebrities, the number could go up to several million).

The workaround for this limit is based on a combination of other endpoints that are more suitable for big batches of data. The `followers/ids` endpoint (`https://dev.twitter.com/rest/reference/get/followers/ids`) can return groups of 5,000 user IDs per request. Despite also being limited to 15 requests in a 15-minute window, it's easy to work out how the final number of user IDs that we can retrieve (75,000 per quarter of an hour) is much better than the previous limitation.

After using the `followers/ids` endpoint, all we have is the list of user IDs corresponding to the user's followers, but we don't have the complete profiles yet. The solution is to use these user IDs as input for the `users/lookup` endpoint (`https://dev.twitter.com/rest/reference/get/users/lookup`), which takes up to 100 IDs as input, providing the corresponding list of complete profiles as output. The rate limits for `users/lookup` are set to 180 every 15 minutes, which corresponds to 18,000 profiles every quarter of an hour. This number is the one that effectively limits our download.

The workaround also works if we want to download a batch of friends' profiles, combining the `friends/ids` endpoint with the aforementioned `users/lookup`. In terms of rate limits, when downloading friends' IDs, we will encounter the same limitations as for the followers. One little mistake to avoid is to consider the two downloading processes completely independent; keep in mind that `users/lookup` is the bottleneck. For a script that downloads both friend and follower profiles, we need to account for the fact that both download processes will need the `users/lookup` endpoint, so the total number of requests to `users/lookup` will be up to the sum of friends and followers. For users who are both friends and followers, only one lookup is needed.

The structure of a user profile

Before digging into the details of how to download a large number of followers and friends profiles, we will consider the case of a single user to understand the structure of a user profile. We can use the `users/show` endpoint as this is a one-off example, so we're not hitting the rate limits (the next section will discuss batch downloads).

The endpoint is implemented in Tweepy by the `API.get_user()` function. We can reuse the authentication code that we defined in Chapter 2, *#MiningTwitter – Hashtags, Topics, and Time Series* (make sure that the environment variables are correctly set up). From the interactive interpreter, we will input the following:

```
>>> from twitter_client import get_twitter_client
>>> import json
>>> client = get_twitter_client()
>>> profile = client.get_user(screen_name="PacktPub")
>>> print(json.dumps(profile._json, indent=4))
```

This code is quite straightforward; once the authentication is performed, a single API call will allow us to download the profile. The object returned by the function call is an instance of the `tweepy.models.User` class, already mentioned in `Chapter 2`, *#MiningTwitter – Hashtags, Topics, and Time Series*, which is a wrapper to store the different user attributes. The original JSON response from Twitter is stored as a Python dictionary in the `_json` attribute that we will output on screen, using `json.dumps()` and the `indent` argument for some pretty printing.

We will observe a piece of JSON similar to the following code (several attributes have been omitted for brevity):

```
{
  "screen_name": "PacktPub",
  "name": "Packt Publishing",
  "location": "Birmingham, UK",
  "id": 17778401,
  "id_str": "17778401",
  "description": "Providing books, eBooks, video tutorials, and
    articles for IT developers, administrators, and users.",
  "followers_count": 10209,
  "friends_count": 3583,
  "follow_request_sent": false,
  "status": { ... },
  "favourites_count": 556,
  "protected": false,
  "verified": false,
  "statuses_count": 10802,
  "lang": "en",
  "entities": {
    "description": {
      "urls": []
    },
    "url": {
      "urls": [
        {
          "indices": [
            0,
            22
          ],
          "display_url": "PacktPub.com",
          "expanded_url": "http://www.PacktPub.com",
          "url": "http://t.co/vEPCgOu235"
        }
      ]
    }
  },
  "following": true,
```

```
    "geo_enabled": true,
    "time_zone": "London",
    "utc_offset": 0,
}
```

The following table provides a description of all the fields we can find:

Attribute Name	Description
_json	This is a dictionary with the JSON response of the user profile
created_at	This is the UTC date time of the user account creation
contributors_enabled	This is the flag to indicate **contributor mode** enabled (rarely true)
default_profile	This is the flag to indicate the user has not altered the profile theme
description	This is the string to describe the user profile
default_profile_image	This is the flag to indicate the user doesn't have a custom profile picture
entities	This is the list of entities in the URL or description
followers_count	This is the number of followers
follow_request_sent	This is the flag to indicate whether a follow request was sent
favourites_count	This is the number of tweets favorited by the user
following	This is the flag to indicate whether the authenticated user is following
friends_count	This is the number of friends
geo_enabled	This is the flag to indicate **geotagging** is enabled
id	This is the unique ID of the user as a big integer
id_str	This is the unique ID of the user as a string
is_translator	This is the flag to indicate the user is part of the Twitter's translator community
lang	This is the language code for the user
listed_count	This is the number of public lists the user is a member of
location	This is the user-declared location as a string
name	This is the name of the user

`profile_*`	This is the amount of profile-related information (refer the following list of profile-related attributes)
`protected`	This is the flag to indicate whether the user protects their tweets
`status`	This is an embedded object with the latest tweet (refer to `Chapter 2`, *#MiningTwitter – Hashtags, Topics, and Time Series*, for all available fields)
`screen_name`	This is the user's screen name, that is, the Twitter handle
`statuses_count`	This is the number of tweets
`time_zone`	This is the user-declared time zone string
`utc_offset`	This is the offset from GMT/UTC in seconds
`url`	This is the URL provided by the user to associate with the profile
`verified`	This is the flag to indicate whether the user is verified

The list of profile-related attributes are as follows:

- `profile_background_color`: This is the hexadecimal color code chosen by the user for their background
- `profile_background_tile`: This is the flag to indicate `profile_background_image_url` should be tiled when displayed
- `profile_link_color`: This is the hexadecimal color code chosen by the user to display links in the Twitter UI
- `profile_use_background_image`: This is the flag to indicate the user wants to use their uploaded background image
- `profile_background_image_url`: This is an HTTP-based URL pointing to the uploaded background image
- `profile_background_image_url_https`: This is same as the previous attribute, but based on HTTPS
- `profile_text_color`: This is the hexadecimal color code chosen by the user to display the text within their Twitter UI
- `profile_banner_url`: This is an HTTPS-based URL of the user's uploaded profile banner
- `profile_sidebar_fill_color`: This is the hexadecimal color code chosen by the user to display sidebar backgrounds within their Twitter UI

- profile_image_url: This is an HTTP-based URL of the user's avatar

- profile_image_url_https: This is same as the previous attribute, but based on HTTPS

- profile_sidebar_border_color: This is the hexadecimal color code chosen by the user to display sidebar borders with their Twitter UI

The following section will discuss how to download user profiles for friends and followers of a given user.

Downloading your friends' and followers' profiles

Given the discussion on the relevant endpoints in the previous section, we can create a script that takes a username (screen name) as input and downloads their complete profile, the list of followers (with complete profiles), and the list of friends (also with complete profiles):

```python
# Chap02-03/twitter_get_user.py
import os
import sys
import json
import time
import math
from tweepy import Cursor
from twitter_client import get_twitter_client

MAX_FRIENDS = 15000

def usage():
    print("Usage:")
    print("python {} <username>".format(sys.argv[0]))

def paginate(items, n):
    """Generate n-sized chunks from items"""
    for i in range(0, len(items), n):
        yield items[i:i+n]

if __name__ == '__main__':
    if len(sys.argv) != 2:
        usage()
        sys.exit(1)
    screen_name = sys.argv[1]
    client = get_twitter_client()
    dirname = "users/{}".format(screen_name)
```

```
max_pages = math.ceil(MAX_FRIENDS / 5000)
try:
  os.makedirs(dirname, mode=0o755, exist_ok=True)
except OSError:
  print("Directory {} already exists".format(dirname))
except Exception as e:
  print("Error while creating directory {}".format(dirname))
  print(e)
  sys.exit(1)

# get followers for a given user
fname = "users/{}/followers.jsonl".format(screen_name)
with open(fname, 'w') as f:
  for followers in Cursor(client.followers_ids,
                          screen_name=screen_name).pages(max_pages):
    for chunk in paginate(followers, 100):
      users = client.lookup_users(user_ids=chunk)
      for user in users:
        f.write(json.dumps(user._json)+"\n")
    if len(followers) == 5000:
      print("More results available. Sleeping for 60 seconds to
            avoid rate limit")
      time.sleep(60)

# get friends for a given user
fname = "users/{}/friends.jsonl".format(screen_name)
with open(fname, 'w') as f:
  for friends in Cursor(client.friends_ids,
                        screen_name=screen_name).pages(max_pages):
    for chunk in paginate(friends, 100):
      users = client.lookup_users(user_ids=chunk)
      for user in users:
        f.write(json.dumps(user._json)+"\n")
    if len(friends) == 5000:
      print("More results available. Sleeping for 60 seconds to
            avoid rate limit")
      time.sleep(60)

# get user's profile
fname = "users/{}/user_profile.json".format(screen_name)
with open(fname, 'w') as f:
  profile = client.get_user(screen_name=screen_name)
  f.write(json.dumps(profile._json, indent=4))
```

The script takes one argument from the command line, which is the screen name of the user you want to analyze. For example, the script can be run with the following command:

```
$ python twitter_get_user.py PacktPub
```

As PacktPub, at the time of this writing, has more than 10,000 followers, the script will take more than 2 minutes to run due to the restriction imposed by the API. As briefly described in `Chapter 2`, *#MiningTwitter – Hashtags, Topics, and Time Series*, this script uses `time.sleep()` to slow down the execution and avoid hitting the rate limits. The number of seconds passed to the `sleep()` function is dictated by the API.

Analysing your network

After downloading the data related to friends and followers of a given profile, we can start some exploratory analysis on the structure of the network created by these connections. *Figure 3.1* shows a fictitious example of a small network of users, with the links between users highlighted from a first-person point of view (that is, from the point of view of the user labeled **ME**, so we'll describe the picture in first person):

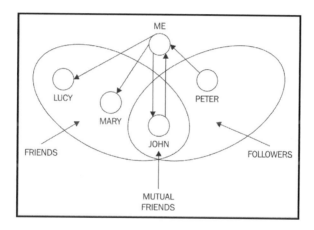

Figure 3.1: An example of your local network: friends, followers, and mutual friends

In this example, I'm connected to four different users: **PETER** and **JOHN** follow me (so they are labeled as **FOLLOWERS**), while I follow **LUCY**, **MARY**, and **JOHN** (so they are labeled as **FRIENDS**). **JOHN** belongs to both groups: the intersection between **FRIENDS** and **FOLLOWERS** is described as **MUTUAL FRIENDS**.

What we don't know from this representation is whether these four users also have connections between them. This is the nature of the data we have downloaded in the previous section: we have information about friends and followers of the given profile, but if we want to discover the connections among them, we need to iterate through all their profiles and download relevant data.

With this data, we have basic statistics on the number of followers and friends, and we can now answer the following basic questions:

- Who are my mutual friends?
- Who is not following me back?
- Whom am I not following back?

The following script reads the JSONL files previously downloaded and computes the statistics to answer these questions:

```python
# Chap02-03/twitter_followers_stats.py
import sys
import json

def usage():
  print("Usage:")
  print("python {} <username>".format(sys.argv[0]))

if __name__ == '__main__':
  if len(sys.argv) != 2:
    usage()
    sys.exit(1)
  screen_name = sys.argv[1]
  followers_file = 'users/{}/followers.jsonl'.format(screen_name)
  friends_file = 'users/{}/friends.jsonl'.format(screen_name)
  with open(followers_file) as f1, open(friends_file) as f2:
    followers = []
    friends = []
    for line in f1:
      profile = json.loads(line)
      followers.append(profile['screen_name'])
    for line in f2:
      profile = json.loads(line)
      friends.append(profile['screen_name'])
    mutual_friends = [user for user in friends
                      if user in followers]
    followers_not_following = [user for user in followers
                               if user not in friends]
    friends_not_following = [user for user in friends
                             if user not in followers]

    print("{} has {} followers".format(screen_name,
          len(followers)))
    print("{} has {} friends".format(screen_name, len(friends)))
    print("{} has {} mutual friends".format(screen_name,
          len(mutual_friends)))
    print("{} friends are not following {}
```

```
      back".format(len(friends_not_following), screen_name))
  print("{} followers are not followed back by
      {}".format(len(followers_not_following), screen_name))
```

The script takes a username as the command-line argument, so you can run it with, for example, the following command:

```
$ python twitter_followers_stats.py PacktPub
```

This will produce the following output:

```
PacktPub has 10209 followers
PacktPub has 3583 friends
PacktPub has 2180 mutual friends
1403 friends are not following PacktPub back
8029 followers are not followed back by PacktPub
```

The data type used to handle friends and followers is a regular Python `list()`, filled in with usernames (`screen_name`, to be precise). The code reads the two JSONL files, adding the screen names to the respective lists. Three list comprehensions are then used to build different statistics.

List comprehension in Python

Python supports a concept called list comprehension, an elegant way to transform one list (or any iterable) into another list. During this process, elements can be conditionally included and transformed by a custom function, for example:

```
>>> numbers = [1, 2, 3, 4, 5]
>>> squares = [x*x for x in numbers]
>>> squares
[1, 4, 9, 16, 25]
```

The preceding list comprehension is equivalent to the following code:

```
>>> squares = []
>>> for x in numbers:
...     squares.append(x*x)
...
>>> squares
[1, 4, 9, 16, 25]
```

A nice aspect of list comprehensions is that they can also be read in plain English, so the code is particularly readable.

Comprehensions are not limited to only lists, in fact, they can be also used to build dictionaries.

There are a couple of considerations about this aspect of implementation. Firstly, the JSONL files will contain unique profiles: each follower (or friend) will be listed only once, so we don't have duplicate entries. Secondly, when computing the preceding statistics, the order of the items is irrelevant. In fact, all we are doing is computing set-based operations (intersection and difference in this example).

We can refactor our code to implement the basic statistics using `set()`; the changes in the script are related to how we can load the data and calculate mutual friends, friends who are not following back, and followers not followed back:

```
with open(followers_file) as f1, open(friends_file) as f2:
  followers = set()
  friends = set()
  for line in f1:
    profile = json.loads(line)
    followers.add(profile['screen_name'])
  for line in f2:
    profile = json.loads(line)
    friends.add(profile['screen_name'])
  mutual_friends = friends.intersection(followers)
  followers_not_following = followers.difference(friends)
  friends_not_following = friends.difference(followers)
```

This will produce the same output as the code using lists. The main advantage of using sets rather than lists is the computational complexity: operations such as containment (that is, a check for `item in list` or `item in set`) run in linear time for lists and in constant time for sets. Containment is used to build `mutual_friends`, `followers_not_following`, and `friends_not_following`, so this simple change will affect the total runtime of the script in a noticeable way, and with a higher number of followers/friends this difference is even clearer due to the linear complexity needed for lists.

Computational complexity

The preceding section used phrases such as *linear time*, *constant time*, and *linear complexity*. The concept of computational complexity is an important one in computer science, as it regards the amount of resources required by an algorithm to run. In this paragraph, we will discuss time complexity and the amount of time taken by an algorithm to run, described as a function of the size of its input.

When an algorithm runs in linear time, for large input size, its running time increases linearly with the size of the input. The mathematical notation (called the Big O notation) to describe this class of algorithm is $O(n)$, where n is the size of the input.

For algorithms that run in constant time instead, the size of the input does not affect the running time. The notation used in this case is O(1). In general, understanding the complexity of different operations and data structure is the key step when developing non-trivial programs, as this can have a huge impact on the performances of our system.

At this point, the reader might be curious about the use of libraries such as NumPy. As already discussed in Chapter 1, *Social Media, Social Data, and Python*, NumPy offers fast and efficient processing for array-like data structures and provides significant performance improvements over simple lists. Despite being optimized for speed, using NumPy in this specific case wouldn't yield any particular benefit in terms of performance, simply because the computational cost of the containment operation would be the same as the one for lists. Refactoring the previous code to employ NumPy produces the following code:

```
with open(followers_file) as f1, open(friends_file) as f2:
    followers = []
    friends = []
    for line in f1:
        profile = json.loads(line)
        followers.append(profile['screen_name'])
    for line in f2:
        profile = json.loads(line)
        friends.append(profile['screen_name'])
    followers = np.array(followers)
    friends = np.array(friends)
    mutual_friends = np.intersect1d(friends,
                                    followers,
                                    assume_unique=True)
    followers_not_following = np.setdiff1d(followers,
                                           friends,
                                           assume_unique=True)
    friends_not_following = np.setdiff1d(friends,
                                         followers,
                                         assume_unique=True)
```

This snippet assumes that NumPy has been imported with the alias np as discussed in Chapter 1, *Social Media, Social Data, and Python*. The library offers some set-like operations- intersect1d and setdiff1d-but the underlying data structure is still an array-like object (like a list). The third argument for these functions, assume_unique, can be used with the assumption that input arrays have unique elements, as in our case. This can help speeding up the calculation, but the bottom line remains the same: with more than hundreds of followers/friends, sets will be faster when performing these operations. The differences in performance will not be noticeable for a small number of followers/friends.

The source code provided with this book offers the three different implementations coded in `twitter_followers_stats.py`, `twitter_followers_stats_set.py`, and `twitter_followers_stats_numpy.py`, which include some timing calculations so that you can experiment with different data.

 To conclude this refactoring interlude, the main message is to choose the most appropriate data structure for the type of operation you're dealing with.

Measuring influence and engagement

One of the most commonly mentioned characters in the social media arena is the mythical *Influencer*. This figure is responsible for a paradigm shift in recent marketing strategies (`htt ps://en.wikipedia.org/wiki/Influencer_marketing`), which focus on targeting key individuals rather than the market as a whole.

Influencers are typically active users within their community; in the case of Twitter, an influencer tweets a lot about topics they care about. Influencers are well connected as they follow and are followed by many other users who are also involved in the community. In general, an influencer is also regarded as an expert in their area and is typically trusted by other users.

This description should explain why influencers are an important part of recent trends in marketing-an influencer can increase awareness or even become an advocate of a specific product or brand and can reach a vast number of supporters.

Whether your main interest is Python programming or wine tasting, regardless how huge (or small) your social network is, you probably already have an idea of who the influencers in your social circles are: a friend, acquaintance, or random stranger on the Internet whose opinion you trust and value because of their expertise in the given subject.

A different, but somehow related, concept is *engagement*. User engagement, or customer engagement, is the assessment of the response to a particular offer, such as a product or service. In the context to the social media, pieces of content are often created with the purpose to drive traffic towards the company website or e-commerce. Measuring engagement is important as it helps in defining and understanding strategies to maximize the interactions with your network, and ultimately bring business. On Twitter, users engage by the means of retweeting or liking a particular tweet, which provides more visibility to the tweet in return.

In this section, we'll discuss some interesting aspects of social media analysis regarding the possibility of measuring influence and engagement. On Twitter, a natural thought would be to associate influence with the number of users in a particular network. Intuitively, a high number of followers means that a user can reach more people, but it doesn't tell us how a tweet is perceived.

The following script compares some statistics for two user profiles:

```python
# Chap02-03/twitter_influence.py
import sys
import json

def usage():
  print("Usage:")
  print("python {} <username1> <username2>".format(sys.argv[0]))

if __name__ == '__main__':
  if len(sys.argv) != 3:
    usage()
    sys.exit(1)
  screen_name1 = sys.argv[1]
  screen_name2 = sys.argv[2]
```

After reading the two screen names from the command line, we will build up a list of followers for each of them, including the number of followers, to calculate the number of reachable users:

```python
followers_file1 = 'users/{}/followers.jsonl'.format(screen_name1)
followers_file2 = 'users/{}/followers.jsonl'.format(screen_name2)
with open(followers_file1) as f1, open(followers_file2) as f2:
  reach1 = []
  reach2 = []
  for line in f1:
    profile = json.loads(line)
    reach1.append((profile['screen_name'],
              profile['followers_count']))
  for line in f2:
    profile = json.loads(line)
    reach2.append((profile['screen_name'],
              profile['followers_count']))
```

We will then load some basic statistics (followers count and statuses count) from the two user profiles:

```python
profile_file1 = 'users/{}/user_profile.json'.format(screen_name1)
profile_file2 = 'users/{}/user_profile.json'.format(screen_name2)
with open(profile_file1) as f1, open(profile_file2) as f2:
```

```
    profile1 = json.load(f1)
    profile2 = json.load(f2)
    followers1 = profile1['followers_count']
    followers2 = profile2['followers_count']
    tweets1 = profile1['statuses_count']
    tweets2 = profile2['statuses_count']

sum_reach1 = sum([x[1] for x in reach1])
sum_reach2 = sum([x[1] for x in reach2])
avg_followers1 = round(sum_reach1 / followers1, 2)
avg_followers2 = round(sum_reach2 / followers2, 2)
```

Then we will load the timelines for the two users to observe the number of times their tweets have been favorited or retweeted:

```
timeline_file1 = 'user_timeline_{}.jsonl'.format(screen_name1)
timeline_file2 = 'user_timeline_{}.jsonl'.format(screen_name2)
with open(timeline_file1) as f1, open(timeline_file2) as f2:
  favorite_count1, retweet_count1 = [], []
  favorite_count2, retweet_count2 = [], []
  for line in f1:
    tweet = json.loads(line)
    favorite_count1.append(tweet['favorite_count'])
    retweet_count1.append(tweet['retweet_count'])
  for line in f2:
    tweet = json.loads(line)
    favorite_count2.append(tweet['favorite_count'])
    retweet_count2.append(tweet['retweet_count'])
```

The preceding numbers are then aggregated into the average number of favorites and retweets, both in absolute terms and per number of followers:

```
avg_favorite1 = round(sum(favorite_count1) / tweets1, 2)
avg_favorite2 = round(sum(favorite_count2) / tweets2, 2)
avg_retweet1 = round(sum(retweet_count1) / tweets1, 2)
avg_retweet2 = round(sum(retweet_count2) / tweets2, 2)
favorite_per_user1 = round(sum(favorite_count1) / followers1, 2)
favorite_per_user2 = round(sum(favorite_count2) / followers2, 2)
retweet_per_user1 = round(sum(retweet_count1) / followers1, 2)
retweet_per_user2 = round(sum(retweet_count2) / followers2, 2)
print("----- Stats {} -----".format(screen_name1))
print("{} followers".format(followers1))
print("{} users reached by 1-degree
      connections".format(sum_reach1))
print("Average number of followers for {}'s followers:
      {}".format(screen_name1, avg_followers1))
print("Favorited {} times ({} per tweet, {} per
      user)".format(sum(favorite_count1), avg_favorite1,
```

```
        favorite_per_user1))
    print("Retweeted {} times ({} per tweet, {} per
        user)".format(sum(retweet_count1), avg_retweet1,
        retweet_per_user1))
    print("----- Stats {} -----".format(screen_name2))
    print("{} followers".format(followers2))
    print("{} users reached by 1-degree
        connections".format(sum_reach2))
    print("Average number of followers for {}'s followers:
        {}".format(screen_name2, avg_followers2))
    print("Favorited {} times ({} per tweet, {} per
        user)".format(sum(favorite_count2), avg_favorite2,
        favorite_per_user2))
    print("Retweeted {} times ({} per tweet, {} per
        user)".format(sum(retweet_count2), avg_retweet2,
        retweet_per_user2))
```

This script takes two arguments from the command line and assumes that the data has already been downloaded. For both users, we need the data about followers (downloaded with `twitter_get_user.py`) and their respective user timelines (downloaded with `twitter_get_user_timeline.py` from `Chapter 2`, *#MiningTwitter – Hashtags, Topics, and Time Series*).

The script is somehow verbose as it computes the same operations for two profiles and prints everything on the terminal. We can break it down into different parts.

Firstly, we will look into the followers' followers. This will provide some information related to the part of the network immediately connected to the given user. In other words, it should answer the question: how many users can I reach if all my followers retweet me? We will achieve this by reading the `users/<user>/followers.jsonl` file and keeping a list of tuples, where each tuple represents one of the followers and is in the `(screen_name, followers_count)` form. Keeping the screen name at this stage is useful in case we want to find out who the users with the highest number of followers are (not computed in the script, but easy to produce using `sorted()`).

In the second step, we will read the user profile from the `users/<user>/user_profile.json` file so that we can get the information about the total number of followers and tweets. With the data collected so far, we can compute the total number of users who are reachable within one degree of separation (follower of a follower) and the average number of followers of a follower. This is achieved via the following lines:

```
sum_reach1 = sum([x[1] for x in reach1])
avg_followers1 = round(sum_reach1 / followers1, 2)
```

The first one uses a list comprehension to iterate through the list of tuples mentioned earlier, while the second one is a simple arithmetic average, rounded up to two decimal points.

The third part of the script reads the user timeline from the `user_timeline_<user>.jsonl` file produced in Chapter 2, *#MiningTwitter – Hashtags, Topics, and Time Series*, and collects information about the number of retweets and favorite for each tweet. Putting everything together allows us to calculate the number of times a user has been retweeted or favorited and the average number of retweets/favorites per tweet and per follower.

To provide an example, I'll perform some vanity analysis and compare my `@marcobonzanini` account with Packt Publishing:

```
$ python twitter_influence.py marcobonzanini PacktPub
```

The script produces the following output:

```
----- Stats marcobonzanini -----
282 followers
1411136 users reached by 1-degree connections
Average number of followers for marcobonzanini's followers: 5004.03
Favorited 268 times (1.47 per tweet, 0.95 per user)
Retweeted 912 times (5.01 per tweet, 3.23 per user)
----- Stats PacktPub -----
10209 followers
29961760 users reached by 1-degree connections
Average number of followers for PacktPub's followers: 2934.84
Favorited 3554 times (0.33 per tweet, 0.35 per user)
Retweeted 6434 times (0.6 per tweet, 0.63 per user)
```

As you can see, the raw number of followers shows no contest, with Packt Publishing having approximatively 35 times more followers than me. The interesting part of this analysis comes up when we compare the average number of retweets and favorites; apparently, my followers are much more engaged with my content than PacktPub's. Is this enough to declare than I'm an influencer while PacktPub is not? Clearly not. What we observe here is a natural consequence of the fact that my tweets are probably more focused on specific topics (Python and data science), hence my followers are already more interested in what I'm publishing. On the other hand, the content produced by Packt Publishing is highly diverse as it ranges across many different technologies. This diversity is also reflected in PacktPub's followers, who include developers, designers, scientists, system administrators, and so on. For this reason, each of PacktPub's tweet is found interesting (that is, worth retweeting) by a smaller proportion of their followers.

Mining your followers

In the real world, a social community is a group of people who share some common conditions. This broad definition includes, for example, communities of people located in a precise geographical area, people with the same political or religious belief, or people sharing a specific interest, such as reading books.

The concept of social communities is also central to social media platforms. The boundaries of a community in a virtual environment can be more blurred than in the real world as, for example, the geographical aspect is less determinant. Just like in a face-to-face situation, a community naturally appears on a social media platform when people with common interest or condition start to interact.

We can make the first distinction between different types of communities depending on whether their members explicitly understand being part of it. In *explicit* communities, members and non-members know exactly whether they belong to the community or not, and usually understand who the other community members are. Interactions between members of the community are more frequent than with non-members.

On the other hand, *implicit* communities come into existence without being explicitly acknowledged. Members of this type of community might share common interests without having clear and strong connections.

This section proposes to analyze user data in order to segment a bunch of user profiles into groups with the purpose of highlighting what these common interests or conditions are.

Clustering, or cluster analysis, is a machine learning technique used to group items in such a way that objects within the same group (that is, *cluster*) are more similar to each other than to objects in other clusters. Clustering belongs to the category of *unsupervised learning* techniques, meaning that the objects we are dealing with are not explicitly labeled. The purpose of unsupervised learning is to discover hidden structures in data.

A common example of an application of clustering is market research, for example, to segment a population of customers with similar behaviors/interests so that they can be targeted with different products or marketing campaigns. Social network analysis is another important field where clustering finds interesting applications as it can be used to recognize the structure of a community within a larger group of people.

Clustering is not just a specific algorithm, but rather a general task that can be approached by different algorithms. The one that we choose for our analysis is **K-Means**, one of the most popular approaches for clustering. K-Means is a convenient choice as it's relatively simple to understand and implement, as well as computationally efficient when compared to other clustering approaches.

K-Means takes essentially two arguments: a number of input vectors in n-dimensional space, which represent the objects we want to cluster, and K as the number of clusters we want to partition our inputs into. As we are in an unsupervised learning setting, we do not have any ground truth information regarding the correct category labels. To be more specific, we don't even know the correct (or ideal) number of clusters. This detail is quite central in cluster analysis, but for the time being, we won't worry too much about it.

The previous paragraph defined the objects that we want to cluster as vectors in the n-dimensional space. In simpler words, this means that each user profile is going to be represented as a vector of n numerical elements called *features*.

The approach we choose to define these features is based on the users' description, that is, the textual information they provide about their interests or occupation. The process of transforming this textual description into a vector of features is called vectorization. Both the K-Means algorithm and the tools for vectorization are implemented with a straightforward interface in scikit-learn, the machine learning toolkit for Python, which was already introduced in `Chapter 1`, *Social Media, Social Data, and Python*.

The vectorization process involves breaking down the user description into tokens and then assigning a particular *weight* to each token. The weighting scheme adopted in this example is the common TF-IDF approach (`https://en.wikipedia.org/wiki/Tf%E2%80%93idf`), which is the combination of **Term Frequency (TF)** and **Inverse Document Frequency (IDF)**. TF is a local statistic as it represent how often a word appears in a document. On the other hand, IDF is a global statistic-it represents how rare a word is across a collection of documents. These statistics, commonly used in search engines and different text mining applications, provide a measure of how important a word is in a given context.

TF-IDF provides a numerical weight behind a simple intuition; if a word is frequent in a document, and rare across the collection, it is probably very representative of this particular document, so it deserves a higher weight. In this application, we are basically treating user descriptions as documents, and we use TF-IDF statistics to represent these user descriptions as vectors. Once we have the n-dimensional vector representation, the K-Means algorithm can use it to calculate the similarity between them.

The following script takes advantage of the facilities offered by scikit-learn, in particular the TfidfVectorizer and KMeans class:

```
# Chap02-03/twitter_cluster_users.py
import sys
import json
from argparse import ArgumentParser
from collections import defaultdict
from sklearn.feature_extraction.text import TfidfVectorizer
from sklearn.cluster import KMeans

def get_parser():
    parser = ArgumentParser("Clustering of followers")
    parser.add_argument('--filename')
    parser.add_argument('--k', type=int)
    parser.add_argument('--min-df', type=int, default=2)
    parser.add_argument('--max-df', type=float, default=0.8)
    parser.add_argument('--max-features', type=int, default=None)
    parser.add_argument('--no-idf', dest='use_idf', default=True,
                        action='store_false')
    parser.add_argument('--min-ngram', type=int, default=1)
    parser.add_argument('--max-ngram', type=int, default=1)
    return parser

if __name__ == '__main__':
    parser = get_parser()
    args = parser.parse_args()
    if args.min_ngram > args.max_ngram:
        print("Error: incorrect value for --min-ngram ({}): it can't
              be higher than --max-value ({})".format(args.min_ngram,
              args.max_ngram))
        sys.exit(1)
    with open(args.filename) as f:
        # load data
        users = []
        for line in f:
            profile = json.loads(line)
            users.append(profile['description'])
        # create vectorizer
        vectorizer = TfidfVectorizer(max_df=args.max_df,
                                     min_df=args.min_df,
                                     max_features=args.max_features,
                                     stop_words='english',
                                     ngram_range=(args.min_ngram,
                                                  args.max_ngram),
                                     use_idf=args.use_idf)
        # fit data
        X = vectorizer.fit_transform(users)
```

```
print("Data dimensions: {}".format(X.shape))
# perform clustering
km = KMeans(n_clusters=args.k)
km.fit(X)
clusters = defaultdict(list)
for i, label in enumerate(km.labels_):
  clusters[label].append(users[i])
# print 10 user description for this cluster
for label, descriptions in clusters.items():
  print('---------- Cluster {}'.format(label+1))
  for desc in descriptions[:10]:
    print(desc)
```

As `TfidfVectorizer` has a number of option to configure the way the vectors are calculated, we will use `ArgumentParser`, part of the Python standard library, to capture these options from the command line. The `get_parser()` function defines the arguments, as follows:

- `--filename`: This is the path to the JSONL filename that we want to analyze
- `--k`: This is the number of clusters
- `--min-df`: This is the minimum document frequency for a feature (the default is 2)
- `--max-df`: This is the maximum document frequency for a feature (the default is 0.8)
- `--max-features`: This is the maximum number of features (the default is None)
- `--no-idf`: This flags whether we want to switch the IDF weight off using only TF (IDF is used by default)
- `--min-ngram`: This is the lower boundary for n-grams to be extracted (the default is 1)
- `--max-ngram`: This is the upper boundary for n-grams to be extracted (the default is 1)

For example, we can run the script with the following command:

```
$ python twitter_cluster_users.py \
  --filename users/marcobonzanini/followers.jsonl \
  --k 5 \
  --max-features 200 \
  --max-ngram 3
```

The only arguments that are mandatory are `--filename` to specify the filename with the profiles to analyze and `--k` to specify the number of cluster. All other parameters are optional and define how `TfidfVectorizer` will create the vectors for `KMeans`.

We can limit the number of features being extracted by `TfidfVectorizer` either explicitly using `--max-features` or specifying the desired range for the document frequency of a feature with `--min-df` and `--max-df`. The minimum document frequency is set to 2 by default, meaning that features that appear in less than two documents will be ignored. On the other hand, the maximum document frequency for a feature is set to `0.8`, meaning that features appearing in more than 80% of the documents will be ignored. Depending on the size of our dataset, we can decide to be more or less conservative with these values. The purpose of excluding features based on their document frequency is to avoid calculations for features that are not representative of the task. Moreover, limiting the total number of features with `--max-features` is also meant to speed up the computing as the input is smaller. When this option is specified, the most frequent features (depending on their document frequency) are chosen.

Different from the other arguments, the `--no-idf` option is not used to specify a particular value, but rather to switch off the use of IDF (meaning that only TF would be considered when computing the feature weights). The argument parser allows us to specify how this argument behaves by providing a variable name as the destination (`dest=use_idf`) and the action to perform when the argument is given: `store_false`, while the variable defaults to `True` if the argument is not provided. IDF is normally used to scale down the weight of terms that are very common across a collection of documents, and hence don't have any particular discriminative power. While, in many applications, it makes perfect sense to adopt IDF in your weighting function, during the exploratory data analysis steps, it's still important to observe its effect and hence the option to switch it off is simply an extra tool in our box.

The last two arguments allow us to go beyond individual words and use *n-grams* as features. Generally speaking, an n-gram is a contiguous sequence of *n* items. In our application, we have a piece of text that is tokenized into a sequence of words. Individual words are also called *unigrams* (n-grams with n = 1). Other commonly used n-grams are bigrams (n = 2) and trigrams (n = 3), while larger sizes can be used depending on the application. For example, given the sentence *the quick brown fox jumped over the lazy dog*, its bigrams are defined as follows: *the quick, quick brown, brown fox, fox jumped,* and so on.

The benefit of using n-grams rather than just unigrams is the possibility of capturing phrases. Consider the following fictitious sentences for example:

- He's a scientist, but he doesn't like data
- He works as a data scientist

By only using unigrams, the terms *data* and *scientists* would be captured in both lines even though they are used in different ways, while with bigrams, we can capture the phrase *data scientist*, which provides a different meaning compared to the two words individually. By default, the lower and upper boundaries for n-grams are set to 1, meaning that we are using only unigrams if not specified differently.

To conclude this description of how `TfidfVectorizer` is configured, we will notice that it also used the `stop_words` argument defined to capture stop words from the English vocabulary. This is a list of common English words such as *the* and *and*, which do not carry particular meaning per se and are probably used in almost every piece of text. While in common English, stop words would probably already be filtered out by the `max_df` options (as their document frequency would be close to 100%), users on Twitter often don't use fluent regular English, but just a list of keywords representing their interests to overcome the limitations with number of characters. `TfidfVectorizer` also allows the `stop_words` attribute to take a custom list of words in case we want to personalize it.

Running the code as described earlier will output some interesting result. For brevity, the output is partially reproduced as shown in *Figure 3.2*:

```
# ---------- Cluster 0
PhD Student #FutureOfNews, #TextMining, Topic Detection & Tracking,
Summarization, Information Retrieval, mostly with Breaking News
Data
PhD candidate - How and what can search engines learn from their
users?
PhD candidate. Information Retrieval. Data Mining. Open Source.
PhD Candidate | Semantic Search in eDiscovery | Information
Retrieval, Text Mining
# ---------- Cluster 1
Co-fundador de Viz Analytics. Diplomado en Ingeniería Informatica
de Gestión y con un Master Universitario en Inteligencia
Artificial.
Lenguas, comunicación y nuevos medios. No tuitear en caso de
incendio.
Lic. en Administración mención informática, promotor del software
libre y las oportunidades que brinda.
# ---------- Cluster 2
I am part time web-developer and I love python
boiling down to Python and Infosec nowadays. Any advices?
Python Padawan, Django noob.
Sherlock of #Data, Love #machinelearning #python
# ---------- Cluster 3
Data Scientist
Data scientist in the making
Data scientist, interested in text analysis, social networks,
artificial and natural intelligence, data, complexity, illusions...
Data Scientist
Wanna be a Data Scientist: using data for good
```

Figure 3.2: Partial output

The output has been shortened for brevity and to highlight the interesting behavior of the K-Means algorithm.

In the first cluster of followers, there's a bunch of academics and PhD students whose work is mainly in text analytics and information retrieval. Finding, for example, both the phrases `PhD candidate` and `Information Retrieval` in two profile descriptions is a strong piece of evidence for user similarity.

The second cluster is composed of Spanish-speaking users. Both K-Means and `TfidfVectorizer` don't have any explicit knowledge about multiple languages. The only linguistic aspect is the use of stop word-removal for common English words. Is K-Means smart enough to recognize a language and use this information as evidence to group these users together? Keep in mind that the vectors we are building are based on a bag-of-words representation (or bag-of-n-grams, to be precise), so the similarity is simply based on word and n-gram overlap. Not being Spanish speakers, we can spot a few words (for example, `en`, `y`, and `de`) that are common between the different profiles. These keywords are probably quite rare across the collection of followers (who are mainly English speaking), so their importance is reflected in a high IDF value. They also happen to be Spanish stop words, but as the stop word list is explicitly designed for English, they are kept as vector features. Besides the language, the connection between these profiles might be quite loose. While the first and third ones mention some computer science-related terms, the second one says *Languages, communication and new media. Don't tweet in case of fire.* The link with the other profiles is quite vague, but this is an interesting result nevertheless.

The third and fourth clusters, just like the first one, are self-explanatory and nicely consistent: cluster 3 is mainly composed of Python developers, while cluster 4 is composed of data scientists.

As the initialization of K-Means has a random component, rerunning the code with exactly the same parameters doesn't guarantee to always obtain the same results. The interested reader is encouraged to play with different values for the script parameters (for example, more or less features, just unigrams versus longer n-grams, narrow versus wide range of document frequency, and so on) and observe how these influence the behavior of the algorithm.

At the beginning of our discussion about K-Means, we mentioned how the number of clusters K is the main input of this algorithm together with the data. Finding the optimal K for a given dataset is a research problem per se, and it's different from how to perform the actual clustering. There's a variety of methodologies that one could employ to achieve this purpose (refer to `https://en.wikipedia.org/wiki/Determining_the_number_of_clusters_in_a_data_set`).

The simplest approach is the rule of thumb, which consists of setting K as the square root of the $n/2$ ratio, where n is the number of objects in the dataset. Different approaches involve some measure of the within-cluster coherence, for example, the Elbow method or Silhouette.

Mining the conversation

After focusing on user profiles and how they are explicitly connected via follower/friend relationships, in this section, we will analyze a different type of interaction-the conversation. On Twitter, users can publish a tweet *in reply to* a particular piece of content. When two or more users follow up with this process, a proper conversation can unfold.

Figure 3.3 shows a conversation represented as a network. Each node of the network is a tweet (uniquely identified by its ID) and each edge represents a *reply to* relationship.

This type of relationship has an explicit direction as it can only go in one way (parent-child relationship). For example, if tweet 2 is a reply to tweet 1, we cannot see tweet 1 being a reply to tweet 2. The cardinality of this relationship is always one, meaning that a given tweet can be a reply to one and only one tweet (but we can have multiple tweets in reply to a given one, making the relationship a one-to-many). Moreover, cycles are not allowed (for example, the sequence of relationships 1 to 2, 2 to 3, 3 to 1 would not be possible). For these reasons, the graph that we are representing falls under the category of directed acyclic graphs or DAG (https://en.wikipedia.org/wiki/Directed_acyclic_graph). More precisely, the type of graph that we are representing here is often referred to as *directed tree*:

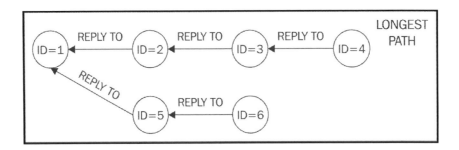

Figure 3.3: An example of conversation represented as a network

While not explicitly described in the figure, we notice that the relationship is time-bound: you can reply to a tweet only if the tweet has been already published.

By describing tweets and replies as a graph, we can use the properties of the graph and algorithms from graph theory to mine the conversation.

For example, the *degree* of a node is the number of nodes in the graph that are the children of the given node. From the point of view of the conversation, the degree of a node corresponds to the number of replies that the node received. In the example of Figure 3.3, node 1 has two nodes directly connected to it, so its degree is two. Nodes 2, 3, and 5 all have a single node connected to them individually, so their degree is one. Finally, nodes 4 and 6 have no node connected to them, so their degree is zero. Nodes 4 and 6 are also called *leaves* of the tree and represent a dead end in the conversation. On the other hand, the beginning of the conversation, node 1, is also called the *root* of the tree.

A fundamental notion in graph theory is the concept of *path*, which is a sequence of edges that connect a sequence of distinct vertices. Given a graph representation of a sequence of tweet, finding a path is the equivalent of following a conversation. An interesting problem is finding the path of maximum length, also called longest path.

In order to apply these graph concepts to our Twitter data, we can employ the **NetworkX** library, already introduced in `Chapter 1`, *Social Media, Social Data, and Python*, as it provides efficient computation of graph structures, as well as a straightforward interface. The following script takes a JSONL file of tweets as input and produces a directed graph as we just discussed:

```
# Chap02-03/twitter_conversation.py
import sys
import json
from operator import itemgetter
import networkx as nx

def usage():
  print("Usage:")
  print("python {} <filename>".format(sys.argv[0]))

if __name__ == '__main__':
  if len(sys.argv) != 2:
    usage()
    sys.exit(1)
  fname = sys.argv[1]
  with open(fname) as f:
    graph = nx.DiGraph()
    for line in f:
      tweet = json.loads(line)
```

```
      if 'id' in tweet:
        graph.add_node(tweet['id'],
                       tweet=tweet['text'],
                       author=tweet['user']['screen_name'],
                       created_at=tweet['created_at'])
      if tweet['in_reply_to_status_id']:
        reply_to = tweet['in_reply_to_status_id']
        if reply_to in graph \
        and tweet['user']['screen_name'] !=
          graph.node[reply_to]['author']:
          graph.add_edge(tweet['in_reply_to_status_id'],
                         tweet['id'])
# Print some basic stats
print(nx.info(graph))
# Find most replied tweet
sorted_replied = sorted(graph.degree_iter(),
                        key=itemgetter(1),
                        reverse=True)
most_replied_id, replies = sorted_replied[0]
print("Most replied tweet ({} replies):".format(replies))
print(graph.node[most_replied_id])
# Find longest conversation
print("Longest discussion:")
longest_path = nx.dag_longest_path(graph)
for tweet_id in longest_path:
  node = graph.node[tweet_id]
  print("{} (by {} at {})".format(node['tweet'],
                                  node['author'],
                                  node['created_at']))
```

The script can be run as follows:

```
$ python twitter_conversation.py <filename>
```

In this script, we will import NetworkX with an alias, `nx`, as discussed in `Chapter 1`, *Social Media, Social Data, and Python*. We will initialize an empty directed graph, which is implemented with the `nx.DiGraph` class. Each line of the input JSONL file represents a single tweet, so we will loop through this file adding one node for each tweet. The `add_node()` function used for this purpose takes one mandatory argument, which is the node ID, followed by the number of optional keyword arguments to provide additional attributes to the node. In our case, we will include the author's screen name, full text of the tweet, and creation timestamp.

After the node creation, we will check whether the tweet was posted in reply to another tweet; if that's the case, we may want to add an edge between the nodes. Before adding the edge, we will first confirm that the tweet being replied to already exists in the graph. This is to avoid including replies to tweets that are not in our dataset (for example, tweets published before we started collecting data with the Streaming API). If the node we're trying to connect to doesn't exist in the graph, the add_edge() function can add it, but we wouldn't have any information about its attributes besides the ID. We also check whether the author of the tweet and the author of its reply are different persons. This is because the Twitter UI automatically groups tweets that are part of a conversation, but some users who are, for example, commenting on a live event or simply writing a comment longer than 140 characters simply reply to their own tweets to easily create a multi-tweet thread. While this can be a nice feature, it's not really a conversation (in fact, it's quite the opposite), so we decide to ignore this kind of thread. If you are interested in finding monologues, you can modify the code to perform the opposite: only adding edges when the author of a tweet and the author of its replies are the same person.

After building the graph, we will first print some basic statistics, which are provided by the nx.info() function. Then we will identify the tweet with the highest number of replies (that is, the node with the highest degree) and the longest conversation (that is, the longest path).

As the degree_iter() function returns an iterator for a sequence of (node, degree) tuples, we will use itemgetter() to sort it according to the degree in reverse order. The first item of the sorted list is the tweet with most replies.

The solution to find the longest conversation is implemented in the dag_longest_path() function, which returns a list of node IDs. To rebuild the conversation, we simply need to iterate through these IDs and print out the data.

The script run with the `stream__RWC2015__RWCFinal_Rugby.jsonl` file created in `Chapter 2`, *#Mining Twitter – Hashtags, Topics, and Time Series*, produces the following output (the output of the longest conversation is omitted for brevity):

```
Name:
Type: DiGraph
Number of nodes: 198004
Number of edges: 1440
Average in degree:   0.0073
Average out degree:   0.0073
Most replied tweet (15 replies):
{'author': 'AllBlacks', 'tweet': 'Get ready for live scoring here, starting
shortly. You ready #AllBlacks fans? #NZLvAUS #TeamAllBlacks #RWC2015',
'created_at': 'Sat Oct 31 15:49:22 +0000 2015'}
Longest discussion:
# ...
```

As you can see, the number of tweets is much higher than the number of edges. This is caused due to many tweets being unconnected to other tweets, that is, only a small portion of tweets are sent in reply to other tweets. This can, of course, vary depending on the data and whether we decide to also include self-replies and older tweets (that is, tweets that have been replied to, but are not in our dataset).

Plotting tweets on a map

This section discusses the visual representation of tweets using maps. Data visualizations are a nice way to provide an easy-to-digest overview of the data as a picture can provide a summary of a particular feature of a dataset.

In a small portion of tweets, we can find details about the geographic localization of the user's device in the form of geographic coordinates. While many users disable this functionality on their mobile, there is still an interesting opportunity in terms of data mining to understand how the tweets are geographically distributed.

This section introduces GeoJSON, a common data format for geographic data structures and the process of building interactive maps of our tweets.

From tweets to GeoJSON

GeoJSON (`http://geojson.org`) is a JSON-based format for encoding geographic data structures. A GeoJSON object can represent a geometry, feature, or collection of features. Geometries only contain the information about the shape; its examples include Point, LineString, Polygon, and more complex shapes. Features extend this concept as they contain a geometry plus additional (custom) properties. Finally, a collection of features is simply a list of features.

A GeoJSON data structure is always a JSON object. The following snippet shows an example of GeoJSON that represents a collection with two different points, each point used to pin a particular city:

```
{
  "type": "FeatureCollection",
  "features": [
    {
      "type": "Feature",
      "geometry": {
        "type": "Point",
        "coordinates": [
          -0.12
          51.5
        ]
      },
      "properties": {
        "name": "London"
      }
    },
    {
      "type": "Feature",
      "geometry": {
        "type": "Point",
        "coordinates": [
          -74,
          40.71
        ]
      },
      "properties": {
        "name": "New York City"
      }
    }
  ]
}
```

In this GeoJSON object, the first key is the `type` of object being represented. This field is mandatory and its value must be one of the following:

- `Point`: This is used to represent a single position
- `MultiPoint`: This represents multiple positions
- `LineString`: This specifies a string of lines that go through two or more positions
- `MultiLineString`: This is equivalent to multiple strings of lines
- `Polygon`: This represents a closed string of lines, that is, the first and the last positions are the same
- `GeometryCollection`: This is a list of different geometries
- `Feature`: This is one of the preceding items (excluding `GeometryCollection`) with additional custom properties
- `FeatureCollection`: This is used to represent a list of features

Given that `type` in the preceding example has the `FeatureCollection` value, we will expect the `features` field to be a list of objects (each of which is a `Feature`).

The two features shown in the example are simple points, so in both cases, the `coordinates` field is an array of two elements: longitude and latitude. This field also allows for a third element to be there, representing altitude (when omitted, the altitude is assumed to be zero).

Once we understand the structure we need, we can extract geographic information from a dataset of tweets. The following script, `twitter_make_geojson.py`, reads a dataset of tweets in the JSON Lines format and produces a GeoJSON file of all the tweets associated with geographic information:

```
# Chap02-03/twitter_make_geojson.py
import json
from argparse import ArgumentParser

def get_parser():
    parser = ArgumentParser()
    parser.add_argument('--tweets')
    parser.add_argument('--geojson')
    return parser

if __name__ == '__main__':
    parser = get_parser()
    args = parser.parse_args()
    # Read tweet collection and build geo data structure
    with open(args.tweets, 'r') as f:
```

```
geo_data = {
  "type": "FeatureCollection",
  "features": []
}
for line in f:
  tweet = json.loads(line)
  try:
    if tweet['coordinates']:
      geo_json_feature = {
        "type": "Feature",
        "geometry": {
          "type": "Point",
          "coordinates": tweet['coordinates']['coordinates']
        },
        "properties": {
          "text": tweet['text'],
          "created_at": tweet['created_at']
        }
      }
      geo_data['features'].append(geo_json_feature)
  except KeyError:
    # Skip if json doc is not a tweet (errors, etc.)
    continue
# Save geo data
with open(args.geojson, 'w') as fout:
  fout.write(json.dumps(geo_data, indent=4))
```

The script makes use of ArgumentParser to read the command-line parameters. It can be run as follows:

```
$ python twitter_make_geojson.py \
  --tweets stream__RWC2015__RWCFinal_Rugby.jsonl \
  --geojson rwc2015_final.geo.json
```

In this example, we will read the stream__RWC2015__RWCFinal_Rugby.jsonl file (using the --tweets argument) collected as described in Chapter 2, *#MiningTwitter – Hashtags, Topics, and Time Series*, while the output will be stored in rwc2015_final.geo.json as passed to the --geojson argument.

The geographic data structure is `FeatureCollection`, represented in the script by the `geo_data` dictionary. While looping through the file containing the dataset of tweets, the script loads each tweet and appends it as a single feature to the feature collection. For each feature, we will store the geometry as a point with the related coordinates, as well as some additional properties such as the text of the tweet and the creation time. If any JSON document in the dataset is not a proper tweet (for example, an error returned by the Twitter API), the lack of the desired attributes will trigger `KeyError`, captured and silenced by the `try/except` block.

The final part of the script simply dumps the geographic information into the given JSON file ready to be used in a custom map.

Easy maps with Folium

This section introduces **Folium** (`https://folium.readthedocs.io/en/latest/`), a Python library that allows generating interactive maps with minimum effort.

Folium offers a bridge between the data processing capabilities of Python and the UI opportunities offered by JavaScript. Specifically, it allows Python developers to integrate GeoJSON and TopoJSON data with the **Leaflet** library, one of the most feature-rich frontend libraries to build interactive maps.

The advantage of using a library such as Folium is that it handles the translation between Python data structures and JavaScript, HTML, and CSS components seamlessly. From the point of view of a Python developer, no knowledge of frontend technologies is required as we can remain in the Python territory and simply dump the output of the library into an HTML file (or visualize it directly from a Jupyter Notebook).

The library can be installed in our virtual environment using `pip`, as follows:

```
$ pip install folium
```

The examples shown in this section are based on version 0.2 of the Folium library, so it's always worth double-checking the documentation, as being a new project, some major changes to the interface are still possible.

The following example shows a simple map centered around Europe that shows two markers, one on top of London and one on top of Paris:

```python
# Chap02-03/twitter_map_example.py
from argparse import ArgumentParser
import folium

def get_parser():
  parser = ArgumentParser()
  parser.add_argument('--map')
  return parser

def make_map(map_file):
  # Custom map
  sample_map = folium.Map(location=[50, 5],
                          zoom_start=5)
  # Marker for London
  london_marker = folium.Marker([51.5, -0.12],
                                popup='London')
  london_marker.add_to(sample_map)
  # Marker for Paris
  paris_marker = folium.Marker([48.85, 2.35],
                               popup='Paris')
  paris_marker.add_to(sample_map)
  # Save to HTML file
  sample_map.save(map_file)

if __name__ == '__main__':
  parser = get_parser()
  args = parser.parse_args()

  make_map(args.map)
```

The script takes one argument using `ArgumentParser` to choose the output file and can be run, for example, with the following command:

```
$ python twitter_map_example.py --map example_map.html
```

Once we run the script, the `example_map.html` file will contain the output that can be visualized in a browser. *Figure 3.4* shows the output of this script:

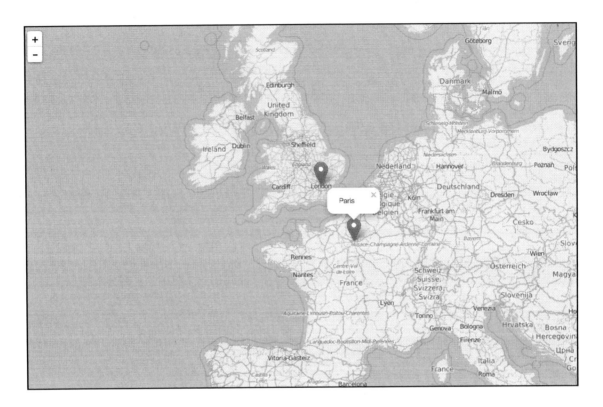

Figure 3.4: An example of the map built with Folium

The core logic of the script is implemented by the `make_map()` function. Firstly, we will create a `folium.Map` object, centered at a specific location (an array of `[latitude, longitude]` coordinates and with a specific zoom. The `zoom_start` attribute accepts an integer-using a lower number means we're zooming out, looking at the bigger picture; while a bigger number is equivalent to zooming in.

Once the map is created, we can attach custom markers to it. The sample script shows how to create markers with a specific location and a balloon-like popup attached to it. In *Figure 3.4*, the marker located in Paris has been clicked and the popup is shown.

After seeing a basic example of how to use Folium, we can apply these concepts to our dataset of tweets. The following example shows how to load a list of markers from a GeoJSON file, similar to the one we previously built:

```python
# Chap02-03/twitter_map_basic.py
from argparse import ArgumentParser
import folium

def get_parser():
  parser = ArgumentParser()
  parser.add_argument('--geojson')
  parser.add_argument('--map')
  return parser

def make_map(geojson_file, map_file):
  tweet_map = folium.Map(location=[50, 5],
                         zoom_start=5)
  geojson_layer = folium.GeoJson(open(geojson_file),
                                 name='geojson')
  geojson_layer.add_to(tweet_map)
  tweet_map.save(map_file)

if __name__ == '__main__':
  parser = get_parser()
  args = parser.parse_args()

  make_map(args.geojson, args.map)
```

The script uses `ArgumentParser` as usual, and it can be run as follows:

```
$ python twitter_map_basic.py \
  --geojson rwc2015_final.geo.json \
  --map rwc2015_final_tweets.html
```

The `--geojson` argument is used to pass the file that is previously created, which contains the GeoJSON information. The `--map` argument is used to provide the name of the output file, in this case, the `rwc2015_final_tweets.html` HTML page that we can observe in *Figure 3.5*.

The main difference between this script and the previous one is the way we implement the `make_map()` function. We start from the initialization of a map object as done earlier. This time, instead of adding the markers one by one, we will use the GeoJSON file to populate a layer, which is added on top of the map. The `folium.GeoJson` object takes care of the translation from JSON data, so the map is populated with minimal effort:

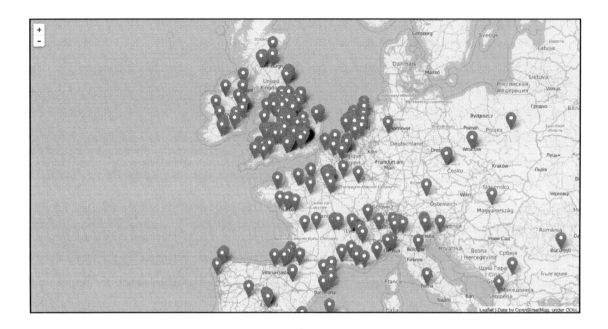

Figure 3.5: A basic map of our tweets

As we did before, the map in *Figure 3.5* is centered in Europe. We can observe that the most crowded area is England (the event was taking place in London), but with the initial zoom, it's difficult to have a better understanding of how the tweets are locally distributed.

One way to approach the problem is to zoom in as the map is interactive. Folium and Leaflet also offer another option to group markers in a dense area.

The following script takes advantage of a `MarkerCluster` object that is dedicated to this purpose:

```
# Chap02-03/twitter_map_clustered.py
from argparse import ArgumentParser
import folium

def get_parser():
```

```
    parser = ArgumentParser()
    parser.add_argument('--geojson')
    parser.add_argument('--map')
    return parser

def make_map(geojson_file, map_file):
    tweet_map = folium.Map(location=[50, 5],
                            zoom_start=5)
    marker_cluster = folium.MarkerCluster().add_to(tweet_map)

    geojson_layer = folium.GeoJson(open(geojson_file),
                                    name='geojson')
    geojson_layer.add_to(marker_cluster)
    tweet_map.save(map_file)

if __name__ == '__main__':
    parser = get_parser()
    args = parser.parse_args()

    make_map(args.geojson, args.map)
```

The script uses `ArgumentParser` as usual, and can be run, for example, with the following command:

```
$ python twitter_map_clustered.py \
  --geojson rwc2015_final.geo.json \
  --map rwc2015_final_tweets_clustered.html
```

The meaning of the arguments is the same as the previous script. This time the output is stored in `rwc2015_final_tweets_clustered.html` that can be opened in a browser.

Figure 3.6 shows a portion of this map after we zoom in to highlight the London area. What we can observe from here is how some markers are grouped together into a cluster, shown as a circular object, which reports the number of elements in it.

When moving the pointer on top of one of the clusters, the map will highlight the region represented by this cluster, so the user can have a better understanding of the local density even before zooming in. In *Figure 3.6*, we will highlight a cluster with 65 items located in South West London (the area where the Twickenham stadium, the location of the event, is based):

Figure 3.6: The example of Folium map with clustered markers

Different features of Folium can be combined to create richer user experience. For example, we could mix the use of GeoJSON, clusters, and popups to allow users to click on the individual markers and see the exact tweet.

An example of map creation that uses clusters and popups is given as follows:

```
def make_map(geojson_file, map_file):
    tweet_map = folium.Map(location=[50, 5],
                           zoom_start=5)
    marker_cluster = folium.MarkerCluster().add_to(tweet_map)
    geodata = json.load(open(geojson_file))
    for tweet in geodata['features']:
        tweet['geometry']['coordinates'].reverse()
        marker = folium.Marker(tweet['geometry']['coordinates'],
```

```
                         popup=tweet['properties']['text'])
    marker.add_to(marker_cluster)
tweet_map.save(map_file)
```

The `make_map()` function as defined earlier can be used to substitute the one in the previous script as the interface is the same.

It's important to note that the `Marker` objects created here expect the coordinates to be given as `[latitude, longitude]`, while the GeoJSON format uses `[longitude, latitude]`. For this reason, the array of coordinates is reversed before being used to define `marker`.

Figure 3.7 shows a sample of the map, after zooming in to highlight the stadium. One of the markers has been clicked on, so the related tweet is shown in a popup:

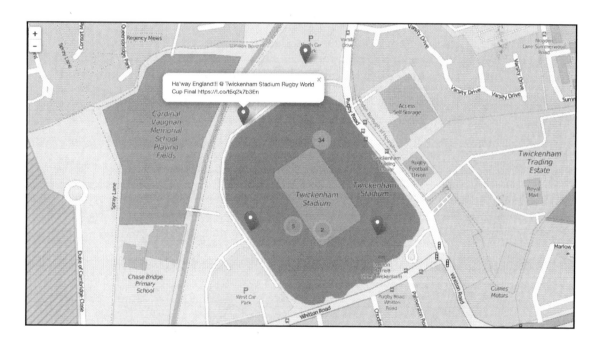

Figure 3.7: The previous map (*Figure 3.6*) has been zoomed in and the clusters become available as single markers

When using a high number of markers, it's important to consider that some performance issues might come up on the UI side. In particular, when combining markers and popups, after a few hundred items, the map might be particularly slow to navigate or the browser could refuse to load it. If this is the case, the suggestion is to experiment with a smaller dataset or reduce the variety of features used in the same map.

Summary

This chapter continued the discussion on mining data from Twitter. After focusing on text and frequencies in Chapter 2, *#MiningTwitter – Hashtags, Topics, and Time Series*, this chapter focused on the analysis of user connections and interactions. We discussed how to extract information about explicit connections (that is, followers and friends) and how to compare influence and engagement between users.

The discussion on user communities has led to the introduction of unsupervised learning approaches for group users according to their profile description, using clustering algorithms.

We have applied network analysis techniques on data related to a live event, in order to mine conversations from a stream of tweets, understanding how to identify the tweets with the highest number of replies and how to determine the longest conversation.

Finally, we have also shown how to understand the geographic distribution of tweets by plotting the tweets onto a map. By using the Python library Folium, we have shown how it is possible to achieve beautiful visualization of geographical data with minimum effort.

In the next chapter, we'll shift our focus onto a different social network, probably nowadays *the* social network: Facebook.

4

Posts, Pages, and User Interactions on Facebook

In a book about social media mining, the reader probably expects a chapter about Facebook. Launched in 2004, and initially limited to Harvard students, today Facebook is a multi-billion dollar company with nearly 1.5 billion monthly active users. Its popularity makes it an extremely interesting playground for data mining.

In this chapter, we will discuss the following topics:

- Creating an app to interact with the Facebook platform
- Interacting with the Facebook Graph API
- Mining posts from the authenticated user
- Mining Facebook Pages, visualizing posts, and measuring engagement
- Building a word cloud from a set of posts

The Facebook Graph API

The Facebook Graph API is at the core of the Facebook platform, and it's one the main components that enable the integration of third parties with Facebook. As the name suggests, it offers a consistent graph-like view of data, representing objects and the connections between them. The different platform components allow developers to access Facebook data and integrate Facebook functionalities into third-party applications.

In terms of data mining opportunities, there was a major shift during 2014 with the release of version 2.0 of the API. One of the main objects of interest in data analysis is the social graph, that is, the list of connections (friendship) between users. Since version 2.0 of the Graph API, applications that want to access this information must explicitly ask for the `user_friends` permission, but the API will only return the list of friends who are also users of the given app.

Effectively, this choice has transformed what used to be a gold mine for data analysis. This section discusses the creation of a Facebook app in Python and the basics of the interaction with the Facebook Graph API.

Registering your app

The access to the Facebook API is offered through a registered app. Developers have to register their app in order to obtain the credentials needed to consume the Graph API. As a Facebook user, you explicitly have to register as a developer in order to create apps, and your account has to be verified via either by mobile phone or credit card.

From the Facebook Developers website (`https://developers.facebook.com`), the procedure is straightforward: clicking on the **Add a New App** link under the **My Apps** menu will open the dialog window as shown in *Figure 4.1*, where we provide `Social Media Mining` as the display name for our sample app (there is a 32-character limit):

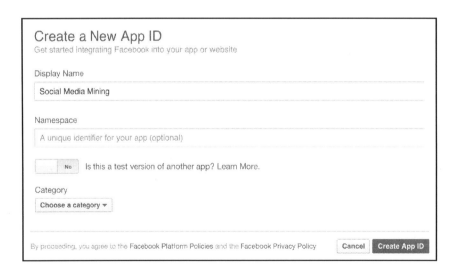

Figure 4.1: The dialog window to create a new Facebook app

Once we have selected a name and category for our app, we can click on **Create App ID** to confirm its creation.

At this point, the name that we have chosen for our app is visible under the **My Apps** menu, and clicking on it will open the app dashboard, as shown in *Figure 4.2*:

Figure 4.2: A view on the app dashboard

This panel provides crucial information such as the **App ID** and **App Secret** that will be necessary to access the API. In order to see the **App Secret**, you'll need to provide your Facebook password to confirm your identity. Needless to say, these details are not to be shared with anyone for obvious security reasons.

Between **App ID** and **App Secret**, there's also a reference to the **API Version** (the example in *Figure 4.2* is using **v2.5**). By default, the API version for a new app will be the latest version available. In the F8 conference in 2014, Facebook announced their decision to provide support for a specific API version for at least two years. This is an important piece of information to keep in mind because when a specific API version is not supported anymore, your app could stop functioning correctly if you don't update it.

Facebook platform versioning

The versioning strategies for the Facebook platform are discussed in the documentation (`https://developers.facebook.com/docs/apps/ver sions`), as well as the sunset dates for specific versions (`https://develo pers.facebook.com/docs/apps/changelog`).

Initially, your app is set up in development mode. This option makes it accessible only to you (as the author) and to any user explicitly designated as **Developers** or **Testers** from the **Roles** menu. It's worth spending some time on the dashboard to understand the basic configuration options and their implications.

Authentication and security

In order to access users' profile information, as well as the information about their interactions with other objects (for example, Pages, places, and so on), your app must obtain an access token with the appropriate permissions.

A token is unique to the user-app combination and handles the permissions that the user has granted to the application. Generating an access token requires user interaction, which means that the users have to confirm to Facebook (usually via a dialog window) that they are granting the required permissions to the application.

For testing purposes, another way to obtain an access token is to use the Graph API Explorer (`https://developers.facebook.com/tools/explorer`), a tool developed by Facebook to provide developers with a convenient interface to interact with the Graph API. *Figure 4.3* showcases the use of the Graph API Explorer, after we have selected our app from the list of available applications, we can click on **Get User Access Token** from the **Get Token** menu:

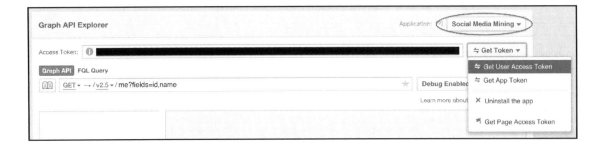

Figure 4.3: Generating an access token from the Graph API Explorer

This action will open a dialog window, like the one in *Figure 4.4*, that we can use to specify what kind of permissions we want to include in the access token. Confirming the permissions for the app will generate the alphanumeric string for the access token, which will be valid for two hours from the time of its creation. Clicking on the small information icon next to the token will show this information.

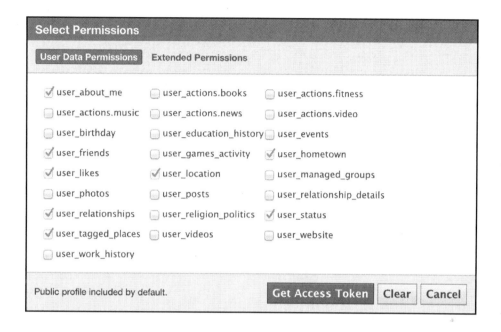

Figure 4.4: Choosing the permissions for the access token from the Graph API Explorer

As we can see from *Figure 4.4*, the permissions for a Facebook app are particularly fine-grained. In this way, the users who install your app will have full visibility of the kind of data they want to share with your app.

For the following examples, we're going to use fields such as the user's full name, location, and posts. For the code to correctly retrieve such information, we need to tick the appropriate permissions (for example, user_location, user_posts, and so on).

The first time an app is accessed by a user, Facebook will show a dialog window to summarize the list of permissions. The user will have the opportunity to review the list of permissions requested by the app.

Accessing the Facebook Graph API with Python

Once the app details are defined, we can programmatically access the Facebook Graph API via Python.

Facebook doesn't provide an official client for Python. Implementing our own client using the **requests** library could be an interesting exercise in order to understand the peculiarities of the API, but fortunately, there are already some options out there to simplify the process.

For our examples, we're going to use **facebook-sdk**, also based on the requests library, which provides an easy-to-use interface to get data from and to a web service. At the time of writing, the latest version of the library available on PyPI is 1.0.0, and it fully supports Python 3. The previous versions have shown some hiccups in terms of Python 3 compatibility. We can install the library using `pip` from our virtual environment, as follows:

```
$ pip install facebook-sdk
```

After we have obtained a temporary token following the steps described in the previous section, we can immediately test the library.

First off, just like we did to configure our access to Twitter in Chapter 2, *#MiningTwitter – Hashtags, Topics, and Time Series*, and Chapter 3, *Users, Followers, and Communities on Twitter*, let's save the token in an environment variable that will be read by the script. From the prompt, use the following command:

```
$ export FACEBOOK_TEMP_TOKEN="your-token"
```

The following script, `facebook_my_profile.py`, connects to the Graph API and queries for the profile of the authenticated user:

```python
# Chap04/facebook_my_profile.py
import os
import json
import facebook

if __name__ == '__main__':
  token = os.environ.get('FACEBOOK_TEMP_TOKEN')

  graph = facebook.GraphAPI(token)
  profile = graph.get_object('me', fields='name,location')

  print(json.dumps(profile, indent=4))
```

The script doesn't take any argument, so it can simply be run with the following command:

```
$ python facebook_my_profile.py
```

The output is a dump of the JSON object returned by the API:

```
{
  "name": "Marco Bonzanini",
  "location": {
    "name": "London, United Kingdom",
    "id": "106078429431815"
  },
  "id": "10207505820417553"
}
```

The `get_object()` function takes the ID or name of a particular object in the Facebook Graph as the first argument and returns the desired information about it. In our example, the `me` ID is just an alias for the authenticated user. Without specifying the second argument and fields, the API would simply return the ID and name of the object. In this case, we explicitly ask for the `name` and `location` to be included in the output. As you can see, `location` is not just a string, but a complex object with its own fields (as nothing else was specified, the fields included for the location are simply `id` and `name`).

The interface to get data from the `GraphAPI` class is quite straightforward. The class also provides facilities to publish and update data on Facebook, allowing the application to interact with the Facebook platform (for example, by posting some content on the authenticated user's wall).

The main methods of interest in our case are the following:

- `get_object(id, **args)`: This retrieves an object given its `id`, and also takes optional keyword arguments
- `get_objects(ids, **args)`: This retrieves a list of objects given a list of `ids`, and also takes optional keyword arguments
- `get_connections(id, connection_name, **args)`: This retrieves a list of objects connected in a `connection_name` relationship to the object identified by `id`, and also takes optional keyword arguments
- `request(path, args=None, post_args=None, files=None, method=None)`: This is a generic method used to implement specific requests to the API, using `path` as defined in the API documentation, the optional arguments define how the API call is performed

The example in the `facebook_my_profile.py` script has used the `get_object()` method to download the profile of the current user. In this case, an optional keyword argument, `fields`, has been given to specify the attributes that we want to retrieve from the API. A complete list of attributes for user profiles is specified in the documentation (`https://dev elopers.facebook.com/docs/graph-api/reference/v2.5/user`).

Following the API specifications, we can see how we could personalize the field's string in order to get more information for the given profile. Particularly, we can also perform nested requests and include details of the objects connected to the given profile. In our example, we retrieved the location, which is an object of type **Page** (`https://developers.faceboo k.com/docs/graph-api/reference/page/`). As each Page has some attributes attached to it, we can also include them in our request, for example, changing the `get_object()` request:

```
profile = graph.get_object("me", fields='name,location{location}')
```

The `first_level{second_level}` syntax allows to query nested objects. In this particular example, the naming might be confusing as `location` is the name of both the first- and second-level attributes that we are retrieving. The solution to make sense of this little puzzle is to understand the data types. The first-level `location` is an attribute of the user profile, and its data type is a Facebook Page (with its own ID, name, and other attributes). The second-level `location` is instead an attribute of the aforementioned Facebook Page, and it's a descriptor of an actual location, made up with attributes such as `latitude` and `longitude`, among others. The output of the previous script with the extra second-level `location` is as follows:

```
{
  "name": "Marco Bonzanini",
  "location": {
    "name": "London, United Kingdom",
    "id": "106078429431815"
  },
  "id": "10207505820417553",
  "location": {
    "id": "106078429431815",
    "location": {
      "city": "London",
      "latitude": 51.516434161634,
      "longitude": -0.12961888255995,
      "country": "United Kingdom"
    }
  }
}
```

The attributes retrieved by default for a `location` object (`https://deve lopers.facebook.com/docs/graph-api/reference/v2.5/locatio n`) are `city`, `country`, `latitude`, and `longitude`.

As mentioned at the beginning of this section, with newer versions of the Facebook Graph API, some data mining opportunities have been limited. Particularly, mining the social graph (that is, friendship relationships) is possible only if all the involved profiles are users of our app. The following script tries to obtain the list of friends for the authenticated user:

```
# Chap04/facebook_get_friends.py
import os
import facebook
import json

if __name__ == '__main__':
  token = os.environ.get('FACEBOOK_TEMP_TOKEN')

  graph = facebook.GraphAPI(token)
  user = graph.get_object("me")
  friends = graph.get_connections(user["id"], "friends")
  print(json.dumps(friends, indent=4))
```

Even though this call to the API requires the `user_friends` permission to be granted to our app, the script is anyway unable to retrieve much data about friends, as the authenticated user (that is, me) is currently the only user of the app. The following is a sample output:

```
{
  "data": [],
  "summary": {
    "total_count": 266
  }
}
```

As we can see, the only information we can retrieve is the total count of friends for the given user, while the friends' data is represented by the empty list. If some friends decide to use our app, we will be able to retrieve their profiles through this call.

We will conclude this section with a brief mention of the rate limits imposed by the Graph API. As discussed in the documentation (`https://developers.facebook.com/docs/gr aph-api/advanced/rate-limiting`), rate limits are rarely encountered. The limits are calculated per app and per user, that is, if the app reaches the daily rate limits, all the calls made by the app will be limited, not only those for a given user. The daily allowance is calculated on the number of users on the previous day and today's loginâ®®this sum gives the base number of users. The app is then given an allowance of 200 API calls per user in a 60-minute window. While this is more than enough for our examples, it's recommended that you take a look at the documentation to understand the possible impact of rate limits in your application.

In the next section, we're going to download all the posts for the authenticated user and start some data analysis on this data.

Mining your posts

After introducing the Python facebook-sdk with a simple example, we will start digging into the data mining opportunities. The first exercise is to download our own posts (that is, the posts published by the authenticated user).

The `facebook_get_my_posts.py` script connects to the Graph API and gets a list of posts published by the authenticated user me. The posts are saved in the `my_posts.jsonl` file using the JSON Lines format that we have already adopted in Chapter 2, *#MiningTwitter – Hashtags, Topics, and Time Series*, and Chapter 3, *Users, Followers, and Communities on Twitter*, (each line of the file is a JSON document):

```
# Chap04/facebook_get_my_posts.py
import os
import json
import facebook
import requests

if __name__ == '__main__':
  token = os.environ.get('FACEBOOK_TEMP_TOKEN')

  graph = facebook.GraphAPI(token)
  posts = graph.get_connections('me', 'posts')

  while True:  # keep paginating
    try:
      with open('my_posts.jsonl', 'a') as f:
        for post in posts['data']:
          f.write(json.dumps(post)+"\n")
```

```
    # get next page
    posts = requests.get(posts['paging']['next']).json()
except KeyError:
  # no more pages, break the loop
  break
```

The script doesn't take any command-line parameter, so it can be run simply with the following command:

```
$ python facebook_get_my_posts.py
```

This script provides an interesting example of pagination, as the list of posts is too long to be collected by a single API call, Facebook provides the pagination information.

The initial API call performed with the `get_connections()` method returns the first page of posts (stored in `posts['data']`), as well as the details needed to loop through the different pages, available in `posts['paging']`. As the pagination functionality is not implemented in the Python facebook-sdk library, we need to fall back by using the requests library directly. Fortunately, the response provided by the Graph API contains the exact URL that we need to request in order to get the next page of posts. In fact, if we inspect the value of the `posts['paging']['next']` variable, we'll see the string representing the precise URL to query, including the access token, API version number, and all the required details.

The pagination is performed inside a `while True` loop, which is interrupted by a `KeyError` exception when we reach the last page. As the last page will not contain a reference to `posts['paging']['next']`, trying to access this key of the dictionary will raise the exception with the only purpose of breaking the loop.

Once the script is executed, we can examine the content of the `my_posts.jsonl` file. Each line of the file is a JSON document, which contains a unique ID, the text of the message attached to the post, and the creation time in the ISO 8601 format. This is an example of a JSON document representing one of the downloaded posts:

```
{
  "created_time": "2015-11-04T08:01:21+0000",
  "id": "10207505820417553_10207338487234328",
  "message": "The slides of my lighting talk at the PyData London
    meetup last night\n"
}
```

Just like the `get_object()` function, `get_connections()` can also take a `fields` argument in order to retrieve more attributes of the desired object. The following script refactors the previous code in order to get more interesting attributes for our posts:

```python
# Chap04/facebook_get_my_posts_more_fields.py
import os
import json
import facebook
import requests

if __name__ == '__main__':
  token = os.environ.get('FACEBOOK_TEMP_TOKEN')

  graph = facebook.GraphAPI(token)
  all_fields = [
    'message',
    'created_time',
    'description',
    'caption',
    'link',
    'place',
    'status_type'
  ]
  all_fields = ','.join(all_fields)
  posts = graph.get_connections('me', 'posts', fields=all_fields)

  while True:  # keep paginating
    try:
      with open('my_posts.jsonl', 'a') as f:
        for post in posts['data']:
          f.write(json.dumps(post)+"\n")
        # get next page
        posts = requests.get(posts['paging']['next']).json()
    except KeyError:
      # no more pages, break the loop
      break
```

All the fields that we want to retrieve are declared in the `all_fields` list, which is then joined in a string of comma-separated attribute names, as the Graph API requires. This value is then passed to the `get_connections()` method via the `fields` keyword argument.

The following section discusses more details about the structure of a post.

The structure of a post

A post is a complex object as it can essentially be any piece of content that a user decides to publish. The following table summarizes the interesting attributes of a post with a brief description of their meaning:

application The App object with information about the app used to publish this post

Attribute Name	Description
id	String representing a unique identifier
status_type	String representing the type of post (for example, added_photos or shared_story)
message	String representing the status message of the post
created_time	String with the date the post has been published in the ISO 8601 format
updated_time	String with the date of last modification in the ISO 8601 format
message_tags	List of profiles tagged in the message
from	Profile that posted the message
to	List of profiles mentioned or targeted in the post
place	Location information attached to the post
privacy	Object with the privacy settings of the post
story_tags	Same as message_tags
with_tags	List of profiles tagged as *being with* the author of the post
properties	List of properties of any attached video (for example, length of the video)

A Post object has even more attributes than the ones represented in the previous table. A complete list of attributes is given in the official documentation (https://developers.facebook.com/docs/graph-api/reference/v2.5/post), where the complexity of this object is even clearer.

Time frequency analysis

After downloading all our posts, we will perform the first analysis based on the creation time of different posts. The purpose of this analysis is to highlight user's behaviors, such as at what time of day the user posts most content on Facebook.

The `facebook_post_time_stats.py` script uses `ArgumentParser` to get a command-line input, that is, the `.jsonl` file with the posts:

```
# Chap04/facebook_post_time_stats.py
import json
from argparse import ArgumentParser
import dateutil.parser
import numpy as np
import pandas as pd
import matplotlib.pyplot as plt
from datetime import datetime

def get_parser():
  parser = ArgumentParser()
  parser.add_argument('--file',
                      '-f',
                      required=True,
                      help='The .jsonl file with all the posts')
  return parser

if __name__ == '__main__':
  parser = get_parser()
  args = parser.parse_args()
  with open(args.file) as f:
    posts = []
    for line in f:
      post = json.loads(line)
      created_time = dateutil.parser.parse(post['created_time'])
      posts.append(created_time.strftime('%H:%M:%S'))
    ones = np.ones(len(posts))
    idx = pd.DatetimeIndex(posts)
    # the actual series (a series of 1s for the moment)
    my_series = pd.Series(ones, index=idx)

    # Resampling into 1-hour buckets
    per_hour = my_series.resample('1H', how='sum').fillna(0)
    # Plotting
    fig, ax = plt.subplots()
    ax.grid(True)
    ax.set_title("Post Frequencies")
    width = 0.8
```

```
ind = np.arange(len(per_hour))
plt.bar(ind, per_hour)
tick_pos = ind + width / 2
labels = []
for i in range(24):
    d = datetime.now().replace(hour=i, minute=0)
    labels.append(d.strftime('%H:%M'))
plt.xticks(tick_pos, labels, rotation=90)
plt.savefig('posts_per_hour.png')
```

The script can be run from the command line as follows:

```
$ python facebook_post_time_stats.py -f my_posts.jsonl
```

The script first produces a list of posts with the creation time of each post. The `dateutil.parser.parse()` function helps to read the ISO 8601 date string into a `datetime` object, which is then converted into a HH:MM:SS string with the `strftime()` function.

The list of creation time is then used to index a pandas Series, which is initially just a sequence of ones. The series is then resampled by the hour, summing up the posts. At this point, we have a series of 24 items, one for each hour of the day, with the number of posts published during that particular hour. The final part of the script has the purpose of plotting the series as a simple bar chart in order to visualize the distribution of posts throughout the day.

Figure 4.5 shows the plot:

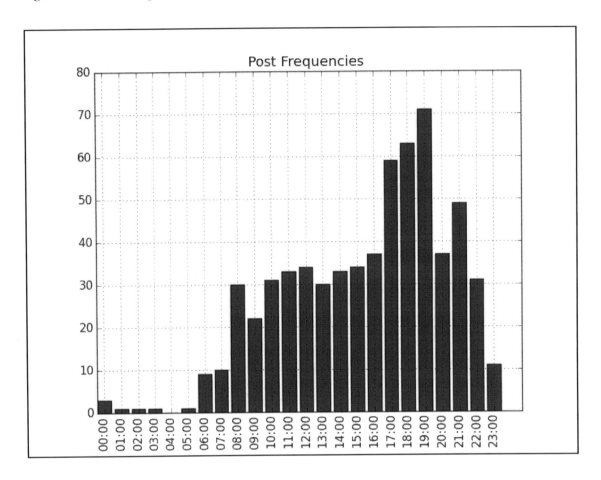

Figure 4.5: Time frequencies of posts

As we can see, the publication time has its peak between late afternoon and evening, but it spreads fairly during the day (with the least frequencies registered during the night and early morning hours). One aspect to consider is that the location is not taken into account, that is, the creation time is normalized to **Coordinated Universal Time (UTC)**, so the original time zone is not considered. For example, if a post has been published on the East Coast of the U.S. at 4 p.m., its creation time will be recorded as 9 p.m. UTC. This is because the **Eastern Standard Time (EST)** is equivalent to UTC – 05:00, that is, it's five hours behind UTC during standard time (autumn/winter, when not observing daylight saving time).

Mining Facebook Pages

Facebook is not only used by individuals who want to connect with their friends and relatives, but also by companies, brands, and organizations who want to engage with people. A Facebook Page is created and managed by a Facebook personal account, and it can be used in a variety of ways:

- To share information about a business (for example, a restaurant or online shop)
- To represent a celebrity (for example, a footballer or rock band)
- To connect with an audience (for example, as an extension of an online community)

Different from personal accounts, Pages can publish posts that are publicly visible. Regular users can like a Page, meaning that they'll receive the content updates published by the Page directly on their news feed, that is, their personalized Facebook home page.

For example, Packt Publishing's Facebook Page is located at `https://www.facebook.com/PacktPub` and it contains general information about PacktPub, as well as the posts related to books, e-books, and video tutorials published by PacktPub.

From the API documentation (`https://developers.facebook.com/docs/graph-api/reference/page`), we can see a variety of information available for a given Page. In particular, interesting attributes about a Page include the following:

- `id`: The numeric identifier for this Page
- `name`: The name of the Page as displayed on Facebook
- `about`: A textual description of the Page
- `link`: The Facebook link to this Page
- `website`: The organization's webpage, if any
- `general_info`: A textual field of general information about the Page
- `likes`: The number of users who like this Page

A `Page` object can also be connected to other objects, and the documentation describes all the possibilities in terms of edges (that is, connections) with other objects. For example:

- `posts`: A list of posts published by the Page
- `photos`: This Page's photos
- `albums`: A list of photo albums published by this Page
- `picture`: This Page's profile picture

Specific types of Pages can also display additional information that is tailored to their type of business (for example, a restaurant can show their opening hours, a band can show the list of band members, and so on).

The following script queries the Facebook Graph API to retrieve some of the basic information about a particular Facebook Page:

```
# Chap04/facebook_get_page_info.py
import os
import json
import facebook
from argparse import ArgumentParser

def get_parser():
  parser = ArgumentParser()
  parser.add_argument('--page')
  return parser

if __name__ == '__main__':
  parser = get_parser()
  args = parser.parse_args()

  token = os.environ.get('FACEBOOK_TEMP_TOKEN')
  fields = [
    'id',
    'name',
    'about',
    'likes',
    'website',
    'link'
  ]
  fields = ','.join(fields)

  graph = facebook.GraphAPI(token)
  page = graph.get_object(args.page, fields=fields)

  print(json.dumps(page, indent=4))
```

The script uses an instance of `ArgumentParser` to get the Page name (or Page ID) from the command line, for example:

```
$ python facebook_get_page_info.py --page PacktPub
```

The output is as follows:

```
{
  "id": "204603129458",
  "website": "http://www.PacktPub.com",
```

```
    "likes": 6357,
    "about": "Packt Publishing provides books, eBooks, video
        tutorials, and articles for IT developers, administrators, and
        users.",
    "name": "Packt Publishing",
    "link": "https://www.facebook.com/PacktPub/"
}
```

We can also use the Facebook Graph API Explorer to get an overview of the available fields.

Getting posts from a Page

After discussing how to get the basic information about a Page, we will examine the procedure to download posts published by a Page and store them in the usual JSON Lines format that allows analyzing the posts later.

The procedure is similar to the one used to download the posts published by the authenticated user, but it also includes information to calculate user engagement:

```python
# Chap04/facebook_get_page_posts.py
import os
import json
from argparse import ArgumentParser
import facebook
import requests

def get_parser():
    parser = ArgumentParser()
    parser.add_argument('--page')
    parser.add_argument('--n', default=100, type=int)
    return parser

if __name__ == '__main__':
    parser = get_parser()
    args = parser.parse_args()

    token = os.environ.get('FACEBOOK_TEMP_TOKEN')

    graph = facebook.GraphAPI(token)
    all_fields = [
        'id',
        'message',
        'created_time',
        'shares',
        'likes.summary(true)',
        'comments.summary(true)'
```

```
]
all_fields = ','.join(all_fields)
posts = graph.get_connections('PacktPub',
                              'posts',
                              fields=all_fields)

downloaded = 0
while True:  # keep paginating
  if downloaded >= args.n:
    break
  try:
    fname = "posts_{}.jsonl".format(args.page)
    with open(fname, 'a') as f:
      for post in posts['data']:
        downloaded += 1
        f.write(json.dumps(post)+"\n")
      # get next page
      posts = requests.get(posts['paging']['next']).json()
  except KeyError:
    # no more pages, break the loop
    break
```

The script uses an instance of ArgumentParser to get the Page name or Page ID from the command line, as well as the number of posts that we want to download. In the sample code, the number of posts is optional (it defaults to 100). As we did earlier when we downloaded the posts from the authenticated user, we will define the list of fields we want to include in the results. In particular, as we'll use this data to perform some analysis related to user engagement, we want the results to contain information about the number of times a post has been liked, shared, or commented on. This is accomplished by adding the shares, likes.summary(true), and comments.summary(true) fields. For likes and comments, the extra summary(true) attribute is necessary to include summary statistics, that is, the aggregated count.

The download is performed in a while True loop using an approach similar to the one used for the posts by the authenticated user. The difference is given by a downloaded counter, which is incremented for each retrieved post. This is used to set a limit to the number of posts that we want to download, mainly because the Pages often publish a huge amount of content.

The script can be run as follows:

```
$ python facebook_get_page_posts.py --page PacktPub --n 500
```

Running the preceding command will query the Facebook Graph API and produce the `posts_PacktPub.jsonl` file with 500 posts, one per line. The following code showcases a pretty-printed example of a single post (that is, one line of the `.jsonl` file):

```
{
  "id": "post-id",
  "created_time": "date in ISO 8601 format",
  "message": "Text of the message",
  "comments": {
    "data": [ /* list of comments */ ],
    "paging": {
      "cursors": {
        "after": "cursor-id",
        "before": "cursor-id"
      }
    },
    "summary": {
      "can_comment": true,
      "order": "ranked",
      "total_count": 4
    }
  },
  "likes": {
    "data": [ /* list of users */ ],
    "paging": {
      "cursors": {
        "after": "cursor-id",
        "before": "cursor-id"
      }
    },
    "summary": {
      "can_like": true,
      "has_liked": false,
      "total_count": 10
    }
  },
  "shares": {
    "count": 9
  }
}
```

As we can see, the post is a complex object, with different nested information. The fields that measure user engagement are `shares`, `likes`, and `comments`. The `shares` field only reports the total count of users who have shared the story. Other details are not included due to privacy settings. When a user shares a piece of content, they are effectively creating their own post, so this new post shouldn't be visible to other users outside their network. The `comments` and `likes` fields, on the other hand, are objects connected to the post itself, so there are more details available for them.

For the `comments` field, the `data` key contains a list of objects with comment-related information. In particular, each comment looks as follows:

```
{
  "created_time": "date in ISO 8601 format",
  "from": {
    "id": "user-id",
    "name": "user-name"
  },
  "id": "comment-id",
  "message": "text of the message"
}
```

The `comments` object also includes a `paging` field, which holds the references to the cursors, in case the number of comments exceeds one page. Given the original request, with an explicit reference to the `summary(true)` attribute, short summary statistics are also included. In particular, we are interested in `total_count`.

The `likes` object is somewhat similar to the `comments` object, although the data is less complex in this case. Specifically, there's a list of user IDs for users who have liked the post. Similarly, we also have summary statistics with the total number of likes as the `summary(true)` attribute was specified in the request.

Once the data has been downloaded, we can perform different types of offline analysis.

Facebook Reactions and the Graph API 2.6

Shortly after this chapter was drafted, Facebook rolled out a new feature called **Reactions**. Born as an extension of the *Like* button, Reactions allow the users to express their feeling towards a particular post, going beyond the mere Like. The new feelings that the users are now able to express are called Love, Haha, Wow, Sad, Angry (as well as Like). *Figure 4.6* shows how the new buttons appear to the users:

Figure 4.6: Visualization of Facebook Reactions

The first version of the Graph API that supports Facebook Reactions is 2.6. The examples in this chapter are mostly based on version 2.5 of the API, so if you are planning to include this feature in your data analysis, you should make sure that you point to the correct version. The information about how to access data related to Reactions can be found in the official documentation (https://developers.facebook.com/docs/graph-api/reference/post/reactions).

From a developer's perspective, Reactions are very similar to Likes. If we request information about Reactions to the API, the structure of the document that we get back for each post is similar to the following code:

```
{
  "message": "The content of the post",
  "created_time": "creation date in ISO 8601",
  "id": "the ID of the post",
  "reactions": {
    "data": [
      {
        "id": "some-user-id",
        "name": "John Doe",
        "type": "WOW"
      },
      {
        "id": "another-user-id",
        "name": "Jane Doe",
        "type": "LIKE"
      },
      /* more reactions... */
    ]
  },
  "likes": {
    "data": /* data about likes as before */
  }
}
```

While the examples in this chapter focus on likes and comments as a way of understanding engagement, they can easily be extended to include this new feature that is supposed to help publishers understand better how their users and friends perceive their content.

Measuring engagement

We start the analysis of posts published by a Facebook Page with some discussion related to user engagement. The data provided by the Graph API includes the following details:

- The number of times the post has been shared
- The number of users who liked the post
- The number of users who reacted to the post
- The number of comments on the post

Sharing, liking, and commenting are all, in fact, the actions that a user can perform with a piece of content published by someone else. While it is difficult to understand the true reasons behind a specific action (for example, how to distinguish between a sarcastic like and a genuine one?), and a deep analysis on the psychology behind such actions is beyond the scope of this book, so for the sake of these data mining examples, we'll assume that posts with more interactions are more *successful*. The term *successful* is in double quotes here as we haven't defined the precise meaning of *success*, so in this section, we are just counting the number of times the users have interacted with the Page.

The following script prints some information about the post published by a Facebook Page that has received the highest number of interactions:

```
# Chap04/facebook_top_posts.py
import json
from argparse import ArgumentParser

def get_parser():
  parser = ArgumentParser()
  parser.add_argument('--page')
  return parser

if __name__ == '__main__':
  parser = get_parser()
  args = parser.parse_args()

  fname = "posts_{}.jsonl".format(args.page)

  all_posts = []
  with open(fname) as f:
```

```
  for line in f:
    post = json.loads(line)
    n_likes = post['likes']['summary']['total_count']
    n_comments = post['comments']['summary']['total_count']
    try:
      n_shares = post['shares']['count']
    except KeyError:
      n_shares = 0
    post['all_interactions'] = n_likes + n_shares + n_comments
    all_posts.append(post)
most_liked_all = sorted(all_posts,
                        key=lambda x: x['all_interactions'],
                        reverse=True)
most_liked = most_liked_all[0]
message = most_liked.get('message', '-empty-')
created_at = most_liked['created_time']
n_likes = most_liked['likes']['summary']['total_count']
n_comments = most_liked['comments']['summary']['total_count']
print("Post with most interactions:")
print("Message: {}".format(message))
print("Creation time: {}".format(created_at))
print("Likes: {}".format(n_likes))
print("Comments: {}".format(n_comments))
try:
  n_shares = most_liked['shares']['count']
  print("Shares: {}".format(n_shares))
except KeyError:
  pass
print("Total: {}".format(most_liked['all_interactions']))
```

The script uses `ArgumentParser` to take the command-line arguments, and it can be run as follows:

```
$ python facebook_top_posts.py --page PacktPub
```

As we loop through the posts, we introduce a `all_interactions` key for each post, computed as the sum of likes, shares, and comments. If the post has not been shared by any user yet, the `shares` key will not be present in the dictionary, so the access to `post['shares']['count']` has been included in the `try/except` block that defaults the number of shares to 0 if the key is not present.

The new `all_interactions` key is used as a sorting option in the `sorted()` function, which returns the list of posts ordered by reversed number of interactions.

The final part of the script simply prints some information. The output is as follows:

```
Post with most interactions:
Message: It's back! Our $5 sale returns!
Creation time: 2015-12-17T11:51:00+0000
Likes: 10
Comments: 4
Shares: 9
Total: 23
```

While finding out the post with the highest number of interactions is an interesting exercise, it doesn't tell us much about the overall picture.

Our next step is to verify whether a particular time of day is more successful than others, that is, whether publishing a post at a given time gives us more interactions.

The following script uses `pandas.DataFrame` to aggregate the statistics of the interactions and plots the results using one-hour buckets, as we did earlier for the authenticated user:

```python
# Chap04/facebook_top_posts_plot.py
import json
from argparse import ArgumentParser
import numpy as np
import pandas as pd
import dateutil.parser
import matplotlib.pyplot as plt
from datetime import datetime

def get_parser():
    parser = ArgumentParser()
    parser.add_argument('--page')
    return parser

if __name__ == '__main__':
    parser = get_parser()
    args = parser.parse_args()

    fname = "posts_{}.jsonl".format(args.page)

    all_posts = []
    n_likes = []
    n_shares = []
    n_comments = []
    n_all = []
    with open(fname) as f:
        for line in f:
            post = json.loads(line)
            created_time = dateutil.parser.parse(post['created_time'])
```

```
    n_likes.append(post['likes']['summary']['total_count'])
    n_comments.append(post['comments']['summary']['total_count'])
    try:
      n_shares.append(post['shares']['count'])
    except KeyError:
      n_shares.append(0)
    n_all.append(n_likes[-1] + n_shares[-1] + n_comments[-1])
    all_posts.append(created_time.strftime('%H:%M:%S'))

  idx = pd.DatetimeIndex(all_posts)
  data = {
    'likes': n_likes,
    'comments': n_comments,
    'shares': n_shares,
    'all': n_all
  }
  my_series = pd.DataFrame(data=data, index=idx)

  # Resampling into 1-hour buckets
  per_hour = my_series.resample('1h', how='sum').fillna(0)
  # Plotting
  fig, ax = plt.subplots()
  ax.grid(True)
  ax.set_title("Interaction Frequencies")
  width = 0.8
  ind = np.arange(len(per_hour['all']))
  plt.bar(ind, per_hour['all'])
  tick_pos = ind + width / 2
  labels = []
  for i in range(24):
    d = datetime.now().replace(hour=i, minute=0)
    labels.append(d.strftime('%H:%M'))
  plt.xticks(tick_pos, labels, rotation=90)
  plt.savefig('interactions_per_hour.png')
```

The script can be run with the following command:

```
$ python facebook_top_posts_plot.py --page PacktPub
```

The output is a matplotlib figure saved in the interactions_per_hour.png file that we can visualize in *Figure 4.7.*

The code loops through the `.jsonl` file, building lists to store various statistics for each post: number of likes, number of shares, number of comments, and their overall sum. Each of these lists will be a column in the data frame, which is indexed using the creation time (just the time, not the date). Using the resampling techniques that are already applied before, all the posts published within a one-hour bucket are aggregated and their frequencies are summed up. For the sake of this exercise, only the overall sum of interactions is considered, but it's also possible to plot the individual statistics separately:

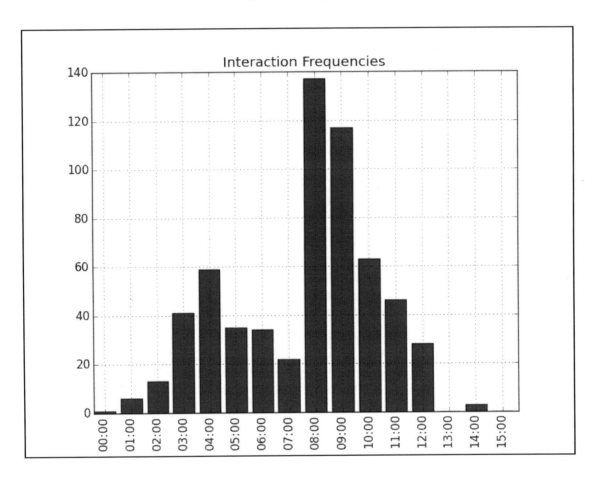

Figure 4.7: The interaction frequency (aggregated per hour)

The plot shows the highest number of interactions in the buckets labeled **08:00** and **09:00** respectively, meaning that in aggregation, the posts published after 8 a.m. and before 10 a.m. received the highest number of interactions.

After observing the dataset, we noticed that the 8 a.m. to 10 a.m. time slot is also when most of the posts are published. If we decided to plot the post frequency, in this case, we would observe a distribution similar to the one observed in *Figure 4.7* (this is left as an exercise for interested readers).

In this case, the core of the matter is the aggregation mode, that is, the `how` attribute in the resampling method. As we are using `sum`, the 8 a.m. to 10 a.m. buckets seem to have more interactions simply because there are more posts to interact with, so the overall sum doesn't really tell us whether these posts are widely successful or not. The fix is simple: rather than `how='sum'`, we can modify the script to `how='mean'` and rerun the code. The output is shown in the following *Figure 4.8*:

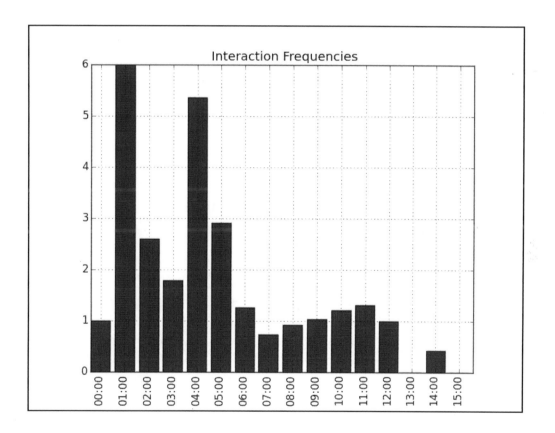

Figure 4.8: The interaction frequency (averaged per hour)

Figure 4.8 shows the distribution of the average number of interactions, aggregated per hour. In this plot, the time slot of 8 a.m. to 10 a.m. doesn't look as successful as earlier. Instead, the highest number of interactions is concentrated between 1 a.m. and 5 a.m. with two peaks.

This simple exercise has shown that aggregating data in different ways can give different results for the same question. Taking the discussion a little bit further, it's important to note that we don't have two important pieces of information in this case. Firstly, we don't have the historical information about how many people like the PacktPub Page, that is, how many people actually see the posts in their news feed. If many people started following the Page only recently, they are less likely to interact with older posts, so the statistics might be biased in favor of the newer posts. Secondly, we don't have the information about the demographics, the location of the users in particular: the 1 a.m. to 5 a.m. time slot seems a bit odd, but as mentioned earlier, the creation times are normalized to the UTC time zone. In other words, 1 a.m. to 5 a.m. UTC corresponds to, for example, morning in India or late afternoon/evening on the Pacific Coast.

If we have this knowledge about the user demographics, we can also understand the best time to publish a new post. For example, if most of our users are located on the Pacific Coast and like to interact during late afternoon (according their time zone), then it's worth to schedule the post publication for 1 a.m. UTC.

Visualizing posts as a word cloud

After analyzing interactions, we move our attention back to the content of the posts.

Word clouds, also called tag clouds (`https://en.wikipedia.org/wiki/Tag_cloud`), are visual representations of textual data. The importance of each word is usually represented by its size in the image.

In this section, we will use the **wordcloud** Python package, which provides an extremely easy way to produce word clouds. Firstly, we need to install the library and its dependency (an imaging library) in our virtual environment using the following commands:

```
$ pip install wordcloud
$ pip install Pillow
```

Pillow is a fork of the old **Python Imaging Library** (PIL) project, as PIL has apparently been discontinued. Among its features, Pillow supports Python 3, so after this brief installation, we're good to go.

The following script reads a `.jsonl` file as the one produced to store the posts from PacktPub, and creates a `.png` file with the word cloud:

```python
# Chap04/facebook_posts_wordcloud.py
import os
import json
from argparse import ArgumentParser
import matplotlib.pyplot as plt
from nltk.corpus import stopwords
from wordcloud import WordCloud

def get_parser():
  parser = ArgumentParser()
  parser.add_argument('--page')
  return parser

if __name__ == '__main__':
  parser = get_parser()
  args = parser.parse_args()

  fname = "posts_{}.jsonl".format(args.page)

  all_posts = []
  with open(fname) as f:
    for line in f:
      post = json.loads(line)
      all_posts.append(post.get('message', ''))
  text = ' '.join(all_posts)
  stop_list = ['save', 'free', 'today',
               'get', 'title', 'titles', 'bit', 'ly']
  stop_list.extend(stopwords.words('english'))
  wordcloud = WordCloud(stopwords=stop_list).generate(text)
  plt.imshow(wordcloud)
  plt.axis("off")
  image_fname = 'wordcloud_{}.png'.format(args.page)
  plt.savefig(image_fname)
```

As usual, the script uses an instance of `ArgumentParser` to get the command-line parameter (the Page name or Page ID).

The script creates a list, `all_posts`, with the textual message of each post. We use `post.get('message', '')` instead of accessing the dictionary directly, as the `message` key might not be present in every post (for example, in the case of images without comment), even though this event is quite rare.

The list of posts is then concatenated into a single string, `text`, which will be the main input to generate the word cloud. The `WordCloud` object takes some optional parameters to define some aspects of the word cloud. In particular, the example uses the `stopwords` argument to define a list of words that will be removed from the word cloud. The words that we include in this list are the standard English stop words as defined in the **Natural Language Toolkit (NLTK)** library, as well as a few custom keywords that are often used in the PacktPub account but that do not really carry interesting meaning (for example, links to `bit.ly` and references to offers for particular titles).

An example of the output image is shown in the following *Figure 4.9*:

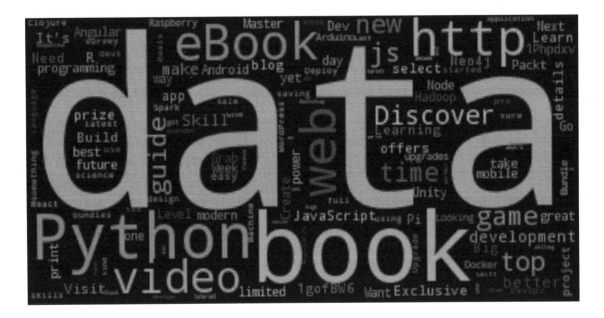

Figure 4.9: Example of word cloud

The preceding image shows some of the products offered by Packt Publishing (books, eBooks, and videos), as well as some of the main technologies discussed in their publications (such as Python, JavaScript, R, Arduino, game development, and so on) with the main keyword being **data**.

Summary

This chapter introduced some data mining applications using Facebook, one of the big players, if not the main player, in the social media arena.

After discussing some aspects of the Facebook Graph API and its evolution, as well as the implications in terms of data mining, we built a Facebook app that we used to interface with the Facebook platform.

The data mining applications shown in this chapter are related to the profile of an authenticated user and Facebook Pages. We saw how to compute statistics related to the publication habits of the authenticated user and to the interactions of users who follow the updates of a given Page. Using simple aggregation and visualization techniques, this type of analysis can be carried out with a relatively small amount of code. Finally, we used a technique called word cloud to visualize the important keywords, which hopefully represent important topics, from a bunch of published posts.

The focus of the next chapter is Google+, one of the most recent social networks, developed by Google.

5

Topic Analysis on Google+

This chapter focuses on Google+ (sometimes called Google Plus or simply G+), one of the most recent big players to join the social network arena. Launched in 2011, it is described as *"a social layer across all of Google's services"* (`https://en.wikipedia.org/wiki/Google%2`
`B`). It experienced an extremely rapid growth in its user base, with 10 million users after its first two weeks. After a number of redesigns, towards the end of 2015, Google revealed their larger focus on communities and collections, moving the service towards interest-based networking.

In this chapter, we will discuss the following topics:

- How to interact with the Google+ API with the help of Python
- How to search for people or pages on Google+
- How to use the web framework, **Flask**, to visualize search results in a web GUI
- How to process content from a user's post to extract interesting keywords

Getting started with the Google+ API

The Google+ API is the programming interface of Google+. This API can be used to integrate your app or website with Google+, similar to what we have already discussed for Twitter and Facebook. This section discusses the process of registering an application and getting started with the Google+ API.

Before starting, we need a Google account (`https://www.google.com/accounts`) if we haven't registered yet. Google offers several services (for example, Gmail, Blogger, and so on) but the account management is centralized. This means that if you are a user of one of these services, your account can be quickly set up for Google+.

Once you are registered and logged in, the starting point is the Google Developers Console (`https://console.developers.google.com/start`). From the console, we need to create our first project. *Figure 5.1* shows the dialog for project creation, all we need to specify is a name for our project:

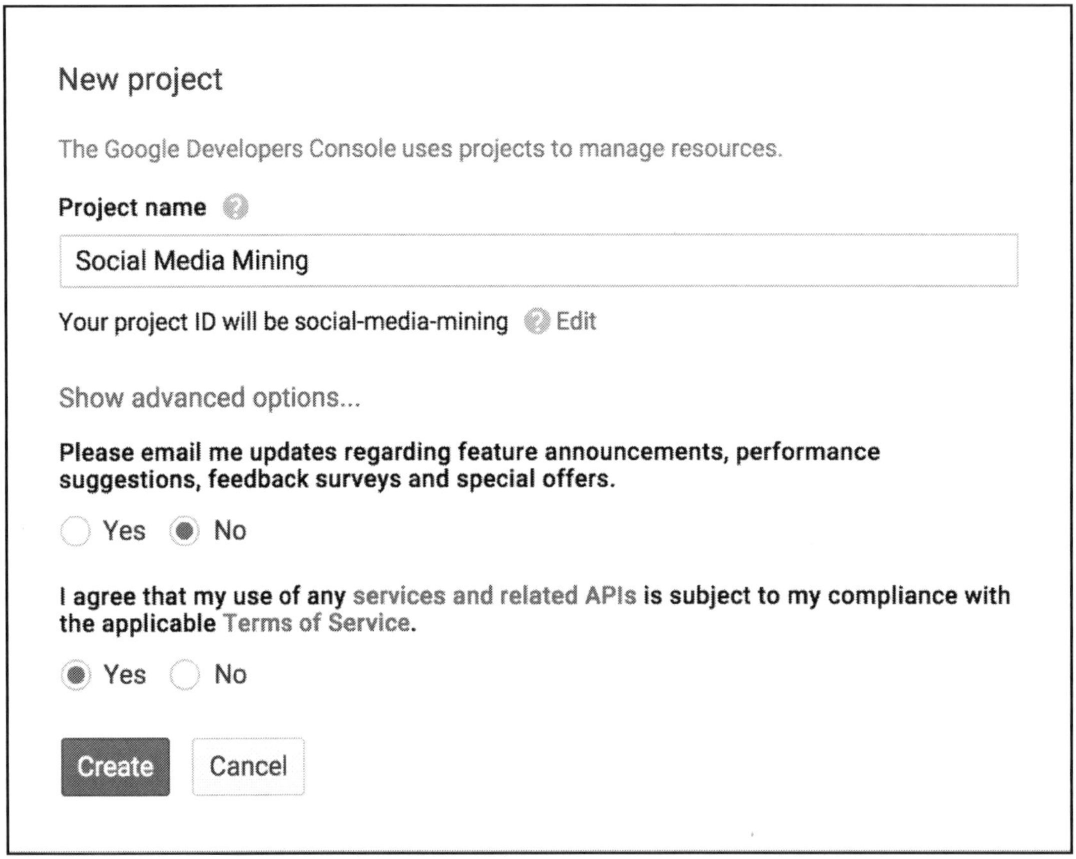

New project

The Google Developers Console uses projects to manage resources.

Project name 🔘

```
Social Media Mining
```

Your project ID will be social-media-mining 🔘 Edit

Show advanced options...

Please email me updates regarding feature announcements, performance suggestions, feedback surveys and special offers.

◯ Yes ◉ No

I agree that my use of any services and related APIs **is subject to my compliance with the applicable** Terms of Service.

◉ Yes ◯ No

[Create] [Cancel]

Figure 5.1: Creating a project in the Google Developers Console

After the project has been created, we need to specifically enable the Google+ API. From the project dashboard, the **Use Google APIs** component allows us to manage API access, create new credentials, and so on. Similar to the way a single Google account can be used to access several Google services, a single project can consume several APIs as long as they are enabled. Once we have located the Google+ API under the **Social APIs** group, we can enable it with a single click. *Figure 5.2* shows the **Overview**, as follows:

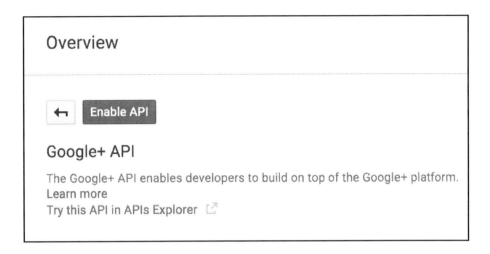

Figure 5.2: Enabling the Google+ API for our project

Immediately after the API is enabled, the system will remind us that, in order to consume the API, we need some sort of credentials, as shown in *Figure 5.3*:

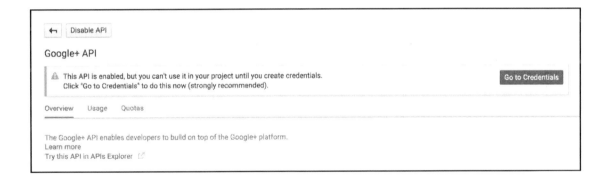

Figure 5.3: After enabling the API, we need to set up the credentials

The **Credentials** tab is easily reachable from the left-hand side menu. There are three different types of credentials: **API key**, **OAuth client ID** or **Service account key** (the latter is needed only for server-to-server use with the Google Cloud APIs).

An **API key** is required for simple API access, that is, an API call that doesn't access any private user data. This key enables an application-level authentication, which is mainly used to measure the project usage for accounting purposes (more details on rate limits are given in the following sections).

An **OAuth client ID** is required for authorized API access, that is, an API call that does access private user data. Before the call, the user who has access to the private data must explicitly grant access to your application. Different Google APIs declare different scopes, that is, the set of permitted operations that have to be approved by the user.

If you are unsure about the type of credentials your application will need, the dashboard also offers a **Help me choose** option (shown in *Figure 5.4*) that will guide you through the choice via a couple of simple questions that will clarify the level of privileges your application needs:

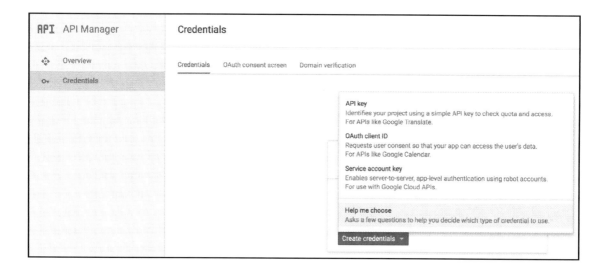

Figure 5.4: The drop-down menu to choose the type of credentials for API access

Once we set up the project and access keys that we need, we can look into how to programmatically access the Google+ API.

Google provides an official Python client for Google APIs, which can be installed in our virtual environment with `pip` using the usual procedure:

```
$ pip install google-api-python-client
```

The client will be available through the `googleapiclient` package, which is also aliased simply as `apiclient`. The following section shows the first working example to test the use of the API.

Searching on Google+

The first example, shown in the `gplus_search_example.py` script, queries the Google+ API searching for people or pages.

This example assumes that you have already set up an API key for simple access through the **Credentials** page on the project dashboard-we're not accessing personal data yet. Similar to what we did with Twitter and Facebook, we will follow the pattern of storing the credentials as environment variables. For example, if we are using the Bash prompt, we can use the following command:

```
$ export GOOGLE_API_KEY="your-api-key-here"
```

The `export` command can also be included in a shell script if we want to:

```python
# Chap05/gplus_search_example.py
import os
import json
from argparse import ArgumentParser
from apiclient.discovery import build

def get_parser():
    parser = ArgumentParser()
    parser.add_argument('--query', nargs='*')
    return parser

if __name__ == '__main__':
    api_key = os.environ.get('GOOGLE_API_KEY')
    parser = get_parser()
    args = parser.parse_args()

    service = build('plus',
                    'v1',
                    developerKey=api_key)

    people_feed = service.people()
    search_query = people_feed.search(query=args.query)
    search_results = search_query.execute()

    print(json.dumps(search_results, indent=4))
```

The script uses an instance of `ArgumentParser` to read the query string from the command line. For example, if we want to query for the term `packt`, we can run the script as follows:

```
$ python gplus_search_example.py --query packt
```

The `--query` argument of the parser is defined with the `nargs='*'` attribute so that multiple terms can be added and used for the search query.

The starting point for using the APIs is to create a `service` object using the `build()` function. From the Google API client, we will import the service builder, which takes the name of the service we want to interact with (`plus`) and the version of its API (`v1`) as mandatory arguments, followed by `developerKey`, that is, the API key that we defined earlier.

 The list of supported APIs and their latest version is shown in the documentation at `https://developers.google.com/api-client-library/python/apis/`.

In general, the service builder is used in the following way:

```
from apiclient.discovery import build
service = build('api_name', 'api_version', [extra params])
```

Once the `service` object is built, it can provide access to different resources (grouped into collections). In the example, we will query the `people` collection.

Once the search query is built and executed, the script simply dumps the JSON output on the screen so that we can have an understanding of the format:

```
{
  "nextPageToken": "token-string",
  "selfLink": "link-to-this-request",
  "title": "Google+ People Search Results",
  "etag": "etag-string",
  "kind": "plus#peopleFeed",
  "items": [
    {
      "kind": "plus#person",
      "objectType": "page",
      "image": {
        "url": "url-to-image"
      },
      "id": "112328881995125817822",
      "etag": "etag-string",
      "displayName": "Packt Publishing",
      "url": "https://plus.google.com/+packtpublishing"
    },
    {
      /* more items ... */
    }
```

```
    ]
  }
```

The output has been simplified for brevity, but the overall structure is clear. The first-level attributes (for example, `title`, `selfLink`, and so on) define some characteristics of the result set. The list of results is included in the `items` list. Each item is uniquely identified by the `id` attribute and it's also represented by its `url`. The results shown in this example can contain a mixture of pages and persons as defined in the `objectType` attribute. The `displayName` attribute is chosen by the user (or the page administrator) and is normally shown in the corresponding G+ page.

Embedding the search results in a web GUI

In this section, we will expand on the first example in order to visualize the results of our search. As a means to show the items, we'll use a web page automatically generated on the fly so that we can display the profile image next to the display name for each person or page using a familiar interface. This visualization can help us disambiguate between different results that share the same display name.

In order to reach this goal, we will introduce **Flask** (`http://flask.pocoo.org/`), a micro framework for web development that allows us to rapidly produce a web interface.

Broadly speaking, Python and web development go hand in hand, and several web-related Python libraries have been around for many years, reaching an interesting level of maturity. Flask is relatively young compared to other frameworks, but it has also reached a level of maturity and has been adopted by a wide community. As web development is not a core concept of this book, we will adopt Flask due to its *micro* nature-it makes no assumptions about the structure of our application and makes it easier to get started with a relatively small amount of code.

Some of the features of Flask include the following:

- Development server and debugger
- Integrated support for unit testing
- Support for templating using the Jinja2 library
- It is Unicode-based
- A large amount of extensions for a variety of use cases

The installation process using `pip` is the usual, as follows:

```
$ pip install flask
```

The preceding command will install the micro framework and the related dependencies.

An interested reader can broaden their knowledge with a variety of titles by *Packt Publishing*, for example, *Learning Flask Framework* by *Matt Copperwaite* and *Charles Leifer* or *Mastering Flask* by *Jack Stouffer* for more advanced use cases. This chapter will keep the discussion about Flask to the minimum by jumping directly onto an example:

```
# Chap05/gplus_search_web_gui.py
import os
import json
from flask import Flask
from flask import request
from flask import render_template
from apiclient.discovery import build

app = Flask(__name__)
api_key = os.environ.get('GOOGLE_API_KEY')

@app.route('/')
def index():
  return render_template('search_form.html')

@app.route('/search', methods=['POST'])
def search():
  query = request.form.get('query')
  if not query:
    # query not given, show an error message
    message = 'Please enter a search query!'
    return render_template('search_form.html', message=message)
  else:
    # search
    service = build('plus',
                    'v1',
                    developerKey=api_key)

    people_feed = service.people()
    search_query = people_feed.search(query=query)
    search_results = search_query.execute()
    return render_template('search_results.html',
                           query=query,
                           results=search_results['items'])

if __name__ == '__main__':
  app.run(debug=True)
```

The `gplus_search_web_gui.py` script implements a basic web application in Flask, showing a simple form to query the Google+ API and display the results.

The application is simply an instance of the `Flask` class and its main method is `run()`, which is used to start the web server (in the example, we will run it in debug mode to simplify the debugging process if needed).

The behavior of the web app is defined by its routes, that is, when a request on a specific URL is performed, Flask routes this request on the desired piece of code, which will produce the response. In the simplest form, routes in Flask are simply decorated functions.

Decorators in Python

While using decorators in Python is extremely simple, understanding them is not if you are new to the topic.

A decorator is simply a function that can be used to enrich the behavior of another function by acting as a wrapper around the target function. This change in behavior is dynamic as it doesn't need any change in the code of the target function, nor the use of subclassing. In this way, a specific functionality can be improved without introducing any particular complexity to the existing code base.

Generally speaking, decorators are a powerful and elegant tool that can prove to be extremely useful in different situations.

In the previous example, `index()` and `search()` are the decorated functions, and in both cases, the decorator is `app.route()`. The decorator is called immediately above the target function, prefixing it with the @ symbol.

Flask routes and templates

The `app.route()` decorator takes the first parameter with the relative URL of the resource we want to access. The second parameter is the list of supported HTTP methods for a specific URL. If the second parameter is not given, it defaults to the GET method.

The `index()` function is used to display the entry page, which contains the search form, available at the relative URL /. All this function does is return the web page stored in the `search_form.html` template by means of the `render_template()` function.

As Flask leverages the Jinja2 template library (`http://jinja.pocoo.org/`), the `render_template()` function reads the code stored in the HTML file, applies the templating directives, and returns the final HTML page as output.

Without going too much into details that are best left for an interested reader to check out in the official documentation, the purpose of using a templating library is to introduce a special syntax embedded into the web pages that can be parsed to generate HTML dynamically.

The source of the `templates/search_form.html` file, positioned relatively to the Python file running Flask, in our case, `gplus_search_web_gui.py`, is shown as follows:

```html
<html>
  <body>

    {% if message %}
    <p>{{ message }}</p>
    {% endif %}

    <form action="/search" method="post">
      Search for:
      <input type="text" name="query" />
      <input type="submit" name="submit" value="Search!" />
    </form>

  </body>
</html>
```

The source contains a basic page (overly simplified for brevity) with a single form. The only templating directive on this page is an `if` block that checks for the `message` variable and shows it in a paragraph if present.

The form action is set to the relative URL `/search` using the POST method. This is the configuration of the second decorated function in the `gplus_search_web_gui.py` file, `search()`.

The `search()` function is where the interaction with the Google+ API happens. Firstly, the function expects a `query` parameter to be passed through the form. This parameter is accessed through the `request.form` dictionary.

The global `request` object in Flask is used in general to access the incoming request data. The `request.form` dictionary provides access to the data that has been passed through a form using a POST method.

If no query is given, the `search()` function will show the search form again, including an error message. The `render_template()` function takes a number of keyword parameters and passes them to the template, in this case, the only parameter is `message`.

On the other hand, if a query is provided, the search() function will perform the interaction with the Google+ API and feed the results to the search_results.html template. The source for the templates/search_results.html file is as follows:

```
<html>
  <link rel="stylesheet"
    href="{{ url_for('static', filename='style.css') }}" />
  <body>

    Searching for <strong>{{ query }}</strong>:

    {% for item in results %}
    <div class="{{ loop.cycle('row_odd', 'row_even') }}">
      <a href="{{ item.url }}">{{ item.displayName }}</a>
      ({{ item.objectType}})<br />
      <a href="{{ item.url }}">
        <img src="{{ item.image.url }}" />
      </a>
    </div>
    {% endfor %}

    <p><a href="/">New search</a></p>

  </body>
</html>
```

The core of the body is a for loop, which iterates over the list of results. For each item in the list, a <div> element with the details for the given item is shown. We notice that the syntax to print the value for a specific variable is constructed with double curly brackets, for example, {{ item.displayName }} will print the display name for each item. On the other hand, the control flow is enclosed in {% and %} symbols.

This example also uses a couple of interesting facilities that allow easy integration with the **Cascading Style Sheet (CSS)** necessary to personalize the look of the result page. The loop.cycle() function is used to cycle between a list of strings or variables and it's used here to assign different CSS classes to the <div> blocks that form the results. In this way, the different rows can be highlighted with different (alternate) colors. The other facility is the url_for() function, used to provide the URL for a particular resource. The static folder, which is similar to the templates folder, has to be placed in the same directory of the gplus_search_web_gui.py file that runs the Flask app. It's used to serve static files, such as images or CSS definitions. The static/style.css file contains the definition of the CSS used in the search result page and is as follows:

```
.row_odd {
  background-color: #eaeaea;
```

```
}
.row_even {
  background-color: #fff;
}
```

While the topic of web development is not strictly related to data mining, it provides an easy way to rapidly prototype some simple user interface. The topic is quite vast and this chapter doesn't aim at a comprehensive discussion. An interested reader is invited to dig into the details of web development and Flask.

The example can be run with the following command line:

```
$ python gplus_search_web_gui.py
```

This will run the Flask app, which will wait for an HTTP request in order to provide a response as defined in the Python code. After running the script, the application should be running in the foreground and the following output should appear on the terminal:

```
* Running on http://127.0.0.1:5000/ (Press CTRL+C to quit)
```

The 127.0.0.1 address is the localhost, while port 5000 is the default for Flask.

Flask server visible through the network
If you are running the Flask application on a virtual machine or machine over the network, you'll need to use the appropriate network address for this machine instead of the localhost address.
Moreover, you'll need to make sure that the server is externally visible so that it's reachable through the network. As this could have security implications, it's first advisable that you consider whether you trust the users of your network.
In order to make the Flask application externally visible, you can either disable the debugging mode or bind the server to the appropriate address, for example:
```
app.run(host='0.0.0.0')
```
Here, 0.0.0.0 means *all addresses on the local machine*.

We can now open a browser window and point to http://127.0.0.1:5000, as shown in *Figure 5.5*:

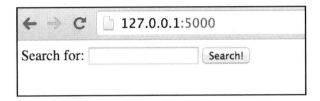

Figure 5.5: The entry page of the Flask application

If we click on the **Search!** button without inserting any input, the app will again show the form with an error message, as shown in *Figure 5.6*:

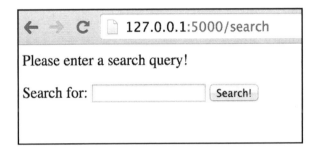

Figure 5.6: The error message if no query is given

On the other hand, if a query is correctly given, the result page will be shown as in *Figure 5.7* (the given query for this figure is `packt`):

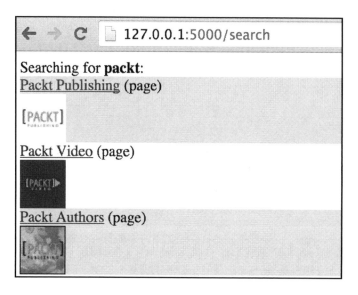

Figure 5.7: The results from a search on the Google+ API

As we can see, each item is displayed in its own block, with alternate background color and the desired information about the item itself. The item names are represented within anchor tags (`<a>`), so they are clickable and linked to the related Google+ page.

Notes and activities from a Google+ page

After searching for a Google+ page and visualizing the results in a web GUI, we will proceed to download a list of activities for a given page. Activities are the Google+ equivalent of Facebook posts. By default, an activity is considered to be a note, that is, a piece of text shared on Google+.

The following script, `gplus_get_page_activities.py`, is used to collect a list of activities from a Google+ page:

```
# Chap05/gplus_get_page_activities.py
import os
import json
from argparse import ArgumentParser
from apiclient.discovery import build
```

```
def get_parser():
  parser = ArgumentParser()
  parser.add_argument('--page')
  parser.add_argument('--max-results', type=int, default=100)
  return parser

if __name__ == '__main__':
  api_key = os.environ.get('GOOGLE_API_KEY')
  parser = get_parser()
  args = parser.parse_args()

  service = build('plus',
                  'v1',
                  developerKey=api_key)

  activity_feed = service.activities()
  activity_query = activity_feed.list(
                                      collection='public',
                                      userId=args.page,
                                      maxResults='100'
                                      )

  fname = 'activities_{}.jsonl'.format(args.page)
  with open(fname, 'w') as f:
    retrieved_results = 0
    while activity_query and retrieved_results < args.max_results:
      activity_results = activity_query.execute()
      retrieved_results += len(activity_results['items'])
      for item in activity_results['items']:
        f.write(json.dumps(item)+"\n")
      activity_query = service.activities().list_next(activity_query,
                                                      activity_results)
```

The script uses `ArgumentParser` to get a couple of input parameters from the command line. The `--page` option is required as it contains the ID of the page (or user) we're looking for. This parameter can either be the numeric ID of the page or its Google+ handle (for example, `+packtpublishing` for the Packt Publishing G+ page). The other parameter is the maximum number of results (that is, activities) that we want to retrieve. This parameter is optional and it defaults to `100`.

The script can be run as follows:

```
$ python gplus_get_page_activities.py --page +packtpublishing
  --max-results 1000
```

After a few seconds, we will find the list of activities in the JSON format in the `activities_+packtpublishing.jsonl` file. The file, as we did for Twitter and Facebook, is formatted according to the JSON Lines specification, meaning that every line is individually a valid JSON document.

The complete description of a single activity is available in the documentation at `https://developers.google.com/+/web/api/rest/latest/activities#resource`. The following list provides an overview of the most significant fields:

- `kind`: This is the item type (that is, `plus#activity`)
- `etag`: This is the entity tag string (refer to `https://en.wikipedia.org/wiki/HTTP_ETag`)
- `title`: This is a short title for the activity
- `verb`: This is either a post or share
- `actor`: This is an object representing the user sharing or posting the activity
- `published`: This is the publication date in the ISO 8601 format
- `updated`: This is the date of the last update in the ISO 8601 format
- `id`: This is the unique identifier of the activity
- `url`: This is the URL of the activity
- `object`: This is a complex object with all the details about the activity, such as content, original actor (if the activity is a share, this will be different from the actor of the activity), information about replies, shares and *plus ones*, list of attachments and related details (for example, images), and information about the geolocation if available

The description of the object has introduced the *plus one* concept, which is somewhat similar to the *Like* button on Facebook. When users like a particular piece of content on Google+, they can *+1* it. The +1 button allows users to share content on Google+ and it also recommends content on Google Search. The details about +1 reactions on a specific object are available in the `plusoners` key in the JSON document. `plusoners.totalItems` contains the number of +1 reactions, while `plusoners.selfLink` contains an API link to the list of +1s. Similarly, `replies` and `resharers` contain the same information about direct comments and shares.

Looking at the gist of the code to download the list of activities, we can see that the starting point is still the `apiclient.discovery.build()` function to build the service object. The following step stores the collection of activities in the `activity_feed` object. In order to query the `activity_feed` object, we will use its `list()` function rather than `search()` as we are retrieving the complete list of activities (at least up to the maximum number of available results). The function requires two mandatory parameters: `collection` and `userId`. While `collection` can accept only `public` as value, the `userId` parameter is the identifier of the user/page whose activities we are retrieving. The parameter can be in the form of a unique numeric identifier or the Google+ handler string. We can also pass `maxResults` as an optional parameter, which is set to `100` in this example. This is the number of items that can be retrieved by a single API call (the default is `20`, the maximum is `100`).

The code also shows how to use pagination with this API. The query is being executed inside a `while` loop, which updates a counter with the number of retrieved results (looping up to the value specified via `--max-results`) and checks whether a next page of results exists. The `list_next()` function, which takes the current query and current list of results as parameters, takes care of the pagination by updating the query object. If a next page of results is not available (that is, the user/page hasn't published more posts than the ones already retrieved), the function will return `None`.

Text analysis and TF-IDF on notes

After discussing how to download a list of notes and activities for a given page or user, we will shift our focus to the textual analysis of the content.

For each post published by a given user, we want to extract the most interesting keywords, which could be used to summarize the post itself.

While this is intuitively a simple exercise, there are a few subtleties to consider. On the practical side, we can easily observe that the content of each post is not always a clean piece of text, in fact, HTML tags can be included in the content. Before we can carry out our computation, we need to extract the clean text. While the JSON object returned by the Google+ API has a clear structure, the content itself is not necessarily a well-formed structured document. Fortunately, there's a nice Python package that comes to the rescue. **Beautiful Soup** is, in fact, able to parse HTML and XML documents, including malformed markup. It is compatible with Python 3 and can be installed from the CheeseShop in the usual way. From our virtual environment, use the following command:

```
$ pip install beautifulsoup4
```

This will install version 4.* of the library. The transition from version 3.* to version 4.* has seen some important changes, so the examples shown here are not compatible with older versions of the library.

The next important question is how do we define the importance of a keyword?

This problem can be tackled from different directions, and the definition of importance can change depending on the application. In our case, we will use an approach based on statistics, where the importance of a keyword is given by its presence within the document and the collection of documents that we are analyzing.

The proposed approach is called **TF-IDF** (`https://en.wikipedia.org/wiki/Tf%E2%80 %93idf`), a combination of two scores (**TF** and **IDF**) based on term frequencies. `Chapter 3`, *Users, Followers, and Communities on Twitter*, on Twitter briefly introduced TF-IDF using the off-the-shelf implementation offered by the scikit-learn library. In general, using an existing implementation is a good idea, especially if it's coming from a high-quality library, such as scikit-learn. In this section, we will propose a custom implementation so that we can showcase the details of TF-IDF to provide the reader with a better understanding of this framework.

The motivation behind TF-IDF is fairly straightforward: a word is a good candidate to represent a document if it shows a high frequency within the document, but is rare across the collection. These two properties are reflected by two scores: **Term Frequency (TF)**, the local frequency of a term within a document, and **Inverse Document Frequency (IDF)**, calculated over the whole collection of documents.

IDF was proposed in 1972 in the context of information retrieval research by Karen Sparck-Jones (`https://en.wikipedia.org/wiki/Karen_Sp%C3%A4rck_Jones`), one of the pioneers of the field. Introduced as a heuristic, it shows a connection between term specificity and Zipf's law (`https://en.wikipedia.org/wiki/Zipf%27s_law`).

Zipf's law and Zipfian distribution

Zipf's law is an empirical law that refers to the fact that many types of data in different fields of science can be approximated by a Zipfian (that is, long-tail) distribution. In `Chapter 2`, *#MiningTwitter – Hashtags, Topics, and Time Series*, we already observed that the words used by Packt Publishing in their tweets follow this distribution. Refer to `Chapter 2`, *#MiningTwitter – Hashtags, Topics, and Time Series*, for more details on Zipf's Law.

From a mathematical point of view, different variations of TF and IDF have been proposed over the years.

Two of the most common options for TF are to simply consider the raw frequency of a word in a document or to normalize it over the number of words in a document (that is, the frequentist interpretation of the probability of observing a word in a document).

On the IDF side, the traditional definition is `log(N/n)`, where `N` is the total number of documents, while `n` is the number of documents that contain the given term. For terms that are present in every document, this will lead to an IDF value of zero (that is, `log(1)`). For this reason, one of the possible normalizations for IDF is `1+log(N/n)`.

Figure 5.8 provides a visual representation of the intuition behind TF-IDF and its connection with Zipf's law-words which are too frequent or too rare are not representative:

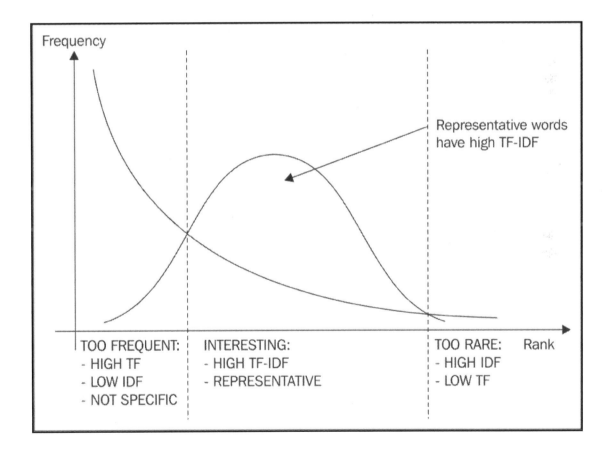

Figure 5.8: The distribution of words and their importance

Frequent words include stop words, for example, terms such as articles, conjunctions, and propositions. Generally speaking, they do not bear any particular meaning on their own, so they can be ignored (that is, removed). On the other hand, very rare words include typos and terms that are too technical. Depending on the application, it's worth exploring the dataset to have a better understanding of whether stop word removal is a good idea.

The `gplus_activities_keywords.py` script reads the list of activities from a given JSON Lines file, computes TF-IDF of every word for the textual content of each activity, and then shows the top keywords next to each post.

 The code uses the NLTK library to perform some text processing operations, such as tokenization and stop word removal. In Chapter 1, *Social Media, Social Data, and Python,* we saw how to download the additional NLTK packages required to perform some of these operations, specifically the `punkt` package for tokenization.

The `gplus_activities_keywords.py` script is as follows:

```
# Chap05/gplus_activities_keywords.py
import os
import json
from argparse import ArgumentParser
from collections import defaultdict
from collections import Counter
from operator import itemgetter
from math import log
from string import punctuation
from bs4 import BeautifulSoup
from nltk.tokenize import word_tokenize
from nltk.corpus import stopwords
```

We will define a list of stop words that include the common English stop words and punctuation symbols:

```
punct = list(punctuation)
all_stopwords = stopwords.words('english') + punct

def get_parser():
    parser = ArgumentParser()
    parser.add_argument('--file',
                        '-f',
                        required=True,
                        help='The .jsonl file of the activities')
    parser.add_argument('--keywords',
                        type=int,
                        default=3,
```

```
                          help='N of words to extract for each post')
        return parser
```

The preprocessing steps are handled by the `preprocess()` function, which orchestrates normalization, data cleaning (using the `clean_html()` helper function) and tokenization:

```python
def clean_html(html):
    soup = BeautifulSoup(html, "html.parser")
    text = soup.get_text(" ", strip=True)
    text = text.replace('\xa0', ' ')
    text = text.replace('\ufeff', ' ')
    text = ' '.join(text.split())
    return text

def preprocess(text, stop=all_stopwords, normalize=True):
    if normalize:
        text = text.lower()
    text = clean_html(text)
    tokens = word_tokenize(text)
    return [tok for tok in tokens if tok not in stop]
```

The following functions deal with word-based statistics. `make_idf()` creates the collection-wide IDF scores, which can be used by `get_keywords()` to calculate the TF-IDF scores for each document, with the purpose of extracting interesting keywords:

```python
def make_idf(corpus):
    df = defaultdict(int)
    for doc in corpus:
        terms = set(doc)
        for term in terms:
            df[term] += 1
    idf = {}
    for term, term_df in df.items():
        idf[term] = 1 + log(len(corpus) / term_df)
    return idf

def get_keywords(doc, idf, normalize=False):
    tf = Counter(doc)
    if normalize:
        tf = {term: tf_value/len(doc)
              for term, tf_value in tf.items()}
    tfidf = {term: tf_value*idf[term]
             for term, tf_value in tf.items()}
    return sorted(tfidf.items(),
                  key=itemgetter(1),
                  reverse=True)

if __name__ == '__main__':
```

```
parser = get_parser()
args = parser.parse_args()
with open(args.file) as f:

  posts = []
  for line in f:
    activity = json.loads(line)
    posts.append(preprocess(activity['object']['content']))

idf = make_idf(posts)

for i, post in enumerate(posts):
  keywords = get_keywords(post, idf)
  print("---------")
  print("Content: {}".format(post))
  print("Keywords: {}".format(keywords[:args.keywords]))
```

As usual, we will take advantage of `ArgumentParser` to read the command-line arguments. In particular, `--file` is used to pass the filename, and `--keywords` is an optional argument to specify the number of keywords that we want to observe for each document (the default is 3).

For example, the script can be run as follows:

```
$ python gplus_activities_keywords.py --file
  activities_+LarryPage.jsonl --keywords 5
```

The command will read the `.jsonl` file of the activities for the user +LarryPage (assuming that we downloaded it previously) and will show the top five keywords for each activity.

For example, one of Larry Page's posts is as follows:

```
---------
Content: ['fun', 'day', 'kiteboarding', 'alaska', 'pretty', 'cold',
'gusty', 'ago']
Keywords: [('alaska', 5.983606621708336), ('gusty', 5.983606621708336),
('kiteboarding', 5.983606621708336), ('cold', 4.884994333040227),
('pretty', 3.9041650800285006)]
```

As we can see, the post appears as a list of terms, while the keywords appear as a list of tuples, with each tuple containing the term itself and the TF-IDF score.

The transition from full text to list of tokens is handled by the `preprocess()` function, which also uses the `clean_html()` function as a helper.

The preprocessing takes care of the following steps:

- Text normalization (that is, lowercasing)
- HTML cleaning/stripping
- Tokenization
- Stop word removal

The `preprocess()` function only takes one mandatory argument, and we can personalize the list of stop words to remove (passing an empty list if we don't want to perform this step), as well as switching off the lowercasing by setting the two keyword arguments, `stop` and `normalize`.

Text normalization is used to group together words that differ only due to the casing used, for example, *The* and *the* would be mapped into *the* by the lowercasing process. Lowercasing makes sense for a lot of applications, but there are situations where it's not helpful, for example, in the case of *us* (pronoun) versus the *U.S.* (acronym for the United States). It's important to keep in mind that lowercasing is not reversible, so if we need to refer to the original text later in the application, we will also need to carry it over.

HTML cleaning is performed with a few lines of code, taking advantage of Beautiful Soup. Once the `BeautifulSoup` object is instantiated with `html.parser` as the second parameter, it's able to handle malformed HTML. The `get_text()` function does exactly what is expected: it only gets the text, leaving the HTML behind. The whitespace, used as the first parameter for this function, is used to replace the stripped HTML tags. This is useful for the following situations:

```
... some sentence<br />The beginning of the next one
```

In this case, just stripping the break-line tag would create the `sentenceThe` token, which is obviously not a real word. Replacing the tag with an empty space solves the problem.

The `clean_html()` function is also enriched with a couple of string replacements for Unicode characters that are whitespaces. Finally, if multiple consecutive whitespaces are present in the text, they are normalized into a single whitespace by splitting the text and rejoining it (for example, `' '.join(text.split())`).

Tokenization, the process of breaking a string down into individual tokens, is handled by NLTK through its `word_tokenize()` function.

Finally, stop word removal is performed with a simple list comprehension, where each token is checked against the `stop` list. The list of English stop words from NLTK and the list of punctuation character from `string.punctuation` are used in a combination as the default stop word list.

The TF-IDF implementation is handled by two functions: `make_idf()` and `get_keywords()`. As IDF is a collection-wide statistic, we will compute this first. The `corpus` argument is a list of lists, that is, a list of tokenized documents as they have already been processed by the `preprocess()` function.

Firstly, we will compute the document frequency using the `df` dictionary. This statistic is simply the number of documents in which a term occurs, that is, we don't consider repetitions. For each document in the corpus, we will cast the document in a set. In this way, the terms are considered only once per document. Secondly, we will iterate over the items of the newly built `df` dictionary and we will use it to compute the IDF score, which is then returned by the function. In this version of IDF, we will use the +1 normalization as discussed earlier.

At this point, we are ready to compute the TF-IDF scores for each term in each document. Iterating over all the posts, we will call the `get_keywords()` function, which takes two parameters: the document (a list of tokens) and the IDF dictionary that was previously built. The third optional parameter is a flag to activate the document-length normalization, which effectively converts the TF into the probability of observing a term in a document, that is, $P(t|d)$.

The `get_keywords()` function firstly build the raw TF by means of `collections.Counter`, which is essentially a dictionary. If the document-length normalization is required, the `tf` dictionary is rebuilt through a dictionary comprehension, dividing the value of each raw TF by the total number of terms in the document (that is, by the document length).

The TF-IDF score is computed by multiplying TF with IDF for each term. Once again, a dictionary comprehension is used to do the trick.

Finally, the function returns the list of terms with their related TF-IDF score, sorted by the score. The `sorted()` function is called with `key=itemgetter(1)` to apply the sorting using the TF-IDF score (the second item in the tuple) and with `reverse=True` to show the values in the descending order.

Capturing phrases with n-grams

TF-IDF provides a simple statistical explanation about the importance of a keyword in a given document. Using this model, each word is considered individually and the order of the words doesn't matter. In reality, words are used in sequence, and often a sequence of words act as a single unit within the structure of a sentence (this is also called constituent in linguistics).

Given a tokenized document (that is, a sequence of tokens), we call *n-grams* a sequence of n adjacent terms taken from the aforementioned document. With n=1, we are still considering single terms (also known as unigrams). With a value greater than one, we will consider sequences of arbitrary length. Typical examples include bigrams (with n=2) and trigrams (with n=3), but potentially any sequence length is possible.

NLTK provides facilities to rapidly compute a list of n-grams, given an input list of tokens. In particular, the function that handles the n-gram generation is `nltk.util.ngrams`:

```
>>> from nltk.util import ngrams
>>> s = 'the quick brown fox jumped over the lazy dog'.split()
>>> s
['the', 'quick', 'brown', 'fox', 'jumped', 'over', 'the', 'lazy', 'dog']
>>> list(ngrams(s, 4))
[('the', 'quick', 'brown', 'fox'), ('quick', 'brown', 'fox', 'jumped'),
('brown', 'fox', 'jumped', 'over'), ('fox', 'jumped', 'over', 'the'),
('jumped', 'over', 'the', 'lazy'), ('over', 'the', 'lazy', 'dog')]
```

As you can see, the function takes two parameters: a sequence of tokens and a number. The value returned by `ngrams()` is a generator object, so in order to visualize it on the prompt, we cast it to a list, but it could be used directly, for example, in a list comprehension.

NLTK also provides two useful shortcuts-`nltk.bigrams()` and `nltk.trigrams()`-that simply call the `ngrams()` function with n=2 and n=3 respectively.

As an exercise for an interested reader, we will close this section with the following questions:

- Can we modify the code proposed in this section so that we can capture interesting bigrams or trigrams, and not just individual keywords?
- When capturing n-grams, what is the effect of stop word removal?

Summary

In this chapter, we looked at the Google+ API. We also discussed how to register a project on the Google Developer Console and how to enable the desired API(s) for our project.

The chapter started with an example that showed how to perform a search using the Google+ API. The discussion was then built upon this example in order to embed the use of the API in a web application. Taking advantage of Flask, a micro framework for web development that allows to get up and running with a few lines of code, we built a web GUI to show the results of a search session.

The next step was to analyze textual notes from a user or page. After downloading the user activities and storing them in the JSON Lines format, we discussed a few details of TF-IDF as a statistical approach to extract interesting keywords from a piece of text.

In the next chapter, we will move our attention to the field of question answering, and we will do so by approaching the Stack Overflow API.

6
Questions and Answers on Stack Exchange

This chapter is about Stack Exchange, the question and answer network, and the broader topic of question answering.

In this chapter, we will discuss the following topics:

- How to create an app that interacts with the Stack Exchange API
- How to search for users and questions on Stack Exchange
- How to deal with data dumps for offline processing
- Supervised machine learning methods for text classification
- How to predict question tags using machine learning
- How to embed a machine learning model in a real-time application

Questions and answers

Looking for answers for a particular information need is one of the main uses of the Web. Over time, technology has evolved and Internet users have been changing their online behaviors.

The way people look for information on the Internet nowadays is quite different from 15-20 years ago. Back in the early days, looking for answers mainly meant using a search engine. A study on query logs from a popular search engine in the late 90s (*Searching the Web: The Public and Their Queries* by *Amanda Spink* and others, *2001*) has shown that in those days, a typical search was very short (on average, 2.4 terms).

In recent years, we started experiencing a transition from short keyword-based search queries to longer conversational queries (or should we say, questions). In other words, search engines have been moving from keyword matching to **Natural Language Processing (NLP)**. For example, *Figure 6.1* shows how Google tries to autocomplete a query/questions from the user. The system uses statistics from popular queries trying to predict how the user intends to complete the question:

Figure 6.1: An example of query autocomplete from Google

A user interface in natural language provides a more natural experience for the end user. The more advanced example is the intelligent personal assistant embedded in our smartphones-applications such as Google Now, Apple's Siri, or Microsoft's Cortana allow users to search the Web, get recommendations about a restaurant, or schedule an appointment.

Asking a question is only part of the story, as the most important part is finding the answer to this question. *Figure 6.2* shows the top of a Google result page that answers the query: why is python called python. The so-called *answer box* is activated when Google interprets the query as a conversational one, that is, a proper question rather than a generic informational query. The box contains a snippet from a web page, which Google thinks to be the answer to the given question. The rest of the page, not shown in the figure, contains the traditional **search engine result page (SERP)**:

Figure 6.2: An example of the answer box as a result of a conversational query

Research on automatic **question answering (QA)** is not limited to the field of search engines. A popular achievement in artificial intelligence is represented by IBM Watson, a question answering system developed by IBM and named after the first CEO of IBM, Thomas Watson (`https://en.wikipedia.org/wiki/Watson_(computer)`). The machine gained popularity when it competed, and won, against human champions in a game of *Jeopardy!*, a popular American game show that features a quiz competition, where the contestants have to find the correct question after being given some clues related to the answer. While the competition is reversing the process, that is, you need to find the question for a given answer, the technology that is necessary to solve the problem can operate in both directions.

While search engines and intelligent personal assistants were improving the way users can find information online, the compelling need to find answers has also promoted the rise of QA websites (refer to `https://en.wikipedia.org/wiki/Comparison_of_Q%26A_sites`). One of the most popular QA network is Stack Exchange (`http://stackexchange.com`). Best known for Stack Overflow (`http://stackoverflow.com`), which features questions and answers on a wide range of programming-related topics, the network nowadays consists of dozens of thematic websites, ranging from technology to science and from business to recreation. Other examples of Stack Exchange websites include Movies & TV (for movie and TV shows enthusiasts), Seasoned Advice (for professional and amateur chefs), English Language & Usage (for linguists, etymologists and English language enthusiasts), and Academia (for academics and those enrolled in higher education). The list of individual websites is long and the themes are fairly diverse (`http://stackexchange.com/sites`).

One of the reasons for the success of Stack Exchange is probably the high-quality content curated by the community. Questions and answers are in fact voted by the users so that the top answers can rise to the top. A mechanism of reputation points, earned through the use of the website, allows us to identify the most active members of the community and their areas of expertise. Users can, in fact, earn (or lose) points when their answers receive an *up* (or *down*) vote, and when they propose a content edit in order to improve the quality of the website. The gamification of the system also includes a series of *badges* that the users can earn for their contributions.

In order to keep the quality of the content high, duplicate questions and low quality questions are usually put on hold, reviewed by moderators, and eventually edited or closed.

Some of the main features of social networking services are not present in Stack Exchange. For example, it's not possible to connect directly with other users (for example, the friend or follower relation on Facebook and Twitter), nor can we have private conversations with other users. The effect of Stack Exchange as a social media platform is still clear as people exchange knowledge and collaborate.

The following section provides an introduction to the Stack Exchange API.

Getting started with the Stack Exchange API

The Stack Exchange API (`https://api.stackexchange.com/docs`) provides a programmatic access to all the Stack Exchange websites. Third-party applications that intend to use the API should be registered at `http://stackapps.com` in order to obtain a request key used to grant more requests per day. Registered apps can also perform authenticated API calls, that is, to interact with Stack Exchange on behalf of the authenticated user. The registration process is fairly straightforward, as shown in *Figure 6.3*- all the details required are an **Application Name** and **Description**:

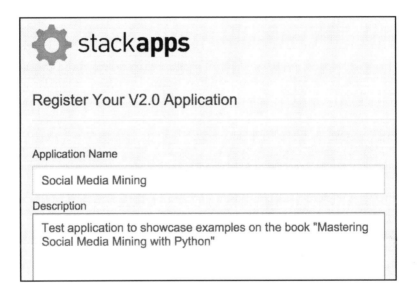

Figure 6.3: An app registration on stackapps.com

The immediate effect of registering our application is the increased number of requests per day that are allowed by the API. It's important to note that rate limits are not only set on a daily basis, but also to prevent flooding (for example, if the same IP is sending more than 30 requests per second, the requests will be dropped). Details on the rate-limit applications are described in the documentation (`https://api.stackexchange.com/docs/throttle`).

After registering the application, we must make note of the keys provided by Stack Exchange. While the *client ID* and *client secret* must be used for the OAuth procedure, in case we need to perform authenticated calls, the key is what we use to enjoy the increased request quota. It's important to note, as detailed in the documentation, that the client ID and key are not secrets; while the client secret, as the name suggests, is sensible information that should not be distributed.

We can configure the use of our application key following the same procedure as the previous chapters, by using environment variables:

```
$ export STACK_KEY="your-application-key"
```

The next tool we need before we can start interacting with the API programmatically is an API client. At the moment, there's mainly one (unofficial) Python Stack Exchange API client called **Py-StackExchange** (https://github.com/lucjon/Py-StackExchange). The client simply binds the API endpoints to Python methods with a straightforward interface.

From our virtual environment, we can install Py-StackExchange following the usual method via the CheeseShop:

```
$ pip install py-stackexchange
```

In order to test the client and showcase its core classes, we can use the Python interactive shell and observe some generic statistics about the Stack Overflow website:

```
>>> import os
>>> import json
>>> from stackexchange import Site
>>> from stackexchange import StackOverflow
>>> api_key = os.environ.get('STACK_KEY')
>>> so = Site(StackOverflow, api_key)
>>> info = so.info()
>>> print(info.total_questions)
10963403
>>> print(info.questions_per_minute)
2.78
>>> print(info.total_comments)
53184453
>>> print(json.dumps(info.json, indent=4))
{
  "total_votes": 75841653,
  "badges_per_minute": 4.25,
  "total_answers": 17891858,
  "total_questions": 10963403,
  "_params_": {
    "body": "false",
    "site": "stackoverflow.com",
    "comments": "false"
  },
  "api_revision": "2016.1.27.19039",
  "new_active_users": 35,
  "total_accepted": 6102860,
  "total_comments": 53184453,
  "answers_per_minute": 4.54,
```

```
    "total_users": 5126460,
    "total_badges": 16758151,
    "total_unanswered": 2940974,
    "questions_per_minute": 2.78
}
```

The core class to interact with the API is `stackexchange.Site`, which can be instantiated with two parameters: the first one is the class definition of the Stack Exchange website that we are interested in (`stackexchange.StackOverflow` in this case), and the second one is the (optional) application key. Once the `Site` object is defined, we can use its methods to access the API.

In this example, we will use the `info()` method to access the `/info` endpoint (`https://api.stackexchange.com/docs/info`). The returned object has a number of attributes. In this example, we will print the values for `total_questions`, `questions_per_minute`, and `total_comments`. The complete list of attributes is visible in the `info.__dict__` dictionary, and more generically, the info object also has an `info.json` attribute, which contains the original response from the API, where all the aforementioned attributes are shown in the JSON format.

Searching for tagged questions

After introducing a basic interaction with the Stack Exchange API, we will use the Python client to search for questions. Specifically, we're going to use the question tags as filters for our keywords.

The following code performs the search:

```python
# Chap06/stack_search_keyword.py
import os
import json
from argparse import ArgumentParser
from stackexchange import Site
from stackexchange import StackOverflow
def get_parser():
  parser = ArgumentParser()
  parser.add_argument('--tags')
  parser.add_argument('--n', type=int, default=20)
  return parser

if __name__ == '__main__':
  parser = get_parser()
  args = parser.parse_args()
  my_key = os.environ.get('STACK_KEY')
```

```
so = Site(StackOverflow, my_key)
questions = so.questions(tagged=args.tags, pagesize=20)[:args.n]

for i, item in enumerate(questions):
  print("{}) {} by {}".format(i,
                              item.title,
                              item.owner.display_name))
```

The code uses `ArgumentParser` to get some parameters from the command line. In particular, the `--tags` option is used to pass the list of tags that we're searching for, separated by a semicolon. The number of results given by the script can be defined using the `--n` flag (with the default being 20 questions).

As an example, we can run the script as follows:

```
$ python stack_search_keyword.py --tags "python;nosql" --n 10
```

The double quotes surrounding the list of tags are needed as the semicolon is the command separator on shells such as Bash, so the line would be interpreted as two separate commands (the second one starting from `nosql`). By using the double quotes, the `python;nosql` string is instead interpreted as a single string, and the whole line as a single command, as we expect.

The list of tags is passed to the API via the `tagged` argument of the `questions()` method. This parameter is used in a Boolean AND query, meaning that the retrieved questions are labelled with both the `python` and `nosql` tags.

Boolean queries
The `questions()` method implements the `/questions` endpoint (`https://api.stackexchange.com/docs/questions`), which uses multiple tags as an AND constrain. The output of a call to this method is a list of questions that contain all the specified tags.
The `search()` method implements instead the `/search` endpoint (`https://api.stackexchange.com/docs/search`), which shows the opposite behavior as multiple tags are plugged into an OR constrain. The output of a call to this method is a list of questions that contain any of the specified tags.

One important detail to note is that the Py-StackExchange client frequently uses lazy lists to minimize the amount of API calls that are performed behind the scenes. This means that methods such as questions() do not return a list, but rather a wrapper around the result set. A direct iteration through such result set would try to access all the items that match the query (if done carelessly, this defeats the purpose of the lazy list), and not only a list of the given page size.

For this reason, we're using the slice operator to explicitly call for a given number of results (specified via the command line with the --n argument, and hence available as args.n).

Slicing and dicing Python lists

The slice operator is a powerful tool, but the syntax could be somewhat confusing for the less experienced Python programmer. The following example summarizes its main uses:

```
# pick items from start to end-1
array[start:end]
# pick items from start to the rest of the array
array[start:]
# pick items from the beginning to end-1
array[:end]
# get a copy of the whole array
array[:]
# pick items from start to not past end, by step
array[start:end:step]
# get the last item
array[-1]
# get the last n items
array[-n:]
# get everything except the n items
array[:-n]
```

For example, consider the following:

```
>>> data = ['one', 'two', 'three', 'four', 'five']
>>> data[2:4]
['three', 'four']
>>> data[2:]
['three', 'four', 'five']
>>> data[:4]
['one', 'two', 'three', 'four']
>>> newdata = data[:]
>>> newdata
['one', 'two', 'three', 'four', 'five']
>>> data[1:5:2]
```

```
['two', 'four']
>>> data[-1]
'five'
>>> data[-1:]
['five']
>>> data[:-2]
['one', 'two', 'three']
```
One important aspect to remember is that the indexes start from zero, so `data[0]` is the first item, `data[1]` the second one, and so on.

The output of the `stack_search_keyword.py` script, run as shown previously, is a sequence of 10 titles for questions related to Python and NoSQL in the following format:

```
n) Question title by User
```

The individual questions (accessed in the `for` loop via the `item` variable) are wrapped into the `stackexchange.model.Question` model class, with attributes such as `title` or `tags`. Each question is also linked to the model of the user who asked it, via the `owner` attribute. In the example, we access `title` of the question and `display_name` of the user.

The result set is sorted by last activity date, meaning that questions with most recent activity (for example, with a new answer) are shown first.

This behavior can be influenced using the `sort` attribute of the `questions()` method, which can take any of the following values:

- `activity` (default): This shows the most recent activity first
- `creation`: This shows the most recent creation date first
- `votes`: This shows the highest score first
- `hot`: This uses the formula for the **hot questions** tab
- `week`: This uses the formula for the **week questions** tab
- `month`: This uses the formula for the **month questions** tab

Searching for a user

After searching for questions, in this section, we will discuss how to search for a specific user. The search procedure is quite similar to the one used to retrieve questions. The following example builds on the previous one as we extend the use of `ArgumentParser` to personalize some search options:

```
# Chap06/stack_search_user.py
import os
import json
from argparse import ArgumentParser
from argparse import ArgumentTypeError
from stackexchange import Site
from stackexchange import StackOverflow
```

The following functions are used to validate the parameters passed via `ArgumentParser`. If the value is not a valid one, they will raise an exception to stop the execution of the script:

```python
def check_sort_value(value):
    valid_sort_values = [
        'reputation',
        'creation',
        'name',
        'modified'
    ]
    if value not in valid_sort_values:
        raise ArgumentTypeError("Invalid sort value")
    return value

def check_order_value(value):
    valid_order_values = ['asc', 'desc']
    if value not in valid_order_values:
        raise ArgumentTypeError("Invalid order value")
    return value
```

The `check_sort_value()` and `check_order_value()` function can then be used in the `ArgumentParser` definition as `type` for the relevant parameters:

```python
def get_parser():
    parser = ArgumentParser()
    parser.add_argument('--name')
    parser.add_argument('--sort',
                        default='reputation',
                        type=check_sort_value)
    parser.add_argument('--order',
                        default='desc',
                        type=check_order_value)
```

```
parser.add_argument('--n', type=int, default=20)
return parser
```

The main logic of the script to implement a user search is fairly straightforward:

```
if __name__ == '__main__':
  parser = get_parser()
  args = parser.parse_args()
  my_key = os.environ.get('STACK_KEY')
  so = Site(StackOverflow, my_key)

  users = so.users(inname=args.name,
                   sort=args.sort,
                   order=args.order)
  users = users[:args.n]

  for i, user in enumerate(users):
    print("{}) {}, reputation {}, joined {}".format(i,
          user.display_name,
          user.reputation,
          user.creation_date))
```

The `stack_search_user.py` script uses `ArgumentParser` as usual to capture command-line arguments. The difference with the previous uses is the personalized data types for some options, such as `--sort` and `--order`. Before digging into the details of the `ArgumentParser` data types, let's see an example of their use.

Let's say that we're searching for the Stack Exchange founders (Jeff Atwood and Joel Spolsky). Sending a query using the given name only can be performed as follows:

```
$ python stack_search_user.py --name joel
```

The output of the preceding command is similar to the following:

```
0) Joel Coehoorn, reputation 231567, joined 2008-08-26 14:24:14
1) Joel Etherton, reputation 27947, joined 2010-01-14 15:39:24
2) Joel Martinez, reputation 26381, joined 2008-09-09 14:41:43
3) Joel Spolsky, reputation 25248, joined 2008-07-31 15:22:31
# (snip)
```

The default behavior of the `Site.users()` method, which implements the `/users` endpoint (`https://api.stackexchange.com/docs/users`) to return a list of users in the descending order of reputation points.

Interestingly, one of the founders of Stack Overflow is not the user with the highest reputation in this result set. We want to find out if he has the oldest registration date. We simply need to add a couple of parameters to the search, as follows:

```
$ python stack_search_user.py --name joel --sort creation --order asc
```

Now the output is different, and as expected, `Joel Spolsky` is the Joel with the oldest registration date:

```
0) Joel Spolsky, reputation 25248, joined 2008-07-31 15:22:31
1) Joel Lucsy, reputation 6003, joined 2008-08-07 13:58:41
2) Joel Meador, reputation 1923, joined 2008-08-19 17:34:45
3) JoelB, reputation 84, joined 2008-08-24 00:05:44
4) Joel Coehoorn, reputation 231567, joined 2008-08-26 14:24:14
# (snip)
```

The use of `ArgumentParser`, as proposed in this example, takes advantage of the fact that we can personalize the data types for the individual arguments. Typically, the `type` parameter passed to the `add_argument()` function uses the built-in data types (such as `int` or `bool`), but in our case, we can move one step further and extend this behavior to perform some basic validation.

The problem we are facing is that the `sort` and `order` parameters to pass to the `/users` endpoint only accept a limited set of strings. The `check_sort_value()` and `check_order_value()` functions simply confirm that the given value is in a list of accepted values. If this is not the case, the functions will raise an `ArgumentTypeError` exception, which will be captured by `ArgumentParser` and used to show a message to the user. For example, use the following command:

```
$ python stack_search_user.py --name joel --sort FOOBAR --order asc
```

This use of the `--sort` argument will produce the following output:

```
usage: stack_search_user.py [-h] [--name NAME] [--sort SORT] [--order
ORDER]
    [--n N]
stack_search_user.py: error: argument --sort: FOOBAR is an invalid sort
value
```

Without implementing a personalized data type, calling the script with the wrong arguments would cause the API to return an error, which would be captured by the Py-StackExchange client and shown as `StackExchangeError` with the related traceback:

```
Traceback (most recent call last):
  File "stack_search_user.py", line 48, in <module>
# (long traceback)
stackexchange.core.StackExchangeError: 400 [bad_parameter]: sort
```

In other words, the personalized data type allows us to handle the error and show a nicer message to the user.

Working with Stack Exchange data dumps

The Stack Exchange network also provides complete dumps of their data, available for download through the Internet Archive (`https://archive.org/details/stackexchange`). The data is available in 7Z, a compressed data format with a high-compression ratio (`http://www.7-zip.org`). In order to read and extract this format, the 7-zip utility for Windows, or one of its ports for Linux/Unix and macOS, must be downloaded.

At the time of writing, the data dumps for Stack Overflow are provided as separate compressed files, with each file representing an entity or table in their dataset. For example, the `stackoverflow.com-Posts.7z` file contains the dump for the Posts table (that is, questions and answers). The size of the first version of this file published in 2016 is about 7.9 GB, which when uncompressed yields a file of 39 GB (approximatively five times bigger than the compressed version). All the other Stack Exchange websites have a much smaller data dump, and they provide a single file for all their tables.

For example, the data from the Movies & TV website (`http://movies.stackexchange.com`), where movie and TV enthusiasts ask and answer questions on this topic, can be downloaded as the single `movies.stackexchange.com.7z` file. Once uncompressed, eight files are produced (one for each entity) as summarized in the following table:

File name	Represented Entity
`movies.stackexchange.com`	Badges
`movies.stackexchange_1.com`	Comments
`movies.stackexchange_2.com`	Post History

`movies.stackexchange_3.com`	Post Links
`movies.stackexchange_4.com`	Posts (questions and answers)
`movies.stackexchange_5.com`	Tags
`movies.stackexchange_6.com`	Users
`movies.stackexchange_7.com`	Votes

The naming convention is the same across different dumps for different sites, for example, for every website, the `website_4.com` filename should contain the list of posts.

The content of the dump file is represented in the XML format. The structure of the file always follows the following template:

```
<?xml version="1.0" encoding="utf-8"?>
  <entity>
    <row [attributes] />
    <!-- more rows -->
  </entity>
```

The first line is a standard XML declaration. The root element of the XML document is the entity type (for example, `posts`, `users`, and so on). Each entry for the specific entity is then represented by a `<row>` element, which has a number of attributes. For example, a small snippet for the `posts` entity looks as follows:

```
<?xml version="1.0" encoding="utf-8"?>
  <posts>
    <row Id="1" PostTypeId="1" ... />
    <row Id="2" PostTypeId="2" ... />
    <row Id="3" PostTypeId="1" ... />
    <!-- more rows -->
  </posts>
```

As the `posts` element is used to represent both questions and answers, the attributes could be different from row to row.

The following table shows a summary of the most important attributes for a `<row>` element used to represent a question:

Attribute name	Description
`Id`	This is the unique identifier for the post
`PostTypeId`	1 for questions

AcceptedAnswerId	This is the ID of the post marked as accepted answer
CreationDate	This is the date the question has been posted in the ISO 8601 format
Score	This is the number of up-votes minus down-votes for the question
ViewCount	This is the number of times the question has been viewed
Title	This is the title of the question
Body	This is the full text of the question
OwnerUserId	This is the ID of the user who posted the question
Tags	This is the list of tags for the question
AnswerCount	This is the number of answers attached to the question
CommentCount	This is the number of comments attached to the question
FavoriteCount	This is the number of users who have labeled the question as favorite

Similarly, the following table shows a list of the main attributes for a `<row>` element used to represent an answer:

Attribute name	Description
Id	This is the unique identifier for the post
PostTypeId	2 for answers
ParentId	This is the ID of the question answered by the post
OwnerUserId	This is the ID of the user who posted the answer
Score	This is the number of up-votes minus down-votes
CommentCount	This is the number of comments attached to the answer
Body	This is the full text of the answer

Throughout this book, we have mainly been working with data in the JSON Lines format as it provides a convenient representation.

The `stack_xml2json.py` script proposed in the following is used to showcase the conversion from the XML of the data dump into a more familiar JSON Lines format. Some basic data cleaning is also performed.

While Python comes with a decent support for XML shipped with the standard library, an interesting package to consider is **lxml** (http://lxml.de). This library provides a Pythonic binding for the low-level C libraries: **libxml2** and **libxslt**, which combine extreme performance and feature completeness with the ease of use of typical well-designed Python libraries.

The only potential downside is the installation procedure, in case things don't go smoothly with the libxml2 and libxslt libraries, which are the required dependencies. The procedure is the usual, using `pip`, like we have done for all the previously installed packages:

```
$ pip install lxml
```

The documentation comes with a detailed discussion (http://lxml.de/installation.html) on the preferred versions of the C libraries, as well as some optimizations. Depending on the platform and on the system configuration, there are many details that could cause the installation to go wrong. A complete troubleshooting goes beyond the scope of this book, but the Web offers plenty of material on this topic (with Stack Overflow itself being a prominent source of information).

Fortunately, lxml has been designed to be as compatible as possible with the **ElementTree** package (part of the Python standard library), so installing lxml is not crucial to follow this section. The suggestion is to try the installation, and if things get too complicated, kicking back without worrying too much about it becomes a concrete option. In fact, if lxml is missing, the script falls back to ElementTree:

```python
# Chap06/stack_xml2json.py
import json
from argparse import ArgumentParser
from bs4 import BeautifulSoup
try:
    from lxml import etree
except ImportError:
    # lxml not installed, fall back to ElementTree
    import xml.etree.ElementTree as etree

def get_parser():
    parser = ArgumentParser()
    parser.add_argument('--xml')
    parser.add_argument('--json')
    parser.add_argument('--clean-post',
                        default=False,
                        action='store_true')
    return parser

def clean_post(doc):
    try:
```

```
      doc['Tags'] = doc['Tags'].replace('><', ' ')
      doc['Tags'] = doc['Tags'].replace('<', '')
      doc['Tags'] = doc['Tags'].replace('>', '')
    except KeyError:
      pass
    soup = BeautifulSoup(doc['Body'], 'html.parser')
    doc['Body'] = soup.get_text(" ", strip=True)
    return doc

if __name__ == '__main__':
  parser = get_parser()
  args = parser.parse_args()

  xmldoc = etree.parse(args.xml)
  posts = xmldoc.getroot()
  with open(args.json, 'w') as fout:
    for row in posts:
      doc = dict(row.attrib)
      if args.clean_post:
        doc = clean_post(doc)
      fout.write("{}\n".format(json.dumps(doc)))
```

The import for lxml is included in a `try/except` block that catches `ImportError`. This type of exception is raised when we try to import a package/module that is not present in the Python path.

The `stack_xml2json.py` script once again uses `ArgumentParser` to capture the command-line arguments. The script can use an optional `--clean-post` flag, so we can differentiate between the `posts` entity, which requires some special treatment described later in this section, and all the other entities.

For example, to convert the tags file of the Movies & TV dataset into JSON, we can use the following command:

```
$ python stack_xml2json.py --xml movies.stackexchange_5.com --json
  movies.tags.jsonl
```

This creates the `movies.tags.jsonl` file, where each tag is represented as a JSON document on a single line. Using the Bash prompt, we can briefly inspect the file:

```
$ wc -l movies.tags.jsonl
```

The preceding command counts the number of lines in the file, hence the number of tags:

```
2218 movies.tags.jsonl
```

If we want to inspect the first JSON document, that is, the first line of the file, we use the following command:

```
$ head -1 movies.tags.jsonl
```

This produces the following output:

```
{"Count": "108", "WikiPostId": "279", "Id": "1", "TagName": "comedy",
"ExcerptPostId": "280"}
```

The script uses lxml.etree to parse the XML document into the xmldoc variable, which holds a tree representation of the document in the form of an ElementTree instance. In order to access a specific object of the tree, we're using the getroot() method as the entry point to start iterating over the rows. This method returns an Element object, stored in the posts variable. As described earlier, each file from the data dump has a similar structure, with the root element holding the entity name (for example, <tags>, <posts>, and so on).

In order to access the individual entries (that is, rows) for the given entity, we can iterate over the root element with a regular for loop. The rows are also instances of the Element class. The conversion from XML to JSON requires dumping the element attributes into a dictionary; this is achieved by simply casting the row.attrib object into a dict in order to make it JSON serializable. This dictionary can then be dumped via json.dumps() into the output file.

As mentioned earlier, the posts entity requires a special treatment. When we use the script to convert the posts into JSON, we need the extra --clean-post argument:

```
$ python stack_xml2json.py --xml movies.stackexchange_4.com --json
    movies.posts.jsonl --clean-post
```

This command produces the movies.posts.jsonl file. The additional flag calls the clean_post() function to perform some data cleaning over the dictionary containing a single post. Specifically, the attributes that require some cleaning are Tags (for questions) and Body (for both questions and answers).

The `Tags` attribute is a string in the `<tag1><tag2>...<tagN>` format, so the angled bracket characters are used as delimiters for the individual tags. By stripping the brackets and adding a space between tag names, we're simplifying the process of retrieving tag names later. For example, a movie question could be labeled as comedy and romance. Before cleaning, the value of the `Tags` attribute in this case would be `<comedy><romance>`, and after cleaning, this is transformed into `comedy romance`. The replacement is enclosed in a `try/except` block that captures `KeyError`; this exception is raised when the `Tags` key is not present in the document, that is, when we are processing an answer (only questions have tags).

The following step consists of using Beautiful Soup to extract the text from the body. In fact, occasionally the body contains some HTML code for paragraph formatting, which we don't need to analyze the textual content of the question. The `get_text()` method from Beautiful Soup strips the HTML code out and returns only the text as we need.

Text classification for question tags

This section is about supervised learning. We define the problem of assigning tags to a question as a text classification problem and we apply it to a dataset of questions from Stack Exchange.

Before introducing the details of text classification, let's consider the following question from the Movies & TV Stack Exchange website (title and body of the question have been merged):

> *"What's the House MD episode where he hired a woman to fake dead to fool the team? I remember a (supposedly dead) woman waking up and giving a high-five to House. Which episode was this from?"*

The preceding question asks for details about a particular episode of the popular TV series *House, M.D.* As described earlier, questions on Stack Exchange are labeled with tags with the purpose of quickly identifying the topic of the question. The tags assigned by the user to this question are `house` and `identify-this-episode`, the first one being a reference to the TV series itself, while the second one describing the nature of the question. One could argue that just using a single tag to label the question (that is, simply using `house`) would be good enough to describe its topic. At the same time, we observe that the two tags are not mutually exclusive, so multiple tags can help to better represent the question.

While the process of assigning labels to documents as described earlier, with the purpose of better understanding the topic of a document, seems to be intuitively straightforward, it is a particular case of the long-standing problem of assigning items (real objects, people, countries, concepts, and so on) to classes. Classification as a field of study spans across multiple disciplines, ranging from philosophy to computer science to business management. In this book, classification is approached as a machine learning problem.

Supervised learning and text classification

Supervised learning is the machine learning field that infers a function from labeled training data. Classification, as a particular case of supervised learning, serves the purpose of assigning the correct class (label) to a new item on the basis of a training set of items whose classes are known.

Practical examples of classification include the following:

- **Spam filtering**: Deciding whether a new e-mail is spam or not
- **Language identification**: Automatically detecting the language of a text
- **Genre identification**: Automatically detecting the genre/topic of a text

These examples describe different variants of classification:

- The spam filtering task is a case of binary classification, as there are only two possible classes, spam or not-spam, of which one must be chosen. It is also a case of single-label classification because a given document can be described with one and only one label.
- Language identification can be approached in different ways. With the assumption of having a document written in only one language, language identification is also a single-label problem. In terms of number of classes, it can be approached as a binary classification problem (for example, is this document written in English or not?), but it's probably best described as a multiclass problem, that is, there is a number of classes greater than two and the document can be assigned to any of them.
- Finally, genre identification (or topic classification) is typically approached as a multiclass and multilabel problem: the number of potential classes is greater than two, and the same document can be assigned to multiple categories (as in the *House, M.D.* question example).

Being a particular case of supervised learning, classification requires training data, that is, instances of the data with the correct label already assigned. A classifier operates in two phases, as pictured in *Figure 6.4*, the learning (or training) step and the prediction step:

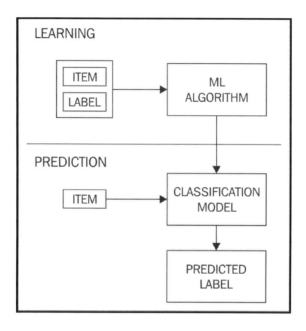

Figure 6.4: A generic framework of supervised learning

During the learning phase, the training data are provided to the machine learning algorithm. The input of the algorithm is hence a series of pairs (item, labels), where the correct label(s) for a given item is known. This process builds the classifier model, which is then used to predict the labels for new unseen data. In this phase, the input is a new item and the output is the label (or labels) assigned to the item by the algorithm.

In the process of building a model for classification, the machine learning algorithm *pays attention* to some elements in order to learn how to classify documents.

In the context of machine learning, a common way to represent documents (and more in general, objects), is with n-dimensional vectors, with each element of the vector being called *feature*. The process of building such vectors from the raw data in a way that is informative is generally called *feature extraction* or *feature engineering* (the latter phrase being used more often when expert knowledge is involved in the procedure).

From a pragmatic point of view, selecting the right features and the right way to represent them can make a huge difference in the performance of the machine learning algorithm. It's often possible to get reasonably decent performance by using a set of obvious features. An iterative trial-and-error process, where different approaches are tested following some intuition, is often what happens in the early stage of development. In the context of text analysis, the starting point is usually the bag-of-words approach, where word frequencies are considered.

To clarify the development from document to vectors, let's consider the following example, where a sample corpus of two documents is shown in raw and vectorized form:

Raw documents	
Doc1	John is a programmer.
Doc2	John likes coding. He also likes Python.
Vectorized documents	
Doc1	[1, 1, 1, 1, 0, 0, 0, 0, 0]
Doc2	[1, 0, 0, 0, 2, 1, 1, 1, 1]
Features	[John, is, a, programmer, likes, coding, he, also, Python]

The vectorized version of each document in the example contains nine elements. This is the number of dimensions used to represent the vectors, that is, the number of different words in the whole corpus. While this representation doesn't really take into account grammar and word order in the original document, the order of the elements in the vectors is important. For example, the first item in each vector represents the word **John**, the second item the word **is**, the fifth item the word **likes**, and so on.

Each word is here represented by its raw frequency, that is, by its count. Other common approaches include the binary representation (all the non-zero counts are set to 1, so it's representing the mere word presence in a document), or some more sophisticated statistics, such as a version of TF-IDF.

From a high-level point of view, the task of creating vectors from documents can look straightforward, but it involves some non-trivial operations, including tokenization and normalization of text.

Fortunately, **scikit-learn** comes to the rescue as it provides some tools to produce document vectors with minimum effort. The `CountVectorizer` and `TfidfVectorizer` classes are the utensils we're looking into. They both belong to the `feature_extraction.text` subpackage, so they can be imported with the following code:

```
from sklearn.feature_extraction.text import CountVectorizer
from sklearn.feature_extraction.text import TfidfVectorizer
```

Specifically, `CountVectorizer` deals with raw frequencies and binary representations (by default, the `binary` attribute is set to `False`), while `TfidfVectorizer` transforms the raw frequencies into TF, TF-IDF, or normalized TF-IDF. The behavior of both vectorizers can be influenced by a number of parameters that can be passed to the constructor.

This is an example of using the `TfidfVectorizer` class:

```
>>> from sklearn.feature_extraction.text import TfidfVectorizer
>>> corpus = [
... "Peter is a programmer.",
... "Peter likes coding. He also likes Python"
... ]
>>> vectorizer = TfidfVectorizer()
>>> vectors = vectorizer.fit_transform(corpus)
>>> vectors
<2x8 sparse matrix of type '<class 'numpy.float64'>'
   with 9 stored elements in Compressed Sparse Row format>
>>> vectors[0]
<1x8 sparse matrix of type '<class 'numpy.float64'>'
   with 3 stored elements in Compressed Sparse Row format>
>>> vectors[1]
<1x8 sparse matrix of type '<class 'numpy.float64'>'
   with 6 stored elements in Compressed Sparse Row format>
>>> print(vectors)
   (0, 6)      0.631667201738
   (0, 3)      0.631667201738
   (0, 5)      0.449436416524
   (1, 7)      0.342871259411
   (1, 0)      0.342871259411
   (1, 2)      0.342871259411
   (1, 1)      0.342871259411
   (1, 4)      0.685742518822
   (1, 5)      0.243955725
>>> vectorizer.get_feature_names()
['also', 'coding', 'he', 'is', 'likes', 'peter', 'programmer', 'python']
```

We can observe that, by default, the vectorizer performs the tokenization as expected, but the word a is not present in the list of features (in fact, the vectors are eight-dimensional rather than being nine-dimensional as previously introduced).

This is because the default tokenization is performed with a regular expression that captures all the tokens of two or more alphanumeric characters, treating punctuation as a token separator similar to whitespaces. By default, tokens are normalized to lowercase.

Some of the interesting attributes that can influence `TfidfVectorizer` are the following:

- `tokenizer`: This is a callable to override the tokenization step.
- `ngram_range`: This is a tuple (`min_n`, `max_n`) to consider n-grams and not only single words as tokens.
- `stop_words`: This is an explicit list of stop words to be removed (by default, stop word removal is not performed).
- `lowercase`: This is a Boolean, which defaults to `True`.
- `min_df`: This defines a minimum document frequency cut-off threshold; it can be an int (for example, 5 would include a token only if it's present in 5 or more documents) or a float in the range [0.0, 1.0] to represent a proportion of documents. By default, it's set to 1, so there is no threshold.
- `max_df`: This defines a maximum document frequency cut-off threshold; like `min_df`, it can be an int or a float. By default, it's set to 1.0 (so 100% of documents), meaning there is no threshold.
- `binary`: This is a Boolean, which defaults to `False`. When `True`, all the non-zero term counts are set to 1, meaning the TF component of TF-IDF is binary, but the final value is still influenced by IDF.
- `use_idf`: This is a Boolean, which defaults to `True`. When `False`, IDF weighting is not enabled.
- `smooth_idf`: This is a Boolean, which defaults to `True`. Enable *Plus one* smoothing of document frequencies to prevent divisions by zero.
- `sublinear_tf`: This is a Boolean, which defaults to `False`. When `True`, apply sub-linear TF scaling, that is, use *1+log(TF)* to replace TF.

The following section describes three common approaches for classification that are available out-of-the-box with scikit-learn.

Classification algorithms

In this section, we will briefly outline three common machine learning approaches that can be used for text classification: **Naive Bayes (NB)**, k-Nearest Neighbor (**k-NN**), and **Support Vector Machine (SVM)**. The purpose is not to dig into the details of the algorithms, but simply to summarize some of the tools that are already available in scikit-learn and can be used straightaway. It's worth taking a look at the scikit-learn documentation as the tool offers support for a rich set of algorithms (for supervised learning algorithms: `http://scikit-learn.org/stable/supervised_learning.html`).

It's important to remember that different algorithms can show different levels of performance with different data, so during the development of a classification system, it's advisable to test different implementations. The interface offered by scikit-learn makes our life fairly easy, as usually we can swap algorithms by simply changing one or two lines of code.

Naive Bayes

We start with Naive Bayes, a family of classifiers based on Bayes' theorem (`https://en.wikipedia.org/wiki/Bayes%27_theorem`), with the (naive) independence assumption between features.

The Bayes' theorem (also known as Bayes' law or Bayes' rule) describes the conditional probability of an event:

$$P(A|B) = \frac{P(B|A)P(A)}{P(B)}$$

The term on the left-hand side of the equation is the probability of observing the event A, given that we have observed the event B.

To put this equation in context, let's consider the spam filtering example:

$$P(\text{Spam}|\text{``money''}) = \frac{P(\text{``money''}|\text{Spam})P(\text{Spam})}{P(\text{``money''})}$$

The equation shows how to calculate the probability of assigning the *Spam* label to a (new, unseen) document that contains the word *"money"*. In terms of conditional probability, the question is often phrased as: given that we observe the word *"money"*, what's the probability of assigning the label *Spam* to this document?

Using the training data, the three probabilities on the right-hand side of the equation can be calculated during the training step.

As the classifier doesn't use a single word/feature to assign a particular class to a document, let's consider the following general case:

$$P(c|d) = \frac{P(d|c)P(c)}{P(d)} \propto P(c) \prod_{t \in d} P(t|c)$$

The last equation describes the probability of assigning a *c* class to an observed document, *d*. The document, according to the independence assumption, is described as a sequence of independent terms, *t*. As the features (and hence their probabilities) are independent, the probability, *P(d|c)*, can be written as the product of *P(t|c)* for each term, *t*, in the document, *d*.

A careful reader has probably realized that the last part of the last equation, where we express the document as a sequence of independent terms, doesn't have the denominator. This is simply an optimization as *P(d)* will be the same across the different classes, hence it doesn't need to be calculated in order to compute and compare the individual class scores. For this reason, the last part of the equation uses a *directly proportional* symbol rather than the *equivalence* symbol.

This is as far as we go in terms of mathematical background, as we don't want to lose sight of the practical aspects of the book. An interested reader is encouraged to dig into deeper details (refer to *Python Machine Learning* by *Sebastian Raschka, Packt Publishing*).

In scikit-learn, the `naive_bayes` subpackage offers support for Naive Bayes methods, for example, the multinomial NB classifier commonly used in text classification is implemented by the `MultinomialNB` class:

```
from sklearn.naive_bayes import MultinomialNB
```

k-Nearest Neighbor

The k-NN algorithm
(https://en.wikipedia.org/wiki/K-nearest_neighbors_algorithm) is a method used for classification and regression. The input of the algorithm consists of the k closest training examples in the feature space, that is, the k most similar documents. The output of the algorithm is the class membership assigned to a particular document obtained via a majority vote of its neighbors.

During the training phase, the multi-dimensional vectors represented the documents in the training set are simply stored with their labels. During the prediction phase, the unseen document is used to query its k most similar documents, with k being a user-defined constant. The class being the most common across these k documents (the nearest neighbors), is assigned to the unseen document.

k-NN belongs to the class of non-parametric methods because the decision of the algorithm is driven directly by the data (that is, the document vectors) and not by a parameter estimated over the data (as in the case of Naive Bayes, where the estimated probabilities are used to assign classes).

The intuition behind the algorithm is quite straightforward, but there are still two open questions:

- How to compute the distance between vectors?
- How to choose the best k?

The first question has different valid answers. A common choice is Euclidean distance (https://en.wikipedia.org/wiki/Euclidean_distance). The default implementation in scikit-learn uses the Minkowski distance, which is equivalent to the Euclidean when using the predefined parameters in scikit-learn.

The answer to the second question is instead a bit more complex and it can vary depending on the data. Choosing a small k means that the algorithm is more influenced by noise. Choosing a big value for k makes the algorithm more computationally expensive. A common approach is to simply choose the squared root of the number of features n, that is, k = sqrt(n); however, experimentation should be required.

The implementation of k-NN for classification is available in the neighbors subpackage of scikit-learn, as follows:

```
from sklearn.neighbors import KneighborsClassifier
```

The `KneighborsClassifier` class takes a number of parameters, including `k` and `distance`. For details about the available options for different distance metrics are described in the documentation of the `sklearn.neighbors.DistanceMetric` class.

Support Vector Machines

Support Vector Machines (SVM)
(`https://en.wikipedia.org/wiki/Support_vector_machine`) are supervised learning models and associated algorithms for classification and regression.

SVM applies a binary classification approach, meaning that unseen documents are assigned to one of two possible classes. The methodology can be extended to a multiclass classification either using a one-versus-all approach, where a given class is compared against a catch-all class, or a one-versus-one approach, where all the possible pairs or classes are considered. In the one-versus-all method, n classifiers are built, with n being the total number of classes. The class with the highest output function is the one assigned to the document. In the one-versus-one method, each classifier increments a counter for the chosen class. At the end, the class with most votes is assigned to the document.

The SVM family of classifiers is known to be effective in text classification tasks, where normally the data are represented in high dimensional space. In cases where the number of dimensions is greater than the number of samples, the classifier can still be effective. If the number of features is much greater of the number of samples (that is, there are few documents in the training set), the method can lose its effectiveness.

Like the other algorithm, an implementation is offered in scikit-learn (via the `svm` sub-package), as follows:

```
from sklearn.svm import LinearSVC
```

The `LinearSVC` class implements a linear kernel, one of the options for the kernel function. Roughly speaking, a kernel function can be seen as a similarity function used to compute similarity between a pair of samples. The scikit-learn library provides common kernels and it's also possible to adopt a custom implementation. The `SVC` class can be instantiated with the `kernel='linear'` parameter; while this classifier is also based on a linear kernel, the implementation under the hood is different, as `SVC` is based on `libSVM`, a general purpose library for SVM, while `LinearSVC` is based on `liblinear`, a much more efficient implementation optimized for the linear kernel.

Evaluation

After the discussion on different classification algorithms, this section tries to address an interesting question: how do we choose the *best* algorithm?

In the context of classification, there are four different categories to define the outcome of a classifier:

- The document belongs to the class C and the system assigns it to the class C (**True Positive**, or **TP**)
- The document doesn't belong to the class C, but the system assigns it to the class C (**False Positive**, or **FP**)
- The document belongs to the class C, but the system doesn't assign it to the class C (**False Negative**, or **FN**)
- The document doesn't belong to the class C and the system doesn't assign it to the class C (**True Negative**, or **TN**)

These outcomes are usually represented in a table called confusion matrix. For the case of binary classification, the confusion matrix looks as follows:

	Predicted label: C	Predicted label: not C
Correct label: C	TP	FN
Correct label: not C	FP	TN

The confusion matrix can be extended for the case of multiclass classification. Once we have the outcome of all the samples in the test set, we can compute different performance metrics. Some of them include:

- **Accuracy**: How often is the classifier correct? *(TP+TN) / total*
- **Misclassification rate**: How often is the classifier wrong? *(FP+FN) / total*
- **Precision**: When assigning to a class C, how often is the classifier correct? *TP / number of predictions for class C*
- **Recall**: What portion of documents in C is correctly identified? *TP / number of labels in C*

All these metrics provide a number between 0 and 1 that can be interpreted as a proportion. Precision and recall are often combined into a single value called harmonic mean (also referred to as F-score or F1).

In the context of multiclass classification, the F-scores across different classes can be averaged in different ways. Typically, the approaches are referred to as micro-F1, where each decision is given equal weight in the average, and macro-F1, where each class is given equal weight in the average (*Machine Learning in Automated Text Categorization, Fabrizio Sebastiani, 2002*).

What we have described so far in terms of evaluation assumes that there is a clear split between training data and test data (the set of data that we run the evaluation against). Some well-known datasets come with a clear annotation about the train/test split, so researchers can replicate the results. Sometimes, this split is not evident, so we need to reserve a portion of the annotated data for test. A small test set means the evaluation could be inaccurate, while a large test set means less data for the training phase.

One possible solution for this problem is called *cross validation*, with the most common approach being called *k-fold validation*. The idea is to repeat the evaluation a number of times using a different train/test split every time and then report an aggregated score (for example, the average).

For example, with a ten-fold validation, we can split the dataset into ten different subsets. Iteratively, we will choose one of these folds to be the test set, while the remaining folds are merged into the train set. Once the evaluation is run on a single fold, we will put the results aside and move on to the next iteration. The second fold now becomes the test set, while the other nine folds are used as training data. After the 10th iteration, we can average all the scores to get a single result. Common approaches for k-folding are ten-fold (a 90/10 train/test split) and five-fold (an 80/20 train/test split). The main advantages of using cross validation is that our confidence on the score being accurate is improved even for small datasets.

Performing text classification on Stack Exchange data

After the long introduction on classification, related algorithms, and evaluation, this section applies what we have discussed to the dataset of questions from the Movies & TV website.

As we're using tag names to represent classes, we will prepare the dataset in order to avoid classes that are too rare, and hence very difficult to capture. Let's say that we set the threshold to 10, that is, tags that appear less than ten times are ignored. This threshold is arbitrary, and we can experiment with different numbers. Moreover, the posts file contains both questions and answers, but here we are considering only the questions (recognizable from the `PostTypeId="1"` attribute), so we can discard all the answers.

The following script reads the JSON Lines files with tags and posts and produces a JSON Lines file with only the tags that are frequent enough according to our threshold:

```
# Chap06/stack_classification_prepare_dataset.py
import os
import json
from argparse import ArgumentParser

def get_parser():
  parser = ArgumentParser()
  parser.add_argument('--posts-file')
  parser.add_argument('--tags-file')
  parser.add_argument('--output')
  parser.add_argument('--min-df', type=int, default=10)
  return parser

if __name__ == '__main__':
  parser = get_parser()
  args = parser.parse_args()

  valid_tags = []
  with open(args.tags_file, 'r') as f:
    for line in f:
      tag = json.loads(line)
      if int(tag['Count']) >= args.min_df:
        valid_tags.append(tag['TagName'])

  with open(args.posts_file, 'r') as fin, open(args.output, 'w') as fout:
    for line in fin:
      doc = json.loads(line)
      if doc['PostTypeId'] == '1':
        doc_tags = doc['Tags'].split(' ')
        tags_to_store = [tag for tag in doc_tags
                         if tag in valid_tags]
        if tags_to_store:
          doc['Tags'] = ' '.join(tags_to_store)
          fout.write("{}\n".format(json.dumps(doc)))
```

The script assumes that we have already converted the tags and posts files from XML to JSON Lines as described earlier.

We can run the script from the command line as follows:

```
$ python stack_classification_prepare_dataset.py \
  --tags-file movies.tags.jsonl \
  --posts-file movies.posts.jsonl \
  --output movies.questions4classification.jsonl \
  --min-df 10
```

The file produced by the script, `movies.questions4classification.jsonl`, contains only questions with frequent tags. We can see the difference in size with the original posts file:

```
$ wc -l movies.posts.jsonl
  28146 movies.posts.jsonl
$ wc -l movies.questions4classification.jsonl
  8413 movies.questions4classification.jsonl
```

We're now ready to perform an experiment over the Movies & TV dataset. Following the discussion on evaluation, we're going to perform a ten-fold cross validation, meaning that the corpus of questions will be split into ten equal folds, and the classification task is going to be run ten times using 90% of the data for training and the remaining 10% for testing, each time using a different fold for testing:

```python
# Chap06/stack_classification_predict_tags.py
import json
from argparse import ArgumentParser
from nltk.corpus import stopwords
from sklearn.feature_extraction.text import TfidfVectorizer
from sklearn.svm import LinearSVC
from sklearn.multiclass import OneVsRestClassifier
from sklearn.metrics import f1_score
from sklearn.preprocessing import MultiLabelBinarizer
from sklearn.cross_validation import cross_val_score
import numpy as np

def get_parser():
  parser = ArgumentParser()
  parser.add_argument('--questions')
  parser.add_argument('--max-df', default=1.0, type=float)
  parser.add_argument('--min-df', default=1, type=int)
  return parser

if __name__ == '__main__':
  parser = get_parser()
  args = parser.parse_args()

  stop_list = stopwords.words('english')

  all_questions = []
  all_labels = []
  with open(args.questions, 'r') as f:
    for line in f:
      doc = json.loads(line)
      question = "{} {}".format(doc['Title'], doc['Body'])
      all_questions.append(question)
```

```
         all_labels.append(doc['Tags'].split(' '))

    vectorizer = TfidfVectorizer(min_df=args.min_df,
                                 stop_words=stop_list,
                                 max_df=args.max_df)
    X = vectorizer.fit_transform(all_questions)
    mlb = MultiLabelBinarizer()
    y = mlb.fit_transform(all_labels)
    classifier = OneVsRestClassifier(LinearSVC())

    scores = cross_val_score(classifier,
                             X,
                             y=y,
                             cv=10,
                             scoring='f1_micro')
    print("Average F1: {}".format(np.mean(scores)))
```

The `stack_classification_predict_tags.py` script accepts three arguments via `ArgumentParser`. The first, `--questions`, is the only mandatory one as we need to specify the `.jsonl` file with the questions. The other two arguments, `--min-df` and `--max-df`, can be used to influence the behavior of the classifier in terms of building the feature vectors. The default values for these two argument does not influence the process of feature extraction as the limits are set to `min_df=1` and `max_df=1.0`, meaning that all the features (words) will be included.

We can run the script with the following command:

```
$ python stack_classification_predict_tags.py \
    --questions movies.questions4classification.jsonl
```

This will produce the following output:

```
Average F1: 0.6271980062798452
```

Digging into the details of the script, after parsing the arguments from the command line, we will load a list of stop words into the `stop_list` variable using NLTK. This is the default list for common English words (approximatively 130 words, including articles, conjunctions, pronouns, and so on). The next step is reading the input file, loading each of the JSON documents in memory, and creating the data structures that will be fed into the classifier. In particular, we will create a list of all documents in the `all_questions` variable by concatenating the title and the body of each question. At the same time, we will keep track of the original tags (that is, the labels/classes for the classifier) in the `all_labels` variable.

For the feature extraction step, we will create an instance of TfidfVectorizer, passing the list of stop words, as well as minimum document frequency and maximum document frequency as parameters to the constructor. The vectorizer will create the feature vectors for the classifier, starting from the raw text, converting each word into a numerical value corresponding to the TF-IDF for the given word. Stop words will not be included in the vectors. Similarly, words with a frequency outside the desired range will be dropped.

The transformation from raw text to vectors is performed via the fit_transform() method of the vectorizer.

As the task we are performing is multilabel, there's an extra step that we need to perform in order to correctly map all the labels into binary vectors. This is needed because the classifier expects a list of binary vectors, rather than a list of class names, as input. To understand how MultiLabelBinarizer performs this transformation, we can examine the following snippet:

```
>>> from sklearn.preprocessing import MultiLabelBinarizer
>>> mlb = MultiLabelBinarizer()
>>> labels = [['house', 'drama'], ['star-wars'], ['drama', 'uk']]
>>> y = mlb.fit_transform(labels)
>>> y
array([[1, 1, 0, 0],
       [0, 0, 1, 0],
       [1, 0, 0, 1]])
>>> mlb.classes_
array(['drama', 'house', 'star-wars', 'uk'], dtype=object)
```

At this point, the corpus and the labels are in a format that can be understood by the classifier. A note on the naming: using uppercase X for the corpus and lowercase y for the labels is simply a common convention in machine learning, which you can frequently find in machine learning textbooks. If you don't like one-letter variables in your code, you can of course rename them.

For the classifier, we will choose LinearSVC, the Support Vector Machine classifier with a linear kernel. An interested reader is encouraged to experiment with a variety of classifiers. As the task is a multilabel one, we will choose the one-versus-all approach, implemented by the OneVsRestClassifier class, which takes an instance of the actual classifier as first parameter and uses it to perform all the classification tasks as described in an earlier section.

The final step is the classification per se. As we want to perform a cross validation, as mentioned earlier, we don't use the classifier object directly, but rather we pass it to the `cross_val_score()` function together with the vectorized data, the labels, and a few more parameters. The purpose of this function is to iterate over the data according to the k-folding strategy declared with the `cv=10` argument (which means we're using ten folds), perform the classification, and finally show the scores for the chosen evaluation metric (in the example, we're using the micro-averaged F1-score).

The return value of the cross-validation function is a NumPy array of scores, one for each fold. By using the `numpy.mean()` function, we can aggregate these scores and show their arithmetic mean.

It's worth noting that the final score, approximatively 0.62, is not good or bad *per se*. It tells us that the classification system is far from perfect, but at this stage we don't have a clear picture of whether there is room for a performance improvement, and in case where this room is. The score doesn't tell us if the classifier is performing *badly* or if the task is just too difficult to achieve a better performance. The aggregated score is a way to compare the behavior of different classifiers, or different runs of the same classifier using different parameters.

To provide an additional example, we can simply rerun the script specifying an extra parameter to filter out all the features that are too rare:

```
$ python stack_classification_predict_tags.py \
    --questions movies.questions4classification.jsonl \
    --min-df 5
```

By setting the minimum document frequency to 5, an arbitrary number that simply cuts the long tail in the feature frequency distribution, we will obtain the following output:

```
Average F1: 0.635184845312832
```

This example shows that a simple tweak in the configuration can yield different (fortunately better, in this case) results.

Embedding the classifier in a real-time application

The previous section has approached the classification problem with an academic mind-set: from a set of pre-labeled documents, we have run a batch experiment, performing a cross validation in order to get an evaluation metric. This is certainly very interesting if all we want to do is experiment with different classifiers, tweak the feature extraction process, and understand which classifier and which configuration works best for the given dataset.

This section moves one step forward and discusses some simple steps to embed the classifier (or more in general, a machine learning model) into an application that can interact with a user in real time. Popular examples of such applications include search engines, recommendation systems, spam filters, and many other intelligent application that we might use on a daily basis, without realizing how they are powered by machine learning techniques.

The application we're going to build in this section performs the following steps:

- Train the classifier (learning step, executed off-line)
- Persist the classifier on disk, so it can be loaded from a real-time app
- Embed the classifier in the application that interacts with the user (prediction step, executed in real-time)

The first two steps are carried out by the following script:

```python
# Chap06/stack_classification_save_model.py
import json
import pickle
from datetime import datetime
from argparse import ArgumentParser
from nltk.corpus import stopwords
from sklearn.feature_extraction.text import TfidfVectorizer
from sklearn.svm import LinearSVC
from sklearn.multiclass import OneVsRestClassifier
from sklearn.preprocessing import MultiLabelBinarizer


def get_parser():
    parser = ArgumentParser()
    parser.add_argument('--questions')
    parser.add_argument('--output')
    parser.add_argument('--max-df', default=1.0, type=float)
    parser.add_argument('--min-df', default=1, type=int)
    return parser
```

```
if __name__ == '__main__':
  parser = get_parser()
  args = parser.parse_args()

  stop_list = stopwords.words('english')

  all_questions = []
  all_labels = []
  with open(args.questions, 'r') as f:
    for line in f:
      doc = json.loads(line)
      question = "{} {}".format(doc['Title'], doc['Body'])
      all_questions.append(question)
      all_labels.append(doc['Tags'].split(' '))

  vectorizer = TfidfVectorizer(min_df=args.min_df,
                               stop_words=stop_list,
                               max_df=args.max_df)
  X = vectorizer.fit_transform(all_questions)
  mlb = MultiLabelBinarizer()
  y = mlb.fit_transform(all_labels)

  classifier = OneVsRestClassifier(LinearSVC())

  classifier.fit(X, y)
  model_to_save = {
    'classifier': classifier,
    'vectorizer': vectorizer,
    'mlb': mlb,
    'created_at': datetime.today().isoformat()
  }
  with open(args.output, 'wb') as f:
    pickle.dump(model_to_save, f)
```

The code is very similar to the off-line classification performed in the previous section. The main difference is that after training the classifier, we don't use it to predict anything, but rather we store it on file.

The output file is opened in the wb mode, meaning that the file pointer is going to have write access to the file, and such file is going to be binary rather than plain text. The pickle package handles the serialization of a complex Python object into a bytecode that can be dumped into a file.

The module has an interface very similar to the `json` package, with simple `load()` and `dump()` functions that perform the conversion between Python objects and files. We don't need only the classifier, but also the vectorizer and the instance of `MultiLabelBinarizer`. For this reason, we use the `model_to_save` variable, a Python dictionary to include all the necessary data. The `created_at` key of this dictionary contains the current system date in the ISO 8601 format, in case we need to keep track of different versions of the classifier, or we have new data and decide to retrain it.

We can execute the script with the following command:

```
$ python stack_classification_save_model.py \
  --questions movies.questions4classification.jsonl \
  --min-df 5 \
  --output questions-svm-classifier.pickle
```

After a few moments, the `questions-svm-classifier.pickle` file is created and it's ready to be used by other applications.

For the sake of simplicity, we're going to implement a basic interface from the command line. The same approach can be easily integrated with a web application (for example, using **Flask** as we did in the previous chapter), in order to offer the prediction capabilities to the users via a web interface.

The `stack_classification_user_input.py` script implements the user-facing application:

```python
# Chap06/stack_classification_user_input.py
import sys
import json
import pickle
from argparse import ArgumentParser

def get_parser():
  parser = ArgumentParser()
  parser.add_argument('--model')
  return parser

def exit():
  print("Goodbye.")
  sys.exit()

if __name__ == '__main__':
  parser = get_parser()
  args = parser.parse_args()

  with open(args.model, 'rb') as f:
```

```
    model = pickle.load(f)
classifier = model['classifier']
vectorizer = model['vectorizer']
mlb = model['mlb']

while True:
  print("Type your question, or type "exit" to quit.")
  user_input = input('> ')
  if user_input == 'exit':
    exit()
  else:
    X = vectorizer.transform([user_input])
    print("Question: {}".format(user_input))
    prediction = classifier.predict(X)
    labels = mlb.inverse_transform(prediction)[0]
    labels = ', '.join(labels)
    if labels:
      print("Predicted labels: {}".format(labels))
    else:
      print("No label available for this question")
```

The script uses `ArgumentParser` to read the command-line parameter, `--model`, which is used to pass the pickle file previously serialized.

The script loads up the pickle file using the pickle interface described previously. The file is a binary one, so it's opened in the `rb` mode (r for read and b for binary). This allows us to get access to the classifier, the vectorizer, and the multilabel binarizer previously produced.

The application then enters an infinite `while True` loop, which is used to continuously ask the user for some input. If we run the following command:

```
$ python stack_classification_user_input.py \
    --model questions-svm-classifier.pickle
```

We are in fact presented with the following prompt:

```
Type your question, or type "exit" to quit.
>
```

Once we type in some input, the `input()` function will read it into the `user_input` variable. This is used to check whether the user has typed the word `exit`, which would cause the application to quit. Otherwise, the classification is performed on whatever text the user has typed in.

The prediction step requires the input to be transformed into feature vectors. This is the job carried out by the vectorizer. It's important to notice that the `vectorizer.transform()` function takes a list (or an iterable) as argument, and not the `user_input` string directly. Once the input is vectorized, it can be passed to the `predict()` function of the classifier and the classification is performed.

The result of the classification is then given back to the user, in a readable format. The prediction at this stage is, in fact, a NumPy array that represents a binary mask over the list of valid labels. `MultiLabelBinarizer`, responsible for producing this mask in the training phase, has the capability of mapping the binary mask back to the original labels, using the `inverse_transform()` function.

The result of this call is a list of tuples. To be precise, as we were passing only one document to classify, the list only has a single tuple (hence the access to the `[0]` index during the inverse transformation).

Before showing the results to the user, the tuple of labels is joined into a string, unless empty (in that case a custom message is shown).

Now we can see the classifier in action:

```
$ python stack_classification_user_input.py \
  --model questions-svm-classifier.pickle
Type your question, or type "exit" to quit.
> What's up with Gandalf and Frodo lately? They haven't been in the Shire
for a while...
Question: What's up with Gandalf and Frodo lately? They haven't been in the
Shire for a while...
Predicted labels: plot-explanation, the-lord-of-the-rings
Type your question, or type "exit" to quit.
> What's the title of the latest Star Wars movie?
Question: What's the title of the latest Star Wars movie?
Predicted labels: identify-this-movie, star-wars, title
Type your question, or type "exit" to quit.
> How old is Tom Cruise?
Question: How old is Tom Cruise?
No label available for this question
Type your question, or type "exit" to quit.
> How old is Brad Pitt?
Question: How old is Brad Pitt?
Predicted labels: character, plot-explanation
Type your question, or type "exit" to quit.
> exit
Goodbye.
```

After calling the script, we are encouraged to type in our question. The highlighted code shows examples of user input mingled with the application response.

Quite interestingly, the classifier can pick up some of the names from *The Lord of the Rings* (Frodo, Gandalf, and the Shire), and correctly label the question without the title being mentioned. For some reason, the question is also interpreted as a request for a plot explanation. More precisely, the features of the questions have led the classifier to label this document as belonging to the plot-explanation class.

The second input contains the phrase Star Wars, so the identification for this label is straightforward as expected. The question also ask for a title, so there are two additional class names, `title` and `identify-this-movie`, which are associated with the question. So far, the classification seems to be pretty accurate.

With the last two questions, we can see that the classifier is not always perfect. When asking about Tom Cruise, the classifier doesn't associate any label to the question. This is likely to be caused by a lack of interesting features in the training data, namely the words *tom* and *cruise*. Slightly better lack with Brad Pitt, whose question is associated to the `character` (a bit stretched) and `plot-explanation` (simply incorrect) labels.

The example is closed with the user input, `exit`, which causes the application to quit.

The experiments in the previous sections have shown that the accuracy of the classifier is far from perfect. With this real-time application, we have tested first-hand the classifier capabilities. Although it can easily be fooled with a vague input, or simply with unseen words, the core message of this section is the fact that we are not limited to academic-like experimentations to test our models. Integrating a machine learning model into a proper user-facing application is almost a straightforward task, especially with Python's elegant and simple interface.

Applications of classification in real time can be countless:

- Sentiment analysis to automatically identify the opinion expressed by a user in a review and show it online
- Spam filtering to block or filter potential spam messages
- Profanity detection to identify users who post nasty messages on a forum and put their messages on hold automatically

The interested reader is invited to reuse what they learned about Flask in Chapter 5, *Topic Analysis on Google+*, and extend it to this context in order to build a simple web application that loads a machine learning model and uses it to classify user questions in real time via a web interface.

Summary

This chapter introduced question answering applications, one of the most popular uses of the Web. The popularity of the Stack Exchange network, and of the Stack Overflow website for programmers, is driven by the high-quality material curated by the community. In this chapter, we discussed how to interact with the Stack Exchange API and how to access the whole data set from Stack Exchange using their data dumps.

The second part of the chapter introduced the task of classification and the related supervised machine learning approaches to tackle it. The availability of labeled data from Stack Exchange has provided the opportunity to build a predictive model. The use case proposed in this chapter was the prediction of labels to be used as question tags, but the techniques can be applied to a variety of applications. The final part of the chapter extended the discussion, showing how a machine learning model can easily be integrated in a real-time user-facing application.

The next chapter focuses on blogs, in particular, on the application of NLP techniques.

7

Blogs, RSS, Wikipedia, and Natural Language Processing

This chapter focuses on **natural language processing** (**NLP**), the field of study that deals with natural language. Before digging into the details of NLP, we'll analyze some options to download textual data from the Web.

In this chapter, we will discuss the following topics:

- How to interact with the WordPress.com and Blogger APIs
- Web feed formats (RSS and Atom) and their use
- How to store data from blogs in the JSON format
- How to interact with the Wikipedia API to search the information about entities
- The core notions of NLP, particularly with regard to text preprocessing
- How to process textual data to identify entities mentioned in the text

Blogs and NLP

Blogs (short for weblogs) are nowadays an important part of the Web, and an incredibly attractive social media platform. Blogs are used by companies, professionals, and hobbyists to reach out to an audience, promote products and services, or simply discuss an interesting topic. Thanks to the abundance of web-publishing tools and services that makes it easy for non-technical users to post their content, setting up a personal blog is a matter of minutes.

From the point of view of a data miner, blogs are the perfect platform to practice text mining. This chapter focuses on two main topics: how to get textual data from blogs and how to apply NLP on such data.

While NLP is a complex field that deserves more than a book just to get started, we're taking a pragmatic approach and introducing the basic theory with practical examples.

Getting data from blogs and websites

Given the abundance of websites with interesting articles, finding textual data to mine shouldn't be a huge problem. Manually, saving one article at a time obviously doesn't scale up very well, so in this section, we will discuss some opportunities to automate the process of getting data from websites.

Firstly, we will discuss two popular free blogging services, WordPress.com and Blogger, which offer a convenient API to interact with their platform. Secondly, we will introduce the RSS and Atom web standards, used by many blogs and news publishers to broadcast their content in a format that is easy to read for a computer. Finally, we will briefly discuss more possible choices, such as connecting to Wikipedia or using web scraping as a last resort if no other option is available.

Using the WordPress.com API

WordPress.com is a blog and web hosting provider, which is powered by the open source WordPress software. The service provides free blog hosting for registered users, as well as paid upgrades and additional paid services. The registration is not required for users who only want to read and comment on blog posts, unless specified otherwise by the blog owner (meaning that a blog can be marked as private by its owner).

WordPress.com and WordPress.org
New WordPress users are often confused by the difference. The open source WordPress software is developed and distributed via WordPress.org; you can download a copy of the software and install it on your own server. On the other hand, WordPress.com is a hosting provider that offers an off-the-shelf solution for users who don't want to install the software on their own and deal with the aspects of server configuration. The domain for a blog hosted at WordPress.com is usually in the `blog-name.wordpress.com` form, unless the blog owner pays for a domain name.
The API discussed in this section is provided by WordPress.com, so the data that we can access through it is the one hosted by this provider.

The Python client support for the WordPress.com API is not particularly well-established. This leaves us with the option of interacting with the API directly (`https://developer.w ordpress.com/docs/api`), or in other words, writing our own client.

Fortunately, the effort required for this task is not overwhelming, and the **requests** Python library makes our life a little bit easier by providing an easy interface to deal with the HTTP side. We're going to use it to set up a bunch of calls to the WordPress.com API, with the purpose of downloading some blog posts from a particular domain.

The first step is to install the library in our virtual environment:

```
$ pip install requests
```

The second step is to take a look at the documentation, particularly for the `/sites/$site/posts` endpoint (`https://developer.wordpress.com/docs/api/1.1/get/sites/%24site/posts/`).

The following script defines the `get_posts()` function that is designed to query the WordPress.com API and handle pagination as required:

```python
# Chap07/blogs_wp_get_posts.py
import json
from argparse import ArgumentParser
import requests

API_BASE_URL = 'https://public-api.wordpress.com/rest/v1.1'

def get_parser():
  parser = ArgumentParser()
  parser.add_argument('--domain')
  parser.add_argument('--posts', type=int, default=20)
  parser.add_argument('--output')
  return parser

def get_posts(domain, n_posts=20):
  url = "{}/sites/{}/posts".format(API_BASE_URL, domain)
  next_page = None
  posts = []
  while len(posts) <= n_posts:
    payload = {'page_handle': next_page}
    response = requests.get(url, params=payload)
    response_data = response.json()
    for post in response_data['posts']:
      posts.append(post)
    next_page = response_data['meta'].get('next_page', None)
    if not next_page:
      break
```

```
    return posts[:n_posts]

if __name__ == '__main__':
  parser = get_parser()
  args = parser.parse_args()

  posts = get_posts(args.domain, args.posts)

  with open(args.output, 'w') as f:
    for i, post in enumerate(posts):
      f.write(json.dumps(post)+"\n")
```

The script uses `ArgumentParser` to accept the command-line parameters. It takes two mandatory arguments: `--domain` to set the blog we're retrieving the data from and `--output` to set the name for the JSON Lines file. Optionally, we can provide a `--posts` argument, which is set to 20 by default, to decide the number of posts we're retrieving from the given domain.

The domain is the complete URL for a given blog, for example, `your-blog-name.wordpress.com`.

For example, we can run the script with the following command:

```
$ python blogs_wp_get_posts.py \
  --domain marcobonzanini.com \
  --output posts.marcobonzanini.com.jsonl \
  --posts 100
```

After a few seconds, the script produces the JSON Lines file with one post per line, which is represented in the JSON format.

Before describing the format of the output, let's analyze the `get_posts()` function in detail, which is the core of our script. The function takes two arguments: the `domain` of the blog and the number of posts, `n_posts`, that we want to retrieve, which is defaulted to 20.

Firstly, the function defines the URL for the relevant API endpoint and initializes the `next_page` variable, which is useful to iterate over multiple pages of results. By default, the API returns 20 results (20 blog posts) per page, so if the blog contains more than this, we'll need to iterate over a few number of pages.

The core of the function is the `while` loop, which is used to retrieve one page of results at a time. The API endpoint is called using the GET method, and it accepts several arguments as defined in the documentation. The `page_handle` argument is what we can use to specify the page of results that we are interested in. At the first iteration, the value of this variable is `None`, so the retrieval starts from the beginning. The response data returned in the JSON format, using the `response.json()` method, contains a list of posts, `response_data['posts']`, as well as some metadata about the request, stored in `response_data['meta']`. If the next page of results is available, the dictionary of metadata will contain a `next_page` key. If this key is not present, we will set it to `None`.

The loop stops either when there is no `next_page`, meaning that we have downloaded all the available posts, or when we have reached enough posts, as declared in `n_posts`. Finally, we will return the sliced list of posts. The slicing is necessary in case the desired number of posts, `n_posts`, is not a multiple of the page size. For example, if we specify 30 as the desired number of posts, the script will download two pages with 20 posts each, hence slicing is required to chop off the last 10 items that were not requested.

Each post object is defined by the attributes listed in the following table:

Attribute	Description
ID	This is the ID of the post within the blog
URL	This is the complete URL of the post
attachment_count	This is the number of attachments (for example, media files, and so on)
attachments	This is the list of attachment objects
author	This is the profile object of the author, including the full name, login name, avatar, gravatar profile URL, and so on
categories	This is the list of categories assigned to this post
content	This is the full content of the post, including the HTML markup
date	This is the publication date in the ISO 8601 format
discussion	This is the information about comments, pings, and so on
excerpt	This is a short summary of the post, usually the first few sentences
feature_image	This is the URL of the feature image, if present
global_ID	This is the global ID for this post
guid	This is the blog domain and post ID combined into a valid URL

`i_like`	This informs whether the logged in user has liked this post
`is_following`	This informs whether the logged in user is following the blog
`is_reblogged`	This informs whether the logged in user has reblogged this post
`like_count`	This is the number of users who have liked this post
`meta`	This is the metadata from the API, for example, hypermedia links for automatic API discovery, and so on
`modified`	This is the last modified date in the ISO 8601 format
`short_url`	This is the short URL (`http://wp.me`) for social media and mobile sharing
`site_ID`	This is the ID of the blog
`slug`	This is the slug of this post
`status`	This is the current status of this post, for example, published, draft, pending, and so on
`sticky`	This informs whether the post is sticky or not (presented on top regardless of the publication date)
`tags`	This is the list of tags associated with the post
`title`	This is the title of the post

As we can see, the structure of a blog post is much more complex than its content, but for the purpose of this chapter, we'll mainly focus on the textual content, including titles and excerpts.

Using the Blogger API

Blogger is another popular blog publishing service, which was bought by Google back in 2003. Blogs hosted by Blogger are generally available at a subdomain of `blogspot.com`, for example, `your-blog-name.blogspot.com`. Country-specific domains are also available for several countries (for example, `blogspot.co.uk` for the United Kingdom), meaning that users from specific countries are redirected to the assigned domain in a transparent fashion.

Being part of Google, the account management is centralized, meaning that once users have registered their Google account, they automatically have access to Blogger. This is also the case for the Blogger API; as developers, we can access it through the Google Developers Console (`https://console.developers.google.com/start`) as we did for Google+ in `Chapter 5`, *Topic Analysis on Google+*, where we have seen the process of creating a project that will require access to (any of) the Google APIs. We can reuse the same project and enable the Blogger API from the Developers Console or we can create a new project from scratch. For these steps, we can refer to the description given in `Chapter 5`, *Topic Analysis on Google+*. Either way, the important part is to *enable the Blogger API for our project*, otherwise we won't have programmatic access to it.

When dealing with the Google Plus API, we also discussed the creation of access keys, particularly a server key, which is also what we'll need to access the Blogger API. If we followed the steps from `Chapter 5`, *Topic Analysis on Google+*, we should already have an available server key that we can store as an environment variable:

```
$ export GOOGLE_API_KEY="your-api-key-here"
```

In terms of client library, we're using the same client library that we used in `Chapter 5`, *Topic Analysis on Google+*, because it's a common interface for all Google's APIs. If we haven't installed it yet, we can add it to our virtual environment using `pip`:

```
$ pip install google-api-python-client
```

Once the environment is all set up, we can start working on the script that will interact with the Blogger API in order to download some posts from a given blog:

```python
# Chap07/blogs_blogger_get_posts.py
import os
import json
from argparse import ArgumentParser
from apiclient.discovery import build

def get_parser():
    parser = ArgumentParser()
    parser.add_argument('--url')
    parser.add_argument('--posts', type=int, default=20)
    parser.add_argument('--output')
    return parser

class BloggerClient(object):

    def __init__(self, api_key):
        self.service = build('blogger',
                             'v3',
                             developerKey=api_key)
```

```
    def get_posts(self, blog_url, n_posts):
      blog_service = self.service.blogs()
      blog = blog_service.getByUrl(url=blog_url).execute()
      posts = self.service.posts()
      request = posts.list(blogId=blog['id'])
      all_posts = []
      while request and len(all_posts) <= n_posts:
        posts_doc = request.execute()
        try:
          for post in posts_doc['items']:
            all_posts.append(post)
        except KeyError:
          break
        request = posts.list_next(request, posts_doc)
      return all_posts[:n_posts]

  if __name__ == '__main__':
    api_key = os.environ.get('GOOGLE_API_KEY')
    parser = get_parser()
    args = parser.parse_args()

    blogger = BloggerClient(api_key)

    posts = blogger.get_posts(args.url, args.posts)

    with open(args.output, 'w') as f:
      for post in posts:
        f.write(json.dumps(post)+"\n")
```

The Google API Client that orchestrates the interaction with all the Google APIs has a concept of service builder, a sort of factory method used to build a service object, the one that we'll use to query the API. In order to provide an easy-to-use interface, we will create a `BloggerClient` class that deals with holding the API key, setting up the service object, and providing a `get_posts()` function, very similar to the one that we defined for the WordPress.com API.

The script, which uses `ArgumentParser` as usual, can be called from the command line with three arguments, as follows:

```
$ python blogs_blogger_get_posts.py \
  --url http://googleresearch.blogspot.co.uk \
  --posts 50 \
  --output posts.googleresearch.jsonl
```

Similar to the WordPress.com example, we're using the `--posts` and `--output` arguments to define the desired number of posts and the name of the output file, respectively. Different from the previous example, the `--url` parameter requires the given string to be the complete URL of the blog and not just the domain name (meaning that it includes the initial `http://`). With the preceding command, after a few moments, we'll obtain the last 50 posts from the Google Research blog.

Taking a deeper look at the `BloggerClient` class, the constructor only takes one argument, which is the developer's API key obtained when registering our application on the Google Developers Console. This is used to set up the `service` object with the `build()` factory function. It's worth noting that we're using the third version of the API, v3, so when referring to the documentation, this detail is important.

The `get_posts()` method does the hard work. The layout is very similar to the `get_posts()` function defined for the WordPress.com API, with two arguments, the blog URL, and the desired number of posts.

Different from the WordPress.com API, the Blogger API requires a blog object first, so we need to convert the URL into a numerical ID. This is performed by the `getByUrl()` method of the object created with `self.service.blogs()`.

Another interesting difference is the fact that the calls to most service functions don't trigger the API call directly, similar to lazily evaluated functions, so we need to explicitly call an `execute()` method in order to perform the API request and obtain the response.

The `request.execute()` call creates the `posts_doc` object, which may or may not contain the `items` key (the list of posts). Wrapping it into a `try/except` block ensures that, if a particular call has no posts, the iteration is stopped with the break call, without raising any error.

Once the desired number of posts is reached, or no other page is available, the list of post is returned using the slicing technique.

The JSON documents returned by the Blogger API are simpler than the WordPress.com ones, but all the key attributes are present. The following table summarizes the main attributes for each post:

Attribute	Description
author	This is the object that represents the author of the post with a display name, user ID, profile image, and URL
blog	This is the object that represents the blog itself (for example, with an ID)
content	This is the complete content of the post, including HTML formatting
id	This is the ID of the post
labels	This is the list of labels associated with the post
published	This is the publication date in the ISO 8601 format
replies	This is the object that represents the comments/replies on the post
selfLink	This is the API-based link to the post
title	This is the title of the post
updated	This is the date of last update in the ISO 8601 format
url	This is the URL of the post

Also in this case, there is more interesting information than just the content of the post, but textual data is our focus in this chapter.

Parsing RSS and Atom feeds

Many blogs, and in general, many websites, offer their content in standard formats that are not meant for the end user to visualize on screen, but rather for third-party publishers to consume. This is the case with **Rich Site Summary (RSS)**, (`https://en.wikipedia.org/wiki/RSS`) and **Atom** (`https://en.wikipedia.org/wiki/Atom_(standard)`), two XML-based formats that we can use to quickly access a variety of information from websites that implement this feature.

RSS and Atom belong to the family of formats generally referred to as web feeds, commonly used to provide users with commonly updated content. The feed providers syndicate the feed, meaning that the users can subscribe to a particular feed via an application and receive updates when new content is released. Several applications, including mail readers, provide features to integrate web feeds into their workflow.

In the context of mining blogs and articles, feeds are interesting as they provide a single point of entry for a given website that offers its content in a machine-readable format.

For example, the **British Broadcasting Corporation** (**BBC**) offers a variety of news feeds, which are grouped by general themes such as world news, technology, sport, and so on. For example, the feed for top news is available at `http://feeds.bbci.co.uk/news/rss.xml` (and is readable in a browser).

The Python support for reading web feeds is pretty straightforward. All we need to do is to install the feedparser library, which takes care of downloading the feed and parsing the raw XML into a Python object.

Firstly, we need to install the library into our virtual environment:

```
$ pip install feedparser
```

The following script is used to download a feed from a given URL and save the news entries in the usual JSON Lines format:

```python
# Chap07/blogs_rss_get_posts.py
import json
from argparse import ArgumentParser
import feedparser

def get_parser():
  parser = ArgumentParser()
  parser.add_argument('--rss-url')
  parser.add_argument('--json')
  return parser

if __name__ == '__main__':
  parser = get_parser()
  args = parser.parse_args()

  feed = feedparser.parse(args.rss_url)
  if feed.entries:
    with open(args.json, 'w') as f:
      for item in feed.entries:
        f.write(json.dumps(item)+"\n")
```

The script takes two arguments defined via `ArgumentParser`: `--rss-url` is used to pass the URL of the feed, while `--json` is used to specify the filename that we're using to save the feed in the JSON Lines format.

For example, in order to download the RSS feed from the BBC top news, we can use the following command:

```
$ python blogs_rss_get_posts.py \
  --rss-url http://feeds.bbci.co.uk/news/rss.xml \
  --json rss.bbc.jsonl
```

The script is pretty self-explanatory. The hard work is done by the `parse()` function of the feedparser library. The function recognizes the format and parses the XML into an object, which contains an `entries` attribute (a list of news items). By iterating over this list, we can simply dump the single items into our desired JSON Lines format and the job is done with just a few lines of code.

The interesting attributes for each of these news items are as follows:

- `id`: This is the URL of the news item
- `published`: This is the publication date
- `title`: This is the title for the news
- `summary`: This is the short summary of the news

Getting data from Wikipedia

Wikipedia probably doesn't need any extended presentation, being one of the most popular websites and reference work. Towards the end of 2015, the English Wikipedia reached around 5 million articles, with the aggregated count across different languages being over 38 million.

Wikipedia offers access to its content by means of an API. Complete data dumps are also regularly provided.

Several projects offer a Python wrapper around the Wikipedia API. A particularly useful implementation is provided by a library called **wikipedia**. From our virtual environment, we can install it in the usual way:

```
$ pip install wikipedia
```

The interface of this library is straightforward; therefore, as its documentation says, we can focus on using the data from Wikipedia rather than on getting it.

Besides accessing the full content of a page, the Wikipedia API also offers features such as search and summarization. Let's consider the following examples:

```
>>> import wikipedia
# Access a Wikipedia page
>>> packt = wikipedia.page('Packt')
>>> packt.title
'Packt'
>>> packt.url
'https://en.wikipedia.org/wiki/Packt'
# Getting the summary of a page
>>> wikipedia.summary('Packt')
"Packt, pronounced Packed, is a print on demand publishing company based in
Birmingham and Mumbai." # longer description
```

In the preceding example, we access the page about Packt Publishing directly, knowing that the name `Packt` is unique.

When we are not sure about the precise page handle of the entity we are interested in, the search and disambiguation features of the Wikipedia API are useful.

For example, the term `London` can be associated to at least two cities (one in the United Kingdom and another in Canada) and several entities or events (for example, Tower of London, Great Fire of London, and so on):

```
>>> wikipedia.search('London')
['London', 'List of bus routes in London', 'Tower of London', 'London,
Ontario', 'SE postcode area', 'List of public art in London', 'Bateaux
London', 'London Assembly', 'Great Fire of London', 'N postcode area']
```

In case of misspelling, the results are quite unexpected:

```
>>> wikipedia.search('Londn')
['Ralph Venning', 'Gladys Reynell', 'GestiFute', 'Delphi in the Ottoman
period']
```

The workaround for the preceding problem is to ask Wikipedia for some suggestions:

```
>>> wikipedia.suggest('Londn')
'london'
```

As we have introduced an example about London, we will also notice that the summary for this entity is particularly long. In case we need a shorter summary, we can specify the number of sentences to the API as shown in *Figure 7.1*:

```
>>> wikipedia.summary('London', sentences=2)
'London /ˈlʌndən/ is the capital and most populous city of England
and the United Kingdom. Standing on the River Thames in the south
east of Great Britain, London has been a major settlement for two
millennia.'
```

Figure 7.1: The short summary

Finally, let's consider an example of homonymy that triggers a disambiguation problem. When visiting a Wikipedia page for a specific name that refers to many different entities, without one being a clear candidate, a disambiguation page is shown.

From the API point of view, the result is an exception, as follows:

```
>>> wikipedia.summary('Mercury')
Traceback (most recent call last):
    # long error
wikipedia.exceptions.DisambiguationError: "Mercury" may refer to:
Mercury (element)
Mercury (planet)
Mercury (mythology)
# ... long list of "Mercury" suggestions
```

To avoid problems with disambiguation, we can wrap the request in a `try`/`except` block:

```
>>> try:
...     wikipedia.summary('Mercury')
... except wikipedia.exceptions.DisambiguationError as e:
...     print("Many options available: {}".format(e.options))
...
Many options available: ['Mercury (element)', 'Mercury (planet)', 'Mercury
(mythology)', ...] # long list
```

Access to Wikipedia can be used to download full articles, but that's not the only useful application. We'll also see how to extract nouns and named entities from a piece of text. In this context, we can take advantage of Wikipedia by augmenting the results of a named entity extraction to explain what the identified entities are with the help of short summaries.

A few words about web scraping

Web scraping is the process of automatically downloading and extracting information from websites. Web scraping software basically simulates a human browsing (and saving) information on a website with the purpose of either harvesting a large amount of data or performing some task that requires interaction in an automatic fashion.

Building a web scraper (also known as a web crawler or simply a bot) is sometimes the answer to situations where a web service does not provide an API or a feed to download the data.

While web scraper is a legitimate application, it's important to keep in mind that automatic scraping could be explicitly against the terms of use of the specific website you intend to scrape. Moreover, there are ethical and legal issues (that could vary from country to country) to consider, as follows:

- Do we have the right to access and download the data?
- Are we overloading the website servers?

The first question is usually answered by the terms of use of the website. The second question is more difficult to answer. In principle, if we perform a huge number of interactions with the website (for example, accessing many pages in a very short time), we are definitely beyond the simulation of a user session and might cause the website performance to degrade. This could even constitute a denial-of-service attack if the website we are connecting to is not able to handle the number of requests.

Given the abundance of available data, and the number of services that provide such data in some easy-to-access way, building a web scraper should be the last resort for these particular cases where an API is not available.

The topic is quite complex. Customized solutions can be built with libraries such as requests and **Beautiful Soup**, although there's a tool particularly tailored for this job-Scrapy (http://scrapy.org). As this topic goes beyond the scope of this book, the reader who is interested in this subject can find a variety of publications, for example, *Web Scraping with Python*, by *Richard Lawson, 2015, Packt Publishing*.

NLP Basics

This section tries to scratch the surface of the complex field of NLP. The previous chapters have mentioned some of the basics that are necessary for dealing with textual data (for example, tokenization) without going too much into the details. Here, we'll try to go one step further into the basic understanding of this discipline. Due to its complexity and many aspects, we're taking a pragmatic approach and only scratching the surface of the theoretical foundations in favor of practical examples.

Text preprocessing

An essential part of any NLP system is the preprocessing pipeline. Before we can perform any interesting task on a piece of text, we must first convert it in a useful representation.

In the previous chapters, we already performed some analysis on the textual data without digging into the details of text preprocessing, but instead using the common tools with a pragmatic approach. In this section, we'll highlight some of the common preprocessing steps and discuss their role in the bigger picture of building an NLP system.

Sentence boundary detection

Given a piece of text (in other words, a string), the task of breaking it into a list of sentences is called **sentence boundary detection** (also *end-of-sentence detection* or simply *sentence tokenization*).

Sentences are linguistic units that group words meaningfully and grammatically to express a complete thought. From the point of view of linguistics (the scientific study of language), a thorough discussion to define all the possible aspects of a sentence would take over several pages. From the point of view of being pragmatic and building an NLP system, this general concept of linguistic unit is more than enough to get started.

It's worth noting that, while sentences can be meaningful in isolation, sometimes they require to be part of a bigger context (for example, a paragraph or section). This is because some words in a sentence might refer to concepts expressed in other sentences. Let's consider the example, *Elizabeth II is the Queen of the United Kingdom. She was born in London in 1926 and her reign began in 1952.*

This simple piece of text contains two sentences. The second sentence uses the pronouns *she* and *her*. If the sentence is taken individually, these two words don't tell us who the subject of this sentence is. When taken in context, a human reader can easily associate these two words with *Elizabeth II*, the subject of the previous sentence. This challenge is called *anaphora resolution* and has been recognized as a very difficult NLP problem. In general, sentences with links to other sentences usually make use of a local context, meaning that the links are pointing to the previous/next sentence rather than to one far away in the text. Recognizing the boundaries of the bigger context (for example, paragraphs and sections of a text) can be useful in some applications, but sentences are the usual starting point.

On the practical side, splitting sentences doesn't seem to be a huge problem, as we can use punctuation (for example, periods, exclamation marks, and so on) to identify the sentence boundaries. This oversimplification leads to some mistakes, as shown in the following example:

```
>>> text = "Mr. Cameron is the Prime Minister of the UK. He serves since 2010."
>>> sentences = text.split('.')
>>> sentences
['Mr', ' Cameron is the Prime Minister of the UK', ' He serves since 2010', '']
```

As we can see, interpreting each *dot* as a period mark breaks the phrase *Mr. Cameron* into two parts, leaving us with the meaningless sentence *Mr* (as well as an empty last sentence). Many other problematic examples can be provided, mainly regarding abbreviations (for example, Dr., Ph.D, U.S.A., and so on).

Fortunately, **Natural Language Toolkit (NLTK)** provides an easy workaround, as follows:

```
>>> from nltk.tokenize import sent_tokenize
>>> sentences = sent_tokenize(text)
>>> sentences
['Mr. Cameron is the Prime Minister of the UK.', 'He serves since 2010.']
```

The sentences are now correctly identified. This example is extremely simple, and there will be cases where NLTK will not perform the correct sentence identification. In general, the library performs well, out of the box, so that we can use it for a variety of applications without worrying too much.

Word tokenization

Given a sentence (that is, a string), the task of breaking it into a list of words is called **word tokenization**, sometimes it is also simply called *tokenization*. In this context, words are often called *tokens*.

Generally speaking, for most European languages, including English, tokenization appears to be an intuitive task as individual words are separated by white spaces. This oversimplification quickly shows its shortcomings:

```
>>> s = "This sentence is short, nice and to the point."
>>> wrong_tokens = s.split()
>>> wrong_tokens
['This', 'sentence', 'is', 'short,', 'nice', 'and', 'to', 'the', 'point.']
```

The tokens `short,` and `point.` (notice the trailing punctuation) are clearly incorrect: the tokenization fails because splitting over white spaces doesn't take the punctuation into account. Building a tokenizer that takes all the nuances of a language into account can be tricky. Things get more complicated for some European languages, such as German or Finnish, that use a huge variety of compounds, for example, two or more words joined together to form a longer word, with a meaning that could be similar to or different from the original meaning of its individual components in isolation. Even more challenges arise from some Asian languages, such as Chinese, which is standardly written without white spaces between words. Specialized libraries might be required when dealing with a particular language, for example, **jieba** (`https://github.com/fxsjy/jieba`) is a Python library dedicated to word segmentation in Chinese.

The reader doesn't need to worry about these aspects of language processing yet as we're focusing on English. Moreover, the NLTK package is already equipped for standard English:

```
>>> from nltk.tokenize import word_tokenize
>>> s = "This sentence is short, nice and to the point."
>>> correct_tokens = word_tokenize(s)
>>> correct_tokens
['This', 'sentence', 'is', 'short', ',', 'nice', 'and', 'to', 'the',
'point', '.']
```

marks are also included in the output as they are considered tokens and can be later useful for processing.

As we can see from this example, individual words are correctly identified. Punctuation marks are also included in the output as they are considered tokens and can be later useful for processing. The word_tokenize() function from NLTK requires the punkt package, an NLTK resource, to be installed. If this function is raising an exception, refer to Chapter 1, Social Media, Social Data, and Python, where the configuration to solve this problem is provided.

Part-of-speech tagging

Once we have a sequence of words, we can assign a grammatical category to each one of them. This process is called **Part-of-speech (POS) tagging** and has useful applications in different text analytics tasks.

Common grammatical categories include nouns, verbs, or adjectives, each of which is identified by a different tag symbol. Different taggers can be based on different tag sets, which means that the list of available tags can differ from tagger to tagger, but also the output of the individual taggers could be fairly different. By default, the NLTK library uses the tag set from the Penn Treebank Project (https://www.cis.upenn.edu/~treebank).

For the complete list of available tags and their meaning, we can consult the online help:

```
>>> nltk.help.upenn_tagset()
```

This will produce a long output, including all the tags, their descriptions, and some examples. Some of the most common tags are NN (common nouns), NNP (proper nouns), JJ (adjectives), and V* (several tags starting with a V, indicating verbs in different tenses).

In order to associate a list of tokens with the relevant tags, we can use the straightforward interface provided by the `nltk.pos_tag()` function. NLTK provides several part-of-speech tagger implementations. In recent versions of the toolkit, the default tagger is the averaged perceptron. As discussed in `Chapter 1`, *Social Media, Social Data, and Python*, some models in NLTK require downloading additional data through the `nltk.download()` interface; this is also the case of the averaged perceptron model shown in *Figure 7.2*:

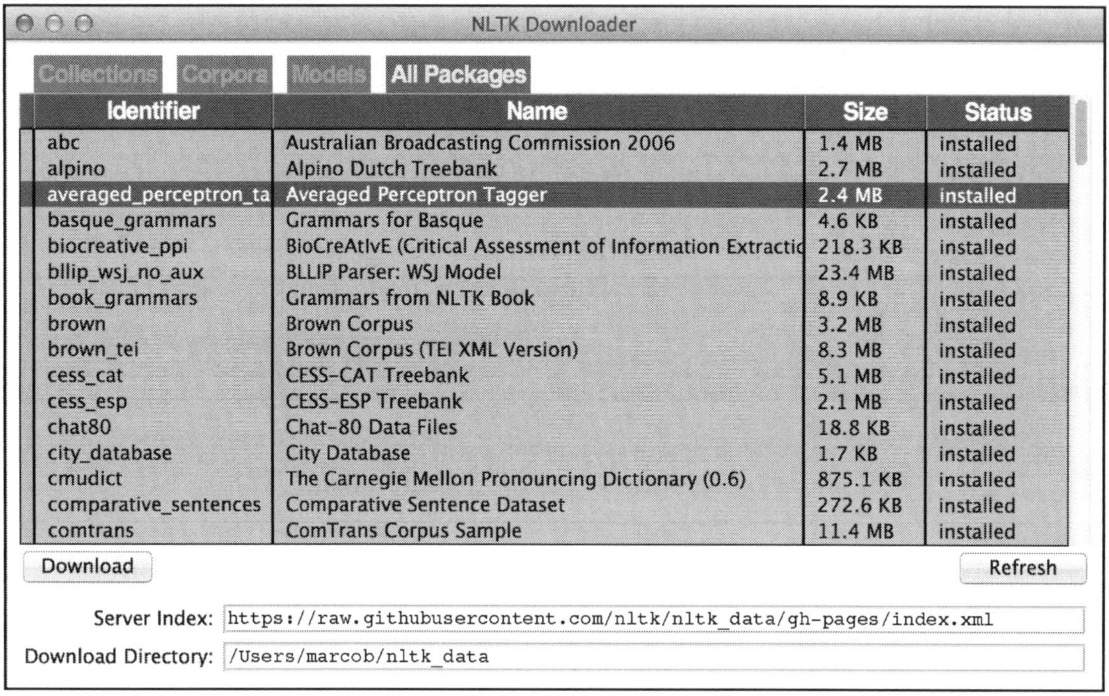
NLTK Downloader
Collections
Corpora
Models
All Packages
Identifier
Name
Size
Status
abc | Australian Broadcasting Commission 2006 | 1.4 MB | installed
alpino | Alpino Dutch Treebank | 2.7 MB | installed
averaged_perceptron_ta | Averaged Perceptron Tagger | 2.4 MB | installed
basque_grammars | Grammars for Basque | 4.6 KB | installed
biocreative_ppi | BioCreAtIvE (Critical Assessment of Information Extracti | 218.3 KB | installed
bllip_wsj_no_aux | BLLIP Parser: WSJ Model | 23.4 MB | installed
book_grammars | Grammars from NLTK Book | 8.9 KB | installed
brown | Brown Corpus | 3.2 MB | installed
brown_tei | Brown Corpus (TEI XML Version) | 8.3 MB | installed
cess_cat | CESS-CAT Treebank | 5.1 MB | installed
cess_esp | CESS-ESP Treebank | 2.1 MB | installed
chat80 | Chat-80 Data Files | 18.8 KB | installed
city_database | City Database | 1.7 KB | installed
cmudict | The Carnegie Mellon Pronouncing Dictionary (0.6) | 875.1 KB | installed
comparative_sentences | Comparative Sentence Dataset | 272.6 KB | installed
comtrans | ComTrans Corpus Sample | 11.4 MB | installed
Download
Refresh
Server Index: https://raw.githubusercontent.com/nltk/nltk_data/gh-pages/index.xml
Download Directory: /Users/marcob/nltk_data

Figure 7.2: The NLTK download interface highlighting the averaged perceptron model for part-of-speech tagging

After we ensured that the relevant model is installed, we can test the `pos_tag()` function on a sample sentence:

```
>>> from nltk import pos_tag
>>> tokens = word_tokenize("This sentence is short, nice and to the point")
>>> pos_tag(tokens)
[('This', 'DT'), ('sentence', 'NN'), ('is', 'VBZ'), ('short', 'JJ'), (',',
','), ('nice', 'JJ'), ('and', 'CC'), ('to', 'TO'), ('the', 'DT'), ('point',
'NN')]
```

The output of the `pos_tag()` function is a list of tuples, where each tuple is in the (`token`, `tag`) format. For example, the first token, `This`, is a determinant (`DT`); the second token, `sentence`, is a common noun (`NN`); and so on.

One common problem with POS tagging is that while there is some agreement among researchers on the basic categories, there is no single correct set of tags, so using different taggers will produce different results. With the ambiguities and nuances of natural language, the same word can be tagged differently depending on the context; in fact, many words in English can be assigned to different categories. For example, words such as fish, walk, and view can be either a verb or a noun.

POS tagging is usually applied as a means to an end. In particular, exploiting POS tag information is useful in at least two cases: when finding the original lemma of a word (see the *Word normalization* section) and when trying to extract structured information from unstructured text (see the *Information extraction* section later in this chapter).

Word normalization

Tokenization and POS tagging are the basic preprocessing steps that are common to many applications. Depending on the task, we might need to apply some additional steps that can be useful for the accuracy of the overall application.

Here, we will use the phrase **word normalization** as an umbrella term to capture all the additional operations that we wish to perform on the individual terms.

Case normalization

To highlight the need for text normalization, we start with the following simple example:

```
>>> "president" == "President"
False
```

While the preceding is probably obvious to most programmers, as `president` and `President` are effectively two different strings, from a linguistic point of view, we often have the need to treat the two words as the same. For example, when we are computing frequencies, we don't want to keep separate counts for two words that are the same.

One way to fulfill this need is to perform a case transformation, mapping the whole text into either lowercase or uppercase:

```
>>> "president".lower() == "President".lower()
True
```

In this example, we will transform all the words via lowercasing so that the original terms can be treated as the same.

It's important to remember that this transformation is not reversible. If we override the text with its lowercased version, the original text cannot be reproduced. In many applications, we might have the need to show the original text to the user, while performing some processing with the normalized text. In this case, it's important to keep a copy of the original text and treat it as immutable data.

It's also worth noting that text normalization doesn't always lead to the desired outcome. A classic example is the acronym for *United States*, *US*, which once normalized is mapped into *us*, an objective personal pronoun. Some trial and error might be necessary to catch some other edge cases.

Stemming

In English, as well as other languages, there are words that are slightly different but bear the same meaning, for example, *fish*, *fishes*, and *fishing*. Mapping these words into a common *conceptual* class can be helpful in some situations where we are interested in matching the aboutness of words rather than their precise spelling.

This mapping process is called *stemming*, and the root (base) form of a word is called the *stem*. A common approach for stemming is *suffix stripping*, a methodology that removes the trailing letters of a word until a root form is reached. A classic example of a suffix-stripping algorithm, still used widely, is the Porter Stemmer (an algorithm for suffix stripping, M.F. Porter, 1980).

NLTK implements the Porter Stemmer and a variety of other stemmers, as follows:

```
>>> from nltk.stem import PorterStemmer
>>> stemmer = PorterStemmer()
>>> stemmer.stem('fish')
'fish'
>>> stemmer.stem('fishes')
'fish'
>>> stemmer.stem('fishing')
'fish'
```

Stemming, like case normalization, is not reversible. If we deal with a stemmed word, it's advisable to keep a copy of the original text in case we need to reproduce it.

Unlike case normalization, stemming is also language-dependent. An alternative stemmer is the Snowball stemmer, which supports multiple languages, so it can be useful if we're dealing with multilingual data:

```
>>> from nltk.stem import SnowballStemmer
>>> SnowballStemmer.languages
('danish', 'dutch', 'english', 'finnish', 'french', 'german', 'hungarian',
'italian', 'norwegian', 'porter', 'portuguese', 'romanian', 'russian',
'spanish', 'swedish')
>>> stemmer = SnowballStemmer('italian')
>>> stemmer.stem('pesce') # fish (noun)
'pesc
>>> stemmer.stem('pesci') # fishes
'pesc'
>>> stemmer.stem('pescare') # fishing
'pesc'
```

One last detail to remember is that a stem is not always a proper word, but simply the root of a word.

Lemmatization

Similar to stemming, lemmatization also groups different inflected forms of a word together so that they can be analyzed as the same one.

Different from stemming, this process is more involved and requires some additional knowledge, such as the correct POS tag associated to each word to lemmatize. The output of lemmatization is called *lemma* and is effectively a proper word. A simple suffix-stripping approach would not work for lemmatization, because, for example, some irregular verb forms have a completely different morphology than their lemma. For example, go, goes, going, and went should all map into go, but a stemmer would fail to recognize the lemma for went:

```
>>> from nltk.stem import PorterStemmer
>>> stemmer = PorterStemmer()
>>> stemmer.stem('go')
'go'
>>> stemmer.stem('went')
'went'
```

Lemmatization in NLTK is implemented with the use of WordNet (`https://wordnet.princeton.edu`), a lexical resource that groups English words into sets of synonyms (also known as *synsets*), and provides definitions and other information related to words:

```
>>> from nltk.stem import WordNetLemmatizer
>>> lemmatizer = WordNetLemmatizer()
>>> lemmatizer.lemmatize('go', pos='v')
'go'
>>> lemmatizer.lemmatize('went')
'went'
>>> lemmatizer.lemmatize('went', pos='v')
'go'
```

The `lemmatize()` function takes a second optional argument, which is the POS tag. Without the POS tag information, the lemmatizer is likely to fail, as follows:

```
>>> lemmatizer.lemmatize('am')
'am'
>>> lemmatizer.lemmatize('am', pos='v')
'be'
>>> lemmatizer.lemmatize('is')
'is'
>>> lemmatizer.lemmatize('is', pos='v')
'be'
>>> lemmatizer.lemmatize('are')
'are'
>>> lemmatizer.lemmatize('are', pos='v')
'be'
```

The available POS tags for the WordNet-based lemmatizer are grouped into macro-categories: adjectives (a), nouns (n), verbs (v), and adverbs (r).

Stop word removal

Stop words are terms that are not particularly content-bearing, at least not when taken in isolation, such as articles and conjunctions, but are very commonly used in most natural languages. Early studies in the field of information retrieval (for example, Luhn, 1958) have shown that the most significant words in a collection were not the most frequent (nor the rarest). Further developments in this line of work showed how it is possible to remove these words without losing significant content. Back in the days when disk space and memory were much more expensive, removing stop words had the benefit of reducing the overall size of the data, hence saving up some space when building an index out of the collection of documents.

Nowadays, when terabytes are much cheaper, the disk space motivation is much weaker than before, but there is still a question of whether removing *uninteresting* words is still beneficial for the specific application at hand.

It's quite easy to find counterexamples where stop word removal would be harmful. Imagine a search engine that doesn't index stop words. How could we find web pages about *The Who* (an English rock band) or the famous verse by Shakespeare, *"To be, or not to be: that is the question?"* All the terms in the band's name and the verse (apart from the question) are common English stop words. As the examples where stop word removal is undesirable are probably countless, modern search engines such as Google or Bing do keep stop words in their indexes.

A different approach for removing uninteresting terms is frequency analysis. By observing the global document frequency of a word (the proportion of documents it appears in), we can define an arbitrary threshold to cut off terms that are too frequent or too rare. This is also implemented in libraries such as scikit-learn, where the constructor of the different vectorizer (for example, the `TfidfVectorizer` class) allows defining arguments such as `max_df` and `min_df`.

In domain-specific collections, some terms are more frequent than they generally are in common English. For example, in a collection of movie reviews, the terms movie or actor are probably present in almost every document. Even though these terms are not stop words per se (in fact, they do bear some meaning, even in isolation), one could be tempted to treat them as such. Automatically removing terms because of their frequencies can open the doors to additional problems: how to capture aspects of language such as *bad movie* or *terrific actor*?

After discussing these examples, this long disquisition on a simple matter like stop word removal can be summarized as follows: whether stop word removal is beneficial or not is highly application-dependent. It's important to test different options and evaluate how our algorithms perform with and without this preprocessing step.

Several lists of common English words are available on the Web, so coming up with a custom list is quite straightforward. NLTK is already equipped with its own list of stop words, as shown in this example:

```
>>> from nltk.corpus import stopwords
>>> stop_list = stopwords.words('english')
>>> len(stop_list)
127
>>> stop_list[:10]   # first 10 words
['i', 'me', 'my', 'myself', 'we', 'our', 'ours', 'ourselves', 'you',
'your']
```

Synonym mapping

The last normalization step that we will discuss in this section is the opportunity to map a group of synonyms into a single item. The motivations are quite similar to case normalization, with the only difference being that synonyms are not exactly the same words, so the mapping could be ambiguous for these terms that carry different meanings depending on the context.

A simple approach can make use of a controlled vocabulary, that is, a lexical resource that provides the mapping. In Python, this takes the form of a dictionary:

```
>>> synonyms = {'big': 'large', 'purchase': 'buy'}
```

In the example, we can use `synonyms` to translate the word `big` into `large` and the word `purchase` into `buy`. The replacement is as simple as accessing the desired key in the dictionary, for example, `synonyms['big']` would return `large`. A dictionary also has a `get(key, default=None)` method, which tries to access a particular key. The method accepts a second argument, which is then used as the default value if the key is not found:

```
>>> text = "I want to purchase a book on Big Data".lower().split()
>>> text
['i', 'want', 'to', 'purchase', 'a', 'book', 'on', 'big', 'data']
>>> new_text = [synonyms.get(word, word) for word in text]
>>> new_text
['i', 'want', 'to', 'buy', 'a', 'book', 'on', 'large', 'data']
```

The preceding snippet uses a list comprehension to iterate over the `text` list. Each `word` in this list is then used to retrieve a potential synonym from the `synonyms` dictionary. If a synonym is not available, using the `get()` method with the second argument will prevent any `KeyError` and keep the original word as it is in the output.

As usual, when dealing with natural language, ambiguities can arise from the simplest situations. On one side, mapping *purchase* into *buy* seems perfectly sensible, but given the preceding example, there is a question of what exactly could *large data* mean. The problem here is that we are not considering the context in which the word *big* is used, while instead it shouldn't be considered in isolation, but as part of the phrase *Big Data*. Besides this particular case, in natural language, we can easily find countless examples of words with multiple meanings (https://en.wikipedia.org/wiki/Polysemy).

Resources such as the previously mentioned WordNet provide rich information about all the potential semantic groups of a word. Just to highlight how the problem is not easy to represent with a simple dictionary, let's consider the following example:

```
>>> from nltk.corpus import wordnet
>>> syns = wordnet.synsets('big', pos='a')
```

```
>>> for syn in syns:
...     print(syn.lemma_names())
...
['large', 'big']
['big']
['bad', 'big']
['big']
['big', 'large', 'prominent']
['big', 'heavy']
['boastful', 'braggart', 'bragging', 'braggy', 'big', 'cock-a-hoop',
'crowing', 'self-aggrandizing', 'self-aggrandising']
['big', 'swelled', 'vainglorious']
['adult', 'big', 'full-grown', 'fully_grown', 'grown', 'grownup']
['big']
['big', 'large', 'magnanimous']
['big', 'bighearted', 'bounteous', 'bountiful', 'freehanded', 'handsome',
'giving', 'liberal', 'openhanded']
['big', 'enceinte', 'expectant', 'gravid', 'great', 'large', 'heavy',
'with_child']
```

As we can see, the word `big` is used in about a dozen different synsets. While they all somehow revolve around the concept of *big*, the nuances of the language require this variety to be properly captured.

In other words, this is not an easy problem. Word sense disambiguation is an active field of research that has impact on several language-related applications. Some applications on a clearly specified data domain will benefit from the use of small controlled vocabularies, but for the general case of common English, synonyms should be handled with care.

Information extraction

One of the most interesting and difficult aspects of NLP is the task of extracting structured information from unstructured text. This process is generally called **information extraction**, and it includes a variety of subtasks, the most popular probably being **Named Entity Recognition (NER)**.

The purpose of NER is to identify mentions of entities, such as persons or companies, in a piece of text and assign them to the correct label. Common entity types include persons, organizations, locations, numerical quantities, expressions of time, and currencies. For example, let's consider the following text:

"The Ford Motor Company (commonly referred to simply as Ford) is an American multinational automaker headquartered in Dearborn, Michigan, a suburb of Detroit. It was founded by Henry Ford and incorporated on June 16, 1903."

The preceding snippet (taken from the Wikipedia page of the Ford Motor Company) contains a number of references to named entities. These are summarized in the following table:

Entity Reference	Entity Type
Ford Motor Company	Organization
Dearborn, Michigan	Location
Detroit	Location
Henry Ford	Person
June 16, 1903	Time

From the point of view of extracting structured information, the same piece of text also describes some relationships between entities, as follows:

Subject	Relationship	Object
Ford Motor Company	Located in	Detroit
Ford Motor Company	Founded by	Henry Ford

Often some additional relationships can be inferred from the text. For example, if Ford is an American company that is located in Detroit, we can infer that Detroit is located in the U.S.

Knowledge representation and reasoning

The Ford example is simplified to provide a clearer presentation. It's important to keep in mind that representing knowledge is a complex topic and a research field on its own, which touches several disciplines, including artificial intelligence, information retrieval, NLP, databases, and the Semantic Web.

While there are standards to represent knowledge (for example, the RDF format), when we design the structure of a knowledge repository, it's important to understand the business domain of our application and how we are going to use such knowledge.

In general, the architecture of an information extraction system follows the structure described in Figure 7.3:

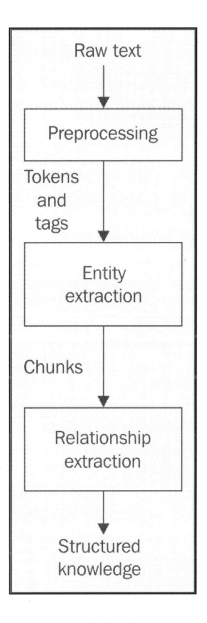

Figure 7.3: An overview of an information extraction system

The first building block is simply labeled **Preprocessing**, but it can include several steps as described in the *Text preprocessing* section. The input is assumed to be the raw text, therefore it is a string. This assumption means that we have already extracted the text from the relevant data format (for example, from a JSON file, from a database entry, and so on). The precise output of the preprocessing stage depends on the chosen steps. For the purpose of extracting entities, stop word removal, stemming, and normalization are not performed as altering the original sequence of word would probably preclude the correct identification of multi-term entities. For example, if the phrase *Bank of America* is transformed into *bank america*, identifying the correct entity wouldn't be possible. For this reason, typically only tokenization and POS tagging are applied at this stage, so the output is formed by a list of tuples `(term, pos_tag)`.

The second step in this pipeline is the **identification of entities**. From the list of tokens, entities are segmented and optionally labeled according to their type. Depending on the application, we might only be interested in proper nouns, or we might also want to include indefinite nouns or noun phrases. The output of this stage is a list of chunks that are short and non-overlapping phrases, which can be organized in trees. Chunking is also called shallow parsing or partial parsing as opposed as full parsing whose purpose is to produce a full parse tree.

The final step is the **identification of relationships** between entities. Relationships are interesting as they allow us to reason out the entities mentioned in the text. This step is often the most difficult one because of the difficult nature of dealing with language. It's also dependent on the quality of the output of the previous steps, for example, if the entity extractor misses an entity, all the relevant relationships will also be missed. The final output can be represented as a list of tuples `(subject, relation, object)` as described in the *Ford Motor* example, or it can be customized to fit the application needs better.

The out-of-the-box implementation from NLTK allows us to perform named-entity extraction very easily. The `nltk.chunk.ne_chunk()` function takes a list of tuples in the `(term, pos_tag)` format and returns a tree of chunks. Each named entity, if recognized correctly, is associated with the relevant entity type (such as person, location, and so on). The function also takes a second optional argument, `binary`, which is `False` by default. When `True`, this argument switches off the entity-type recognition, so the entities are simply labeled as NE (named entity) and their type is omitted.

The following example puts everything together using the Wikipedia API to get short summaries of the identified entities.

We will define the imports and the `ArgumentParser` definition as usual:

```
# Chap07/blogs_entities.py
from argparse import ArgumentParser
from nltk.tokenize import word_tokenize
from nltk import pos_tag
from nltk.chunk import ne_chunk
import wikipedia

def get_parser():
  parser = ArgumentParser()
  parser.add_argument('--entity')
  return parser
```

We will then define a function that iterates a list of POS-tagged tokens and returns a list of noun phrases. Noun phrases are sequences of tokens labeled with the same noun-related tag (for example, NN or NNP). The list of nouns can be compared to the actual named entities as identified by NLTK:

```
def get_noun_phrases(pos_tagged_tokens):
  all_nouns = []
  previous_pos = None
  current_chunk = []
  for (token, pos) in pos_tagged_tokens:
    if pos.startswith('NN'):
      if pos == previous_pos:
        current_chunk.append(token)
      else:
        if current_chunk:
          all_nouns.append((' '.join(current_chunk),
                           previous_pos))
        current_chunk = [token]
    else:
      if current_chunk:
        all_nouns.append((' '.join(current_chunk),
                         previous_pos))
      current_chunk = []
    previous_pos = pos
  if current_chunk:
    all_nouns.append((' '.join(current_chunk), pos))
  return all_nouns
```

Then, we will define a function that takes a tree of chunks and an entity type and returns the list of entities from the given tree according to the specified entity type:

```
def get_entities(tree, entity_type):
    for ne in tree.subtrees():
        if ne.label() == entity_type:
            tokens = [t[0] for t in ne.leaves()]
            yield ' '.join(tokens)
```

Finally, the core logic of the script: we will query Wikipedia for a particular entity, retrieving its short summary. The summary is then tokenized and POS-tagged. Noun phrases and named entities are identified in the short summary. Each named entity will then be shown with a short summary next to it (again from Wikipedia):

```
if __name__ == '__main__':
    parser = get_parser()
    args = parser.parse_args()

    entity = wikipedia.summary(args.entity, sentences=2)

    tokens = word_tokenize(entity)
    tagged_tokens = pos_tag(tokens)
    chunks = ne_chunk(tagged_tokens, binary=True)

    print("-----")
    print("Description of {}".format(args.entity))
    print(entity)
    print("-----")
    print("Noun phrases in description:")
    for noun in get_noun_phrases(tagged_tokens):
        print(noun[0])  # tuple (noun, pos_tag)
    print("-----")
    print("Named entities in description:")
    for ne in get_entities(chunks, entity_type='NE'):
        summary = wikipedia.summary(ne, sentences=1)
        print("{}: {}".format(ne, summary))
```

We can run the preceding script with, for example, the following command:

```
$ python blogs_entities.py --entity London
```

The output of the script is partially shown in *Figure 7.4*:

```
-----
Description of London
London /ˈlʌndən/ is the capital and most populous city of England and
the United Kingdom. Standing on the River Thames in the south east of
Great Britain, London has been a major settlement for two millennia.
-----
Noun phrases in description:
London
/ˈlʌndən/
capital
# more nouns ...
-----
Named entities in description:
London: London /ˈlʌndən/ is the capital and most populous city of
England and the United Kingdom.
England: England /ˈɪŋglənd/ is a country that is part of the United #
# more entities ...
```

Figure 7.4: The output of the script

The complete list of identified noun phrases is shown in *Figure 7.5*:

```
London, /ˈlʌndən/, capital, city, England, United Kingdom, Standing,
River Thames, south east, Great Britain, London, settlement, and
millennia.
```

Figure 7.5: Identified noun phrases

In this case, only the term `Standing` is incorrectly labeled as a noun, probably because of the capital `S`, as it is the word at the beginning of the sentence. Whether all the terms are interesting (for example, `standing`, `settlement`, and `millennia`) is questionable, but all the nouns are there. On the other hand, the list of identified named entities seems pretty good: `London`, `England`, `United Kingdom`, `River Thames`, `Great Britain`, and `London`.

Summary

In this chapter, we introduced the field of NLP, a complex field of study with many challenges and opportunities.

The first part of the chapter focused on how to get textual data from the Web. Blogs were a natural candidate for text mining, given the abundance of textual data out there. After dealing with two of the most popular free blogging platforms, WordPress.com and Blogger, we generalized the problem by introducing the XML standard for web feed, specifically RSS and Atom. Given its strong presence on the Web, and probably in everyday life of many Internet users, Wikipedia also deserved to be mentioned in a discussion about textual content. We saw how it's easy to interact with all of these services in Python either by using available libraries or by quickly implementing our own functions.

The second part of the chapter was about NLP. We already introduced some NLP concepts throughout the book, but this was the first time we took time to provide a more formal introduction. We described an NLP pipeline that goes from raw text to named entity identification, walking through all the necessary preprocessing steps that make advanced applications possible.

The next chapter will focus on other social media APIs in order to provide an even wider horizon in terms of data mining possibilities.

8
Mining All the Data!

This chapter provides an outlook on some of the social media APIs available out there. In particular, we will discuss the following topics:

- How to mine videos from YouTube
- How to mine open source projects from GitHub
- How to mine local businesses from Yelp
- How to use the requests library to call any web-based API
- How to wrap your requests calls into a custom client

Many social APIs

Each of the previous chapters focused on a particular social media platform that has been popular in the recent years. Fortunately, the story is not over. Many platforms provide social networking functionalities, as well as a nice API to mine data from. On the other hand, providing a comprehensive description of all the possible APIs with exhaustive examples and interesting use cases would go far beyond the scope of this book.

In order to provide food for thought, this chapter tackles two aspects of social media mining. Firstly, we'll walk through a few interesting APIs in order to search or mine complex entities such as videos, open source projects, or local businesses. Secondly, we'll discuss what to do if a nice Python client is not available for a particular API.

Mining videos on YouTube

YouTube (http://youtube.com) probably doesn't need much introduction nowadays, being one of the most visited websites in the world (ranked second in March 2016 in Alexa rank). The video-sharing service features a wide spectrum of content material is, in fact, produced and shared by a range of different authors, from amateur video bloggers to big corporations. YouTube's registered users can upload, rate, and comment on videos. Viewing and sharing doesn't require the users to register a profile.

YouTube was acquired by Google in 2006, so today they are part of the larger Google platform. In Chapter 5, *Topic Analysis on Google+*, and Chapter 7, *Blogs, RSS, Wikipedia and Natural Language Processing*, we have already introduced other services by Google, especially Google+ and Blogger. YouTube provides three different APIs to integrate your applications with the YouTube platform: YouTube Data, YouTube Analytics, and YouTube Reporting. We'll focus on the first one to retrieve and mine data from YouTube as the other two are tailored for content creators.

The first steps to access the YouTube Data API are very similar to what we have already seen, so the reader is encouraged to take a look at Chapter 5, *Topic Analysis on Google+*, to go through the procedure of accessing the Google Developers Console (https://console.developers.google.com). If you have already registered your credentials on the Google Developers Console, you simply need to enable the YouTube Data API as shown in *Figure 8.1*:

YouTube Data API v3

The YouTube Data API v3 is an API that provides access to YouTube data, such as videos, playlists, and channels.
Learn more
Try this API in APIs Explorer

Figure 8.1: Enabling the YouTube Data API from the Google Developers Console

From the **Credentials** tab in the Google Developers Console, we can reuse the API key that we obtained from the Google+ project discussed in Chapter 5, *Topic Analysis on Google+*. Once the credentials are sorted out, we can store our Google API key as an environment variable:

```
$ export GOOGLE_API_KEY="your-api-key"
```

We are also going to reuse the same Python client used for the other Google services, which can be installed via the CheeseShop:

```
$ pip install google-api-python-client
```

As a refresher, we will remind the user that the package that we just installed is available as googleapiclient, but it's also aliased simply as apiclient (used in the code examples).

The API is rate limited using a quota system. Each application has a daily cap of 1,000,000 units. Different calls to different endpoints will have a different quota cost, but the rate limit of one million units is far beyond what we need to get started and experiment with the API. The usage and quota can be seen in the Google Developers Console.

The first example of interaction with the YouTube Data API is a generic search application. The youtube_search_video.py script implements a call to the search.list API endpoint (https://developers.google.com/youtube/v3/docs/search/list). A single call to this endpoint has a quota cost of 100 units:

```python
# Chap08/youtube_search_video.py
import os
import json
from argparse import ArgumentParser
from apiclient.discovery import build

def get_parser():
  parser = ArgumentParser()
  parser.add_argument('--query')
  parser.add_argument('--n', type=int, default=10)
  return parser

if __name__ == '__main__':
  parser = get_parser()
  args = parser.parse_args()

  api_key = os.environ.get('GOOGLE_API_KEY')
  service = build('youtube',
                  'v3',
                  developerKey=api_key)
```

```
search_feed = service.search()
search_query = search_feed.list(q=args.query,
                                 part="id,snippet",
                                 maxResults=args.n)
search_response = search_query.execute()

print(json.dumps(search_response, indent=4))
```

The script, as seen before, uses the `ArgumentParser` approach to parse the command-line parameters. The `--query` argument allows us to pass the query string for the API call, while the `--n` argument (optional, default to `10`) is used to define the number of results we want to retrieve.

The core of the interaction with the YouTube API is handled by the `service` object, instantiated by a call to the `apiclient.discovery.build()` function, similar to what we did for Google+ and Blogger. The two positional arguments of this function are the service name (`youtube`) and the version of the API (`v3`). The third keyword argument is the API key that we defined as the environment variable. After instantiating the `service` object, we can call its `search()` function to build the search feed object. This is the object that allows us to call the `list()` function, defining the actual API call.

The `list()` function only takes keyword-based arguments. The `q` argument is the query that we want to pass to the API. The `part` argument allows us to define a comma-separated list of properties that the API response should include. Finally, we can execute the call to the API, which results in a response object (that is, a Python dictionary) that, for simplicity, we pretty print using the `json.dumps()` function.

The `search_response` dictionary has several first-level attributes, as listed in the following:

- `pageInfo`, including `resultsPerPage` and `totalResults`
- `items`: This is a list of search results
- `kind`: This is the type of result object (`youtube#searchListResponse` in this case)
- `etag`
- `regionCode`: This is the two-letter country code, for example, GB
- `nextPageToken`: This is a token to build a call to the next page of results

In the `items` list, each item is a search result. We have the ID of the item (which could be a video, channel, or playlist) and a snippet that contains several details.

For videos, some of the interesting details include the following:

- `channelId`: This is the ID of the video creator
- `channelTitle`: This is the name of the video creator
- `title`: This is the title of the video
- `description`: This is the textual description of the video
- `publishedAt`: This is a string with the publication date in the ISO 8601 format

The basic query can be extended to customize the outcome of the search request. For example, the query from the `youtube_search_video.py` script retrieves not only the videos, but also the playlists or channels. If we want to restrict the results to a particular type of objects, we can use the `type` argument in the `list()` function, which takes one of the possible values: `video`, `playlist`, and `channel`. Moreover, we can influence how the results are sorted using the `order` attribute. This attribute takes one of several accepted values:

- `date`: This sorts the results in reverse chronological order (the most recent ones will be first)
- `rating`: This sorts the results from the highest to lowest rating
- `relevance`: This is the default option to sort results according to their relevance to the query
- `title`: This sorts the results alphabetically by title
- `videoCount`: This sorts channels in the descending order of uploaded videos
- `viewCount`: This sorts videos from the highest to lowest number of views

Finally, we can also restrict the search to a particular range of publication dates using the `publishedBefore` and `publishedAfter` parameters.

Let's consider the following example in order to put this information together and build a custom query to the search API endpoint. Let's say that we are interested in retrieving the videos published in January 2016 in order of relevance. The call to the `list()` function can be refactored as follows:

```
search_query = search_feed.list(
                            q=args.query,
                            part="id,snippet",
                            maxResults=args.n,
                            type='video',
                            publishedAfter='2016-01-01T00:00:00Z',
                            publishedBefore='2016-02-01T00:00:00Z')
```

The `publishedAfter` and `publishedBefore` arguments expect the date and time to be formatted according to RFC 3339.

In order to handle a higher arbitrary number of search results, we need to implement a pagination mechanism. The simplest way to achieve this goal is to wrap the call to the search endpoint into a custom function that iterates over the different pages until the desired number of results is reached.

The following class implements a custom YouTube client with a method tailored for video search:

```python
class YoutubeClient(object):

    def __init__(self, api_key):
        self.service = build('youtube',
                                'v3',
                                developerKey=api_key)

    def search_video(self, query, n_results):
        search = self.service.search()
        request = search.list(q=query,
                                part="id,snippet",
                                maxResults=n_results,
                                type='video')
        all_results = []
        while request and len(all_results) <= n_results:
            response = request.execute()
            try:
                for video in response['items']:
                    all_results.append(video)
            except KeyError:
                break
            request = search.list_next(request, response)
        return all_results[:n_results]
```

On initialization, the `YoutubeClient` class requires `api_key` that will be used to call the `apiclient.discovery.build()` method and set up the service.

The core of the search logic is implemented in the search_video() method, which takes two arguments: the query and the desired number of results. We will first set up the request object using the list() method as we did before. The while loop checks whether the request object is not None and we haven't reached the number of results yet. The execution of the query retrieves the results in the response object, which is a dictionary as seen before. The data about the videos is listed in response['items'], appended to the all_results list. The last operation of the loop is a call to the list_next() method, which overrides the request object, making it ready to retrieve the next page of results.

The YoutubeClient class can be used as follows:

```
# Chap08/youtube_search_video_pagination.py
import os
import json
from argparse import ArgumentParser
from apiclient.discovery import build

def get_parser():
    parser = ArgumentParser()
    parser.add_argument('--query')
    parser.add_argument('--n', type=int, default=50)
    parser.add_argument('--output')
    return parser

class YoutubeClient(object):
    # as defined in the previous snippet

if __name__ == '__main__':
    parser = get_parser()
    args = parser.parse_args()

    api_key = os.environ.get('GOOGLE_API_KEY')

    youtube = YoutubeClient(api_key)
    videos = youtube.search_video(args.query, args.n)

    with open(args.output, 'w') as f:
        for video in videos:
            f.write(json.dumps(video)+"\n")
```

The script can be called with the following example:

```
$ python youtube_search_video_pagination.py \
  --query python \
  --n 50 \
  --output videos.jsonl
```

Executing the preceding command will generate the `videos.jsonl` file that contains the data of 50 videos relevant to the query `python`. The file is saved in the JSON Lines format as we have seen in all the previous chapters.

This section showcased some examples of interaction with the YouTube Data API. The patterns are very similar to the ones already seen with the Google+ and Blogger APIs, so once the approach is understood for one of the Google services, it can be easily translated to others.

Mining open source software on GitHub

GitHub (`https://github.com`) is a hosting service for Git repositories. While private repositories are one of the key features for paying plans, the service is well known for hosting many open source services. On top of the source control management functionalities of Git, GitHub offers a bunch of features that make the management of an open source project easier (for example, bug tracking, wikis, feature requests, and so on).

Source control management software
A source control system (also known as version control or revision control) is one of the most important tools in software management as it keeps track of how the software under development is evolving. This aspect is often neglected by novice or solo developers, but it is crucial when working on complex projects, either in a team or independently. Among the advantages, there's the possibility of rolling back an undesirable change (for example, storing and restoring different versions of the software), as well as the efficient collaboration with team members. Git, originally developed by Linus Torvalds (author of Linux), is one of the most popular tools for version control. Knowing the basics of version control systems is going to be beneficial for novice developers, analysts, and researchers alike.

GitHub offers access to their data via an API (`https://developer.github.com/v3`), using the common mechanism of registering an app on their platform. App authentication is required only when accessing private information that is available only to the authenticated users.

The API has some strict rate limits. Unauthenticated calls are limited to 60 per hour, which is a fairly low number. Implementing the authentication, the limit is upgraded to 5,000 per hour. The search API also has custom rate limit rules (10 requests per minute if not authenticated and 30 if authenticated). The authentication can be performed in the following three different ways:

- Basic username/password authentication
- Via Oauth2 token
- Via Oauth2 client ID and client secret

The basic authentication requires sending the actual username and password to the API endpoints as defined by HTTP standards. Authentication via Oauth2 token, on the other hand, requires acquiring the token programmatically (`https://developer.github.com/v3/oauth_authorizations/#create-a-new-authorization`) and then sending it to the API endpoints either via the header or the URL parameter. The last option is to pass the client ID and client secret to the API. These details can be obtained by registering an application on the GitHub platform (`https://github.com/settings/applications/new`). *Figure 8.2* shows the registration form to create a new application:

Figure 8.2: Registering a new application in GitHub

Once the application is registered, we can store the credentials as environment variables:

```
$ export GITHUB_CLIENT_ID="your-client-id"
$ export GITHUB_CLIENT_SECRET="your-client-secret"
```

Now that everything is set up, we are ready to interact with the GitHub API. There are several Python libraries that can be used as clients, all of which are third parties, that is, not officially supported by GitHub (`https://developer.github.com/libraries`). The library that we chose for the examples in this section is PyGithub (`https://github.com/PyGithub/PyGithub`), but the readers are encouraged to test other libraries if they wish.

To install the library from our virtual environment, use the following command:

```
$ pip install PyGithub
```

The following script can be used to look up for a particular username in order to obtain some basic information about their profile and their GitHub repositories:

```
# Chap08/github_get_user.py
import os
from argparse import ArgumentParser
from github import Github
from github.GithubException import UnknownObjectException

def get_parser():
  parser = ArgumentParser()
  parser.add_argument('--user')
  parser.add_argument('--get-repos', action='store_true',
                      default=False)
  return parser

if __name__ == '__main__':
  parser = get_parser()
  args = parser.parse_args()
  client_id = os.environ['GITHUB_CLIENT_ID']
  client_secret = os.environ['GITHUB_CLIENT_SECRET']

  g = Github(client_id=client_id, client_secret=client_secret)

  try:
    user = g.get_user(args.user)
    print("Username: {}".format(args.user))
    print("Full name: {}".format(user.name))
    print("Location: {}".format(user.location))
    print("Number of repos: {}".format(user.public_repos))
    if args.get_repos:
      repos = user.get_repos()
```

```
        for repo in repos:
            print("Repo: {} ({} stars)".format(repo.name,
                    repo.stargazers_count))
    except UnknownObjectException:
        print("User not found")
```

The script uses `ArgumentParser` to capture the parameters from the command line: `--user` is used to pass the username to search, while the optional `--get-repos` argument is a Boolean flag to state whether we want to include the list of the user's repositories in the output (notice that pagination is not included for simplicity).

The script can be run with the following command:

```
$ python github_get_user.py --user bonzanini --get-repos
```

This will produce the following output:

```
Username: bonzanini
Full name: Marco Bonzanini
Location: London, UK
Number of repos: 9
Repo: bonzanini.github.io (1 stars)
Repo: Book-SocialMediaMiningPython (3 stars)
# more repositories ...
```

The `Github.get_user()` function assumes that we already know the exact username that we are looking for.

Some of the most interesting attributes of the user object are listed in the following table:

Attribute Name	Description
avatar_url	This is the URL of the avatar image
bio	This is the short biography of the user
blog	This is the user's blog
company	This is the user's company
created_at	This is the creation date of the profile
email	This is the e-mail of the user
followers	This is the number of followers of the user
followers_url	This is the URL to retrieve the list of followers of the user
following	This is the number of profiles followed by the user

following_url	This is the URL to retrieve the list of profiles followed by the user
location	This is the geographic location of the user
login	This is the login name
name	This is the full name
public_repos	This is the number of public repositories
public_gists	This is the number of public gists
repos_url	This is the URL to retrieve repositories

After retrieving a user profile using the precise username, we can look at the option of searching for a user. The GitHub API provides an endpoint accessed by the `Github.search_users()` function, which allows us to specify a query and some sorting and ordering arguments. The following script implements the search:

```python
# Chap08/github_search_user.py
import os
from argparse import ArgumentParser
from argparse import ArgumentTypeError
from github import Github

def get_parser():
    parser = ArgumentParser()
    parser.add_argument('--query')
    parser.add_argument('--sort',
                        default='followers',
                        type=check_sort_value)
    parser.add_argument('--order',
                        default='desc',
                        type=check_order_value)
    parser.add_argument('--n', default=5, type=int)
    return parser

def check_sort_value(value):
    valid_sort_values = ['followers', 'joined', 'repositories']
    if value not in valid_sort_values:
        raise ArgumentTypeError('"{}" is an invalid value for
                                "sort"'.format(value))
    return value

def check_order_value(value):
    valid_order_values = ['asc', 'desc']
    if value not in valid_order_values:
```

```
        raise ArgumentTypeError('"{}" is an invalid value for
                             "order"'.format(value))
    return value

if __name__ == '__main__':
    parser = get_parser()
    args = parser.parse_args()
    client_id = os.environ['GITHUB_CLIENT_ID']
    client_secret = os.environ['GITHUB_CLIENT_SECRET']

    g = Github(client_id=client_id, client_secret=client_secret)

    users = g.search_users(args.query,
                           sort=args.sort,
                           order=args.order)
    for i, u in enumerate(users[:args.n]):
        print("{}) {} ({}) with {} repos ".format(i+1, u.login,
            u.name, u.public_repos))
```

The script uses ArgumentParser to parse the parameters from the command line. The search query can be passed via the --query option. The API also accepts two arguments that allow customizing the sorting and ordering. These two values, implemented as --sort and --order arguments, only accept specific values, so we have to specify a particular type for each one of them. More precisely, the check_sort_value() and check_order_value() helper functions implement the following logic: if the given value is a valid one, it is returned to be passed to the API, otherwise an ArgumentTypeError exception is raised. Lastly, ArgumentParser also accepts a --n parameter to specify the desired number of results (defaulted to 5).

The script can be run with the following command:

```
$ python github_search_user.py \
  --query [your query here] \
  --sort followers \
  --order desc
```

The output is a list of the five (default) most popular users, that is, the ones with the highest number of followers.

A very similar script can be implemented to search for popular repositories. The implementation is shown in the following script:

```
# Chap08/github_search_repos.py
import os
from argparse import ArgumentParser
from argparse import ArgumentTypeError
```

```python
from github import Github

def get_parser():
  parser = ArgumentParser()
  parser.add_argument('--query')
  parser.add_argument('--sort',
                      default='stars',
                      type=check_sort_value)
  parser.add_argument('--order',
                      default='desc',
                      type=check_order_value)
  parser.add_argument('--n', default=5, type=int)
  return parser

def check_sort_value(value):
  valid_sort_values = ['stars', 'forks', 'updated']
  if value not in valid_sort_values:
    raise ArgumentTypeError('"{}" is an invalid value for
                            "sort"'.format(value))
  return value

def check_order_value(value):
  valid_order_values = ['asc', 'desc']
  if value not in valid_order_values:
    raise ArgumentTypeError('"{}" is an invalid value for
                            "order"'.format(value))
  return value

if __name__ == '__main__':
  parser = get_parser()
  args = parser.parse_args()
  client_id = os.environ['GITHUB_CLIENT_ID']
  client_secret = os.environ['GITHUB_CLIENT_SECRET']

  g = Github(client_id=client_id, client_secret=client_secret)

  repos = g.search_repositories(args.query,
                                sort=args.sort,
                                order=args.order)
  for i, r in enumerate(repos[:args.n]):
    print("{}) {} by {} ({} stars)".format(i+1, r.name,
          r.owner.name, r.stargazers_count))
```

The github_search_repos.py script is very similar to the previous one as it also uses ArgumentParser with custom types for the parsed --sort and --order arguments. In order to search for repositories, it uses the Github.search_repositories() method, which takes a query and some keyword-based arguments.

The script can be run with the following command:

```
$ python github_search_repos.py \
  --query python \
  --sort stars \
  --order desc
```

The `python` query issues some interesting results:

```
1) oh-my-zsh by Robby Russell (36163 stars)
2) jQuery-File-Upload by Sebastian Tschan (23381 stars)
3) awesome-python by Vinta (20093 stars)
4) requests by Kenneth Reitz (18616 stars)
5) scrapy by Scrapy project (13652 stars)
```

While there are some popular Python projects in the list (such as the **requests** and Scrapy libraries), the first two results don't seem to be related to Python. This is because calling the search API by default issues a query against the title/description fields, so this particular call has captured some repositories that mention the keyword `python` in their description, but they are not implemented in Python.

We can refactor the search in order to only retrieve repositories that are written in a specific language, which use that language as the main one. The only piece of code that needs to be changed is the call to `Github.search_repositories()`, using the `language` qualifier, as follows:

```
repos = g.search_repositories("language:{}".format(args.query),
                              sort=args.sort,
                              order=args.order)
```

After this minimal change in the query, the results look quite different:

```
1) httpie by Jakub Roztoĉil (22130 stars)
2) awesome-python by Vinta (20093 stars)
3) thef*** by Vladimir Iakovlev (19868 stars)
4) flask by The Pallets Projects (19824 stars)
5) django by Django (19044 stars)
```

At this point, all the results are projects mainly implemented in Python.

The following table summarizes the main attributes of repository objects:

Attribute Name	Description
name	This is the name of the repo as it appears in the URL
full_name	This is the complete name of the repo (that is, user_name/repo_name)
owner	This is the object representing the user owning the project
id	This is the numeric ID of the repo
stargazers_count	This is the number of stargazers
description	This is the textual description of the repo
created_at	This is the datetime object of the creation time
updated_at	This is the datetime object of the last update
open_issues_count	This is the number of open issues
language	This is the main language for the repo
languages_url	This is the URL to retrieve other language information
homepage	This is the URL of the homepage for the project

There are many attributes and details about a particular repository. The documentation of the API (https://developer.github.com/v3/repos) provides an exhaustive description.

This section showed some examples of data retrieval from the GitHub API. Potential applications include the analysis to understand the programming languages that are most commonly used by extracting, for example, the highest number of projects written in a specific language, the most active projects per language, the highest number of issues opened in a given time frame, and so on.

Mining local businesses on Yelp

Yelp is an online service that hosts crowd-sourced reviews about local businesses, such as bars and restaurants (https://www.yelp.com). Visited by 135 million monthly users, its content is mainly community-driven.

Yelp offers three APIs that can be used to search for and interact with data about local businesses. The three APIs are grouped depending on their purpose. The search API is the entry point for keyword-based search. The business API is used to look for information about a specific business. The phone search API is used to search for a business by phone number.

The Yelp API has the rate limit of 25,000 calls per day.

This section describes the basic steps to set up an application that searches the Yelp database for particular keywords.

The access to the APIs is protected by tokens. The first step to access any of the APIs, after registering an account on Yelp, is to obtain the tokens on the developers' website (`https://www.yelp.com/developers`). *Figure 8.3* shows the form that we need to fill in order to access the API. In the example, the **Your website URL** field points to the localhost:

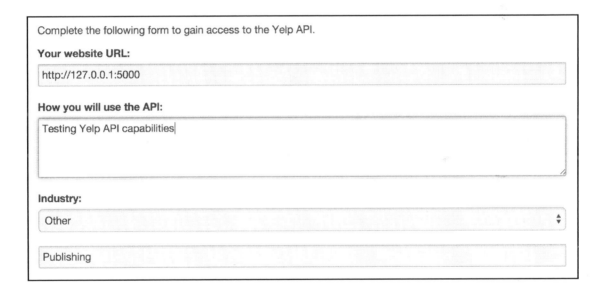

Figure 8.3: The access to the Yelp API

Once we have completed this first step, we'll obtain four different access keys. These strings should be kept protected and never be shared. The access keys are called consumer key, consumer secret, token, and token secret. These strings are used for the OAuth authentication process that is necessary before calling the API.

Following the convention used throughout the book, we can store these configuration details as environment variables:

```
$ export YELP_CONSUMER_KEY="your-consumer-key"
$ export YELP_CONSUMER_SECRET="your-consumer-secret"
$ export YELP_TOKEN="your-token"
$ export YELP_TOKEN_SECRET="your-token-secret"
```

In order to access the API programmatically, we will need to install the official Python client. From our virtual environment, use the following command:

```
$ pip install yelp
```

The following script, `yelp_client.py`, defines a function that we will use to set up our calls to the API:

```
# Chap08/yelp_client.py
import os
from yelp.client import Client
from yelp.oauth1_authenticator import Oauth1Authenticator

def get_yelp_client():
  auth = Oauth1Authenticator(
    consumer_key=os.environ['YELP_CONSUMER_KEY'],
    consumer_secret=os.environ['YELP_CONSUMER_SECRET'],
    token=os.environ['YELP_TOKEN'],
    token_secret=os.environ['YELP_TOKEN_SECRET']
    )

  client = Client(auth)
  return client
```

Once everything is in place, we can perform our first search for a local business. The `yelp_search_business.py` script calls the search API using the provided location and the keywords:

```
# Chap08/yelp_search_business.py
from argparse import ArgumentParser
from yelp_client import get_yelp_client

def get_parser():
  parser = ArgumentParser()
  parser.add_argument('--location')
  parser.add_argument('--search')
  parser.add_argument('--language', default='en')
  return parser

if __name__ == '__main__':
```

```
client = get_yelp_client()
parser = get_parser()
args = parser.parse_args()

params = {
    'term': args.search,
    'lang': args.language,
    'limit': 20,
    'sort': 2
}

response = client.search(args.location, **params)
for business in response.businesses:
    address = ', '.join(business.location.address)
    categories = ', '.join([cat[0] for cat in
                            business.categories])
    print("{} ({}, {}); rated {}; categories
          {}".format(business.name,
          address,
          business.location.postal_code,
          business.rating,
          categories))
```

An `ArgumentParser` object is used to parse the arguments passed via the command line. In particular, two arguments are mandatory: `--location`, which is the name of the city or local neighborhood, and `--search`, which allows us to pass specific keywords for the search. An optional `--language` argument can also be provided to specify the desired language for the output (particularly for the reviews). The value of this argument has to be a language code (for example, `en` for English, `fr` for French, `de` for German, and so on). We will also provide two more optional arguments. The `--limit` parameter is the number of results we desire (defaulted to 20), while the `--sort` argument defines how the results are sorted (0 for best match, 1 for distance, and 2 for highest rated).

In the main part of the script, we will set up the Yelp client and the parser. We will then define a dictionary of parameters to be passed to the Yelp client. These parameters include the ones defined via the command line.

The script can be called with the following command:

```
$ python yelp_search_business.py \
  --location London \
  --search breakfast \
  --limit 5
```

The output is a list of (five, in this case) local businesses printed on the console:

```
Friends of Ours (61 Pitfield Street, N1 6BU); rated 4.5; categories Cafes,
Breakfast & Brunch, Coffee & Tea
Maison D'Ãªtre (154 Canonbury Road, N1 2UP); rated 4.5; categories Coffee &
Tea, Breakfast & Brunch
Dishoom (5 Stable Street, N1C 4AB); rated 4.5; categories Indian, Breakfast
& Brunch
E Pellicci (332 Bethnal Green Road, E2 0AG); rated 4.5; categories Italian,
Cafes, Breakfast & Brunch
Alchemy (8 Ludgate Broadway, EC4V 6DU); rated 4.5; categories Coffee & Tea,
Cafes
```

When searching for multiple keywords, the query has to be wrapped around double quotes so that it can be interpreted correctly, as follows:

```
$ python yelp_search_business.py \
  --location "San Francisco" \
  --search "craft beer" \
  --limit 5
```

The `location` objects returned by the API have several properties. The following table summarizes the most interesting ones:

Attribute Name	Description
id	This is the business identifier
name	This is the business name
image_url	This is the URL of the photo of the business
is_claimed	This is a Boolean attribute that informs us whether the business owner has claimed the page
is_closed	This is a Boolean attribute that informs us whether the business has permanently closed
url	This is the Yelp URL of the business
mobile_url	This is the Yelp mobile URL of the business
phone	This is the string with the phone number in international format
display_phone	This is the string with the phone number formatted for display

categories	This is the list of categories associated with the business. Each category is a tuple (`display_name`, `filter_name`), where the first name can be used for presentation and the second name can be used to filter the query
review_count	This is the number of reviews for this business
rating	This is the rating for the business, rounded (for example, 1, 1.5 ... 4.5, 5)
snippet_text	This is the short description of the business
snippet_image_url	This is the URL of the snippet image associated with the business
location	This is the `location` object associated with the business

The `location` object provides the following attributes:

- `address (list)`, only contains address fields
- `display_address (list)`, formatted for display, includes cross streets, city, state code, and so on
- `city (string)`
- `state_code (string)`, the ISO 3166-2 state code for the business
- `postal_code (string)`
- `country_code (string)`, the ISO 3166-1 country code for the business
- `cross_streets (string)`, the cross streets for the business (US)
- `neighborhoods (list)`, neighborhood information for the business
- `coordinates.latitude (number)`
- `coordinates.longitude (number)`

Besides the search API, Yelp also provides a business API that is tailored for the retrieval of information about a given business. The API assumes that you already have the specific ID for the business.

The following script shows how to use the Python client to access the business API:

```
# Chap08/yelp_get_business.py
from argparse import ArgumentParser
from yelp_client import get_yelp_client

def get_parser():
  parser = ArgumentParser()
```

```
        parser.add_argument('--id')
        parser.add_argument('--language', default='en')
        return parser

if __name__ == '__main__':
    client = get_yelp_client()
    parser = get_parser()
    args = parser.parse_args()

    params = {
        'lang': args.language
    }

    response = client.get_business(args.id, **params)
    business = response.business
    print("Review count: {}".format(business.review_count))
    for review in business.reviews:
        print("{} (by {})".format(review.excerpt, review.user.name))
```

One major limitation of the business API is the fact that the list of reviews for a given business is not completely provided. In fact, only one review is given. This single review is the only additional information provided by the business API that the search API doesn't show, so there is not much more room for data mining in this case.

It is interesting to notice that Yelp provides a dataset, which is updated and enriched from time to time, for academic research (`https://www.yelp.com/dataset_challenge`). The dataset includes details about businesses, users, reviews, pictures, and connections between users. This data can be used for applications of Natural Language Processing, graph mining, and machine learning in general. The dataset is also associated with a challenge where students are awarded for the technical quality of their submission.

Building a custom Python client

Throughout the book, we accessed different social media platform through Python libraries, either officially supported by the social media server themselves or provided by third parties.

This section answers the question: what if they don't provide a Python client for their API (and there is no unofficial library either)?

HTTP made simple

In order to implement the calls to the desired API, the recommended library for easy HTTPinteractions is **requests**. From our virtual environment, use the following command:

```
$ pip install requests
```

The requests library offers a straightforward interface to perform HTTP calls. In order to test the library, we're going to implement a simple client for the httpbin.org service, a web service, that offers basic request/response interactions, perfect for our educational purposes.

The httpbin.org web page (http://httpbin.org/), explains the various endpoints and their meaning. To showcase the use of the requests library, we will implement a HttpBinClient class with the methods to call some of the basic endpoints:

```
class HttpBinClient(object):

    base_url = 'http://httpbin.org'

    def get_ip(self):
        response = requests.get("{}/ip".format(self.base_url))
        my_ip = response.json()['origin']
        return my_ip

    def get_user_agent(self):
        response = requests.get("{}/user-agent".format(self.base_url))
        user_agent = response.json()['user-agent']
        return user_agent

    def get_headers(self):
        response = requests.get("{}/headers".format(self.base_url))
        headers = HeadersModel(response.json())
        return headers
```

The client has a base_url class variable, which is used to store the base URL to call. The implementations of the get_ip(), get_user_agent(), and get_headers() methods call the /ip, /user-agent and /headers endpoints respectively, building the complete URL using the base_url variable.

The interaction with the requests library is very similar for the three methods. The endpoint is called using requests.get(), which sends the HTTP GET request to the endpoint and returns the response object. This object has some attributes such as status_code (which stores the response status) and text (which stores the raw response data), as well as the json() method that we will use to load the JSON response into a dictionary.

While IP and user-agent are simple strings, the headers object is a bit more complex as there are several attributes. For this reason, the response is wrapped into a custom `HeadersModel` object, defined as follows:

```
class HeadersModel(object):

    def __init__(self, data):
        self.host = data['headers']['Host']
        self.user_agent = data['headers']['User-Agent']
        self.accept = data['headers']['Accept']
```

If we save the preceding classes in a file called `httpbin_client.py`, we can use the custom client from our sample application, as follows:

```
>>> from httpbin_client import HttpBinClient
>>> client = HttpBinClient()
>>> print(client.get_user_agent())
python-requests/2.8.1
>>> h = client.get_headers()
>>> print(h.host)
httpbin.org
```

The simplicity of the web API and the proposed example shouldn't mislead the reader to think that we're just adding a layer of complexity to an otherwise straightforward task. We could, in fact, interact directly with the web API from our application using the requests library. On one hand, this might be true for this particular example, but on the other hand, social media APIs are extremely dynamic in their own nature. New endpoints are added, response formats are changed, and new features are constantly developed. For example, after Chapter 4, *Posts, Pages, and User Interactions on Facebook*, was drafted, Facebook introduced the new reactions feature, which also triggered a change in their API response.

In other words, the custom Python client adds a layer of abstraction that allows us to focus on the interface of the client rather than on the web API. From the application point of view, we will focus on calling the client's methods, such as `HttpBinClient.get_headers()`, and hide the details of how the `/headers` API endpoint sends a response inside such method. If the response format from the web API is going to change in the future, all we need to do is update the client to reflect the new changes, but all our applications interacting with the web API are not affected, thanks to this extra layer of abstraction.

The `httpbin.org` service is really uncomplicated, so real implementations of a client for a social media API are probably not so straightforward, but all in all, this is the gist of it: hide implementation details with a layer of abstraction. This is what all the Python clients that we have adopted so far do.

HTTP status codes

In order to have a broader understanding of how HTTP interactions work, we must mention the importance of the response status code. At the low level, each response from a HTTP server is opened with a numeric status code, followed by a reason phrase that describes the motivation behind the status code. For example, when we point our browser to a particular URL, the web server can reply with a status code 200, followed by the reason phrase OK. The response then includes the actual web page that we're requesting, which can be displayed by the browser. A different option for the web server is to respond with a status code 404, followed by the reason phrase Not Found. The browser can understand this response and display the appropriate error message to the user.

Web APIs are not different from the brief interaction described earlier. Depending on the request, the server could send a successful response (status code 2xx) or an error (status code 4xx for client errors and 5xx for server errors). The client-side implementation should be able to correctly interpret the different status codes as provided by the web API, and behave accordingly. It's also worth mentioning that some services introduce non-standard status codes, such as Twitter's error code 420, *Enhance your calm*, used when the client is sending too many requests and it has to be rate-limited.

A complete list of status codes and their meaning is available at https://en.wikipedia.org/wiki/List_of_HTTP_status_codes with a simplified description, but the official documentation is included in the appropriate RFC documents.

Given the availability of open source libraries, the need to implement a client from scratch should be fairly rare nowadays. If this is the case, the reader should now be equipped to get started.

Summary

This chapter discussed some more options to mine data on social media. Beyond the usual popular social networks, such as Twitter, Facebook, and Google+, many other platforms offer APIs to access their data.

When a Python client is not available for a particular platform, we can implement a custom client, exploiting the simplicity of the requests library. The implementation of a custom client seems to add unnecessary complexity at first, but it provides an important layer of abstraction that pays off in terms of design in the long run.

Besides the instructions for a custom client implementation, we also examined some other popular services to mine complex objects. We retrieved data about videos from YouTube, open source projects from GitHub, and local businesses such as restaurants from Yelp.

Many more social media platforms remain unexplored in this book, because providing a comprehensive discussion would be unrealistic, but I hope that the readers have a good taste of the many possibilities that are out there.

The next chapter is the last chapter of the book. It provides a discussion on the Semantic Web and serves as an outlook for the readers to understand the importance of semantically marked up data.

9
Linked Data and the Semantic Web

This chapter provides an overview about the Semantic Web and related technologies. In this chapter, we will discuss the following topics:

- Discussing the foundations of the Semantic Web as a Web of Data
- Discussing microformats, Linked Data, and RDF
- Mining semantic relations from DBpedia
- Mining geographic information from Wikipedia
- Plotting geographic information into Google Maps

A Web of Data

The **World Wide Web Consortium (W3C)**, an international organization that works to develop Web standards, suggests a simple definition for the Semantic Web (`https://www.w3.org/standards/semanticweb/data`, retrieved April 2016):

> *"The Semantic Web is a Web of Data"*

Both, the term *Semantic Web* and this definition, were coined by the inventor of the Web himself, Sir Tim Berners-Lee (`https://en.wikipedia.org/wiki/Tim_Berners-Lee`), who is also the director of the W3C. When he talks about his greatest invention, he often stresses its social implications and how the Web is more a social creation than a technical one (*Weaving the Web, Tim Berners-Lee, 1999*).

The vision of the Web as a social platform becomes even clearer if we briefly analyze its evolution. One of the keywords (or buzzwords) that became popular in the first decade of the millennium is *Web 2.0*, coined in the late 1990s, but later popularized by Tim O'Reilly. The term suggests a new version of the Web, but it doesn't refer to any particular technical update or change in the specifications, instead it concerns the gradual evolution from the old static Web 1.0 towards a user-centric approach of understanding the Web and a rich user experience.

The evolution from Web 1.0 to Web 2.0 can be summarized in one word—collaboration. Tim Berners-Lee disagrees on this distinction because the technologies and standards used in Web 2.0 are essentially the same as those used in the old Web 1.0. Moreover, collaboration and connecting people were the original goals since the beginning of the Web. Despite this distinguished opinion, the term Web 2.0—jargon or not—has become part of our vocabulary, often in conjunction with the term social web (which, to complicate things further, is sometimes referred to as Web 2.X).

So where do we place the Semantic Web? According to the Web's creator, that's one further step on the evolutionary scale, that is, Web 3.0.

The natural evolution of the Web is to become a Web of Data. Paramount to this progression are data models and data representations that allow knowledge to be shared in a machine-understandable way. Using data that is shared in a consistent and semantic format, a machine can take advantage of this information and support complex information needs of the users, as well as decision making.

The mainstream format for documents on the World Wide Web is HTML. This format is a markup convention used to describe the structure of a document, which combines text, multimedia objects such as images or videos, and links between documents.

HTML allows content curators to specify some metadata in the header of the document. Such information is not necessarily for display purposes, as a browser typically only shows the body of the document. The metadata tags include the author's name, copyright information, a short description of the documents, and keywords to describe the document. All these details can be interpreted by a computer to categorize the document. HTML falls short in specifying more complex information.

For example, using the HTML metadata, we can describe that a document is about Woody Allen, but the language doesn't support the disambiguation of more convoluted concepts such as, is the document about a character in movie played by Woody Allen, a movie directed by Woody Allen, or a documentary about Woody Allen directed by someone else? Since the purpose of HTML is to describe the structure of a document, it's probably not the best tool to represent knowledge at this level of granularity.

Semantic Web technologies, on the other hand, allow us to move a step further and describe the concepts that characterize our world in terms of its entities, their attributes, and the relationships between them. As an example, part of Allen's filmography can be represented in the following table:

Artist	Role	Movie
Woody Allen	Director	Manhattan
Woody Allen	Actor	Manhattan
Woody Allen	Director	Match Point

The table explicitly shows the link between the entity types called *Artist* and *Movie*. Representing this kind of structured knowledge is the territory of Semantic Web technologies.

The remainder of this section provides a broad overview on the main concepts and terminology related to the topics of Semantic Web and knowledge representation. It introduces the technologies that aim at answering complex query like the one in the Woody Allen's example.

Semantic Web vocabulary

This section briefly introduces and recaps some of the basic vocabulary commonly used in the wider picture of semantic technologies.

Markup language: This is a system used to annotate documents. Given a piece of text, or more in general, a piece of data, a markup language allows content curators to label chunks of text (data) according to the specific meaning of the markup language. A well-known markup language that we have already come across is HTML. Markup languages can include both presentational annotations as well as descriptive annotations. The former has to do with the way documents are displayed, whereas the latter provides a description of the annotated data. In the case of HTML, both presentation and description tags are available. For example, the `<b>` or `<i>` tags represent a style, a content designer can use them to state that a particular piece of text has to be displayed in bold or italics. On the other hand, the `<strong>` and `<em>` tags provide a specific semantic as they indicate that a piece of text should be provided as strong or emphasized, respectively, in some way. In regular browsers, `<b>` and `<strong>` are both displayed in bold, just as `<i>` and `<em>` are both displayed in italics. Blind users don't benefit from visualizing a bold style, but labeling a phrase as `<strong>` allows a screen reader to understand how the phrase itself should be read.

Semantic markup: As described previously, there is a distinction between the way things should be presented and the way things should be understood. Semantic markup is all about describing the meaning of the information being presented rather than its look. In HTML and XHTML, presentational markup tags are not explicitly deprecated, although they are not recommended. HTML5 has moved one step forward towards semantic markup, introducing some semantic tags such as `<article>` or `<section>`. At the same time, presentational tags such as `<b>` and `<i>` have been preserved with a precise meaning (that is, to be stylistically different from regular prose without conveying any particular importance).

Ontology: One of the pillars of the Semantic Web are ontologies. They are formal naming and definition of types, attributes, and relationships of the entities of a particular business domain. Examples of ontologies include WordNet (`https://wordnet.princeton.edu/`), a lexical resource where terms are categorized into concepts according to their meaning, and SNOMED CT (`http://www.ihtsdo.org/snomed-ct`), a medical vocabulary.

Wikipedia shows a small extract from WordNet
(`https://en.wikipedia.org/wiki/WordNet`):

```
dog, domestic dog, Canis familiaris
  => canine, canid
    => carnivore
      => placental, placental mammal, eutherian, eutherian mammal
        => mammal
          => vertebrate, craniate
            => chordate
              => animal, animate being, beast, brute, creature, fauna
                => ...
```

In this example, representing one of the senses of the word `dog`, we can appreciate the level of details employed to represent this piece of knowledge: a dog is not simply an animal, but it's also classified according to its belonging to a particular biological family (canids) or order (carnivore).

Ontologies can be described using semantic markup, for example, the **Web Ontology Language** (**OWL**, `https://en.wikipedia.org/wiki/Web_Ontology_Language`) allows content curators to represent knowledge. The challenges of building ontology include the vastness of the domains to represent, as well as the inherent ambiguity and uncertainty that surrounds human knowledge and natural language as a vehicle for transmitting knowledge. Manually building an ontology requires a deep-level understanding of the domain being modeled. Describing and representing knowledge has been one of the fundamental problems of humanity since the early days of philosophy, so we can look at Semantic Web ontologies as a practical application of philosophical ontology.

Taxonomy: Narrower than ontologies, taxonomies refers to the hierarchical representation of knowledge. In other words, they are used to categorize well-defined classes of entities, defining **is a** and **has a** relationships between classes. The main difference between ontologies and taxonomies is that ontologies model a larger variety of relationships.

Folksonomy: This is also called social taxonomy. The practice of building folksonomy refers to social tagging. Users can label a piece of content using a particular tag, given such tag is the interpretation of a particular category. The results are a sort of democratization of taxonomy, which results in displaying information in the way users perceive it, without a superimposed rigid structure. The other side of the coin is that folksonomies in the wild can be totally disorganized and harder to use. It might also represent a particular trend rather than a deep understanding of the business domain being described.

In the context of social media, a classic example of folksonomy is given by Twitter. Using hashtags, users can label their tweets as belonging to a particular topic. In this way, other users can search for specific topics or follow an event. The characteristics of folksonomies are quite visible in the use of Twitter hashtags—they are chosen by the user who publishes a tweet, they are not hierarchical, they are not formally organized, and only those that are seen as meaningful can be picked up by the crowd can become trendy (democratization).

Inference and reasoning: In the field of logic, inference is the process of deriving logical conclusions from facts that are known (or assumed) to be true. Another term that often appears in this context is *reasoning*. One way to look at this dichotomy is to consider reasoning as the goal and inference as the implementation.

One classic example of inference is the Socrates syllogism. Let's consider the following facts (assertions that are considered to be true):

- Every man is mortal
- Socrates is a man

From these premises, a reasoning system should be able to answer the question: *is Socrates mortal?* The thrilling answer is *yes*.

The general case for a syllogisms is as follows:

- Every A is B
- C is A
- Therefore, C is B

Here, *A*, *B*, and *C* can be categories or individuals. Syllogisms are a classic example of deductive reasoning. In general, the verbs *inferring from*, *making inference from*, or *reasoning over* are pretty much synonyms in our context as they all require to produce new knowledge from some known (true) facts.

Given the preceding knowledge base about Socrates and other men, in order to answer questions such as *is Plato mortal?*, we need to consider the following paragraph.

Closed-world and open-world assumptions: A reasoning system can embrace either a closed-world or open-world assumption about the universe. This difference is crucial in the way conclusions are drawn from the (limited) set of known facts. In systems based on closed-world assumptions, every unknown fact is considered to be false. Systems based on the open-world assumption, on the other hand, assume that unknown facts may or may not be true, so they don't force the interpretation of the unknown to be false. In this way, they can deal with incomplete knowledge, in other words, with knowledge bases that are only partially specified or are refined over time.

For example, the classic logic programming language Prolog (derived from **Programming in Logic**) is based on the closed-world assumption. The knowledge base about Socrates is expressed in the Prolog syntax as follows:

```
mortal(X) :- man(X).
man(socrates).
```

The question whether Plato is a mortal would be answered with a *No*. This is because the system doesn't have any knowledge about Plato, so it can't infer any further fact.

The dualism between closed- and open-world assumptions also has repercussions in the way different knowledge bases are merged. If two knowledge bases provide facts that are in contrast, a system based on closed-world assumption would trigger an error as the system wouldn't be able to deal with this type of inconsistency. On the other hand, system based on the open-world assumption would try to recover from the inconsistency by producing more knowledge and trying to find a way to sort the inconsistency. An approach for this is to assign probabilities to facts: to simplify, two facts that are contradicting each other could be 50% true.

As an example of closed-world assumption, we can consider an airline booking database. The system has complete information about the specific domain. This leads it to answer some questions in a clear way: if seats are assigned when checking in, and a passenger is booked for a flight, but doesn't have a seat assigned, we can infer that the passenger hasn't checked in yet and send an e-mail to remind the passenger about the online check-in option.

On the other hand, the open-world assumption applies when the system does not have complete information on the given domain. For example, a Web-based platform for advertising job vacancies online knows the specific location of a given job and where an applicant is based. If a company advertises a position for their office in New York, and they receive an application from a professional based in Europe, the system cannot infer whether the professional has the right to work in the U.S. by just using the knowledge described in this section. For this reason, such system might need to explicitly ask the applicant this question before they can proceed with the application.

Logic and logic programming are vast research areas, so it would be impossible to distill all the knowledge that is essential to appreciate all the facets of the topic in a short section. For the purpose of this chapter, we limit ourselves to mentioning that, generally speaking, on the Web, it's safer to assume a knowledge base to be incomplete, because the Web is a system with incomplete information. In fact, frameworks such as **Resource Description Framework (RDF)** are based on the open-world assumption.

Microformats

Microformats (`http://microformats.org`) extend HTML and allow an author to specify machine-readable semantic annotations about persons, organizations, events, and pretty much any different type of object. They are essentially conventions that offer content creators the opportunity to embed unambiguous structured data inside their web pages. The most recent developments are incorporated in microformat2 (`http://microformats.org/wiki/microformats2`).

Examples of interesting microformats include the following:

- `h-card`: This represents people, organizations, and related contact information
- `h-event`: This represents event information, such as location and starting time
- `h-geo`: This represents geographical coordinates, which are used in conjunction with `h-card` and `h-event`
- **XHTML Friends Network (XFN)**: This is used to represent human relationships via hyperlinks
- `h-resume`: This publishes resumes and CVs on the Web, including education, experience, and skills
- `h-product`: This describes product-related data such as brand, price, or description

- h-recipe: This represents recipes on the Web, including ingredients, quantities, and instructions
- h-review: This publishes reviews about any item (for example, referencing h-card, h-event, h-geo, or h-product), including rating information and description

The following snippet includes an example of the XFN markup used to represent human relationships via hyperlinks:

```
<div>
  <a href="http://marcobonzanini.com" rel="me">Marco<a>
  <a href="http://example.org/Peter" rel="friend met">Peter<a>
  <a href="http://example.org/Mary" rel="friend met">Mary<a>
  <a href="http://example.org/John" rel="friend">John<a>
</div>
```

XFN augments regular HTML through the rel attribute. Some HTML links have been labeled according to the relationship between people. The first link is labeled as me, meaning that the link is related to the author of the document. The other links are labeled using the friend and met classes, with the latter indicating someone met in person (as opposed to being an online-only connection). Other classes include, for example, spouse, child, parent, acquaintance, or co-worker.

The following snippet includes an example of h-geo markup used to represent the geographic coordinates of London:

```
<p class="h-geo">
  <span class="p-latitude">51.50722</span>,
  <span class="p-longitude">-0.12750</span>
</p>
```

While h-geo is the latest version of this microformat, the old version (simply called geo) is still widely used. The preceding example could be rewritten in the old format as follows:

```
<div class="geo">
  <span class="latitude">51.50722</span>,
  <span class="longitude">-0.12750</span>
</div>
```

If these examples of microformats seem quite simple to understand, it's because microformats are meant to be simple. The *micro* in microformat stands for their characteristic of being extremely focused on a very specific domain. Individually, microformat specifications solve a very well-defined problem in a restricted domain (such as describing human relationships or providing geographical coordinates) and nothing more. This aspect of microformats also makes them highly composable—a complex document can employ several microformats to enrich the provided information in different ways. Moreover, some microformats can embed others to provide richer data—`h-card` can include `h-geo`, `h-event` can include `h-card` and `h-geo`, and so on.

Linked Data and Open Data

The term *Linked Data* refers to a set of principles for publishing structured data on the Web using W3C standards in a way that favors specialized algorithms to exploit the connections between data.

As the Semantic Web is not only about putting data on the Web, but also about allowing people (and machines) to take advantage of this data and exploring it, Tim Berners-Lee suggested a set of rules to promote the publication of Linked Data and move towards, what he defines as, Linked Open Data, that is, Linked Data available through an open license (`https://www.w3.org/DesignIssues/LinkedData.html`).

Similar to the Web as network of documents linked together via hyperlinks, the Web of Data is also based on documents published on the Web and linked together. On the other hand, the Web of Data is about data in the most general-purpose form, and not only about documents. The format of choice to describe arbitrary *things* is the RDF rather than (X)HTML.

There are four rules suggested by Berners-Lee that can be used as implementation guidelines to build Linked Data, are as follows:

- Use URIs as names for things
- Use HTTP URIs so that people can look up these names
- When someone looks up a URI, provide useful information using the standards (RDF*, SPARQL)
- Include links to other URIs so that they can discover more things

These basic principles provide a set of expectations that content publishers should meet in order to produce Linked Data.

In order to encourage people to embrace Linked Data, a five-star rating system has been developed so that people can self-assess their Linked Data and understand the importance of Linked Open Data. This is especially for government-related data owners, in a general effort to move towards transparency. The five-star rating system is described as follows:

- **One-star**: This is available on the Web (any format), but with an open license to be Open Data
- **Two-star**: This is available as machine-readable structured data (for example, in Excel instead of image scan of a table)
- **Three-star**: This is available as a two-star, plus non-proprietary format (for example, CSV instead of Excel)
- **Four-star**: This is available as all of the preceding ratings, but it also uses open standards from W3C (RDF and SPARQL) to identify things so that people can point at your stuff
- **Five-star**: This is available as all the preceding ratings, but it also links your data to other people's data to provide context

After reaching the five stars, the next step for a dataset is to provide additional metadata (data about the data), and in case of governmental data, to be listed in a major data catalog such as https://www.data.gov/, https://data.gov.uk/, or http://data.europa.eu/euodp/en/data for the U.S., UK, and European Union, respectively.

It is very clear that Linked Data is a fundamental concept of Semantic Web. One of the well-known examples of dataset implementing Linked Data is DBpedia (http://dbpedia.org), a project that aims at extracting structured knowledge from the information published on Wikipedia.

Resource Description Framework

Resource Description Framework (RDF) is from the W3C specifications family, originally designed as metadata model and used to model structured knowledge (https://en.wikipedia.org/wiki/Resource_Description_Framework).

Similar to classical conceptual modeling frameworks such as the entity-relationship model that is popular in database design, RDF is based on the idea of declaring statements about resources. Such statements are expressed as *triples* (also called *triplets*) as they have three essential components: subject, predicate, and object.

The following is an example of statements expressed as subject-predicate-object triples:

```
(Rome, capital_of, Italy)
(Madrid, capital_of, Spain)
(Peter, friend_of, Mary)
(Mary, friend_of, Peter)
(Mary, lives_in, Rome)
(Peter, lives_in, Madrid)
```

The preceding syntax is arbitrary and doesn't follow a particular RDF specification, but it serves as an example to understand the simplicity of the data model. A triplet-based approach to store statements allows representing any kind of knowledge. A collection of RDF statements can be naturally seen as a graph (https://en.wikipedia.org/wiki/Graph_theory), and particularly as labeled directed multigraph; labeled because the nodes (resources) and edges (predicates) are associated with information, such as the name of the edges; directed because the subject-predicate-object relationships have a clear direction; multigraph because multiple parallel edges between the same nodes are possible, meaning that two identical resources can be in several different relationships with each other, all of which with different semantics.

Figure 9.1 allows us to visualize the knowledge expressed in the previous example in a graph-oriented way:

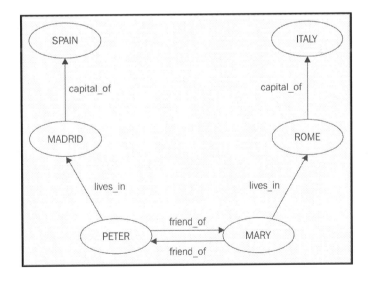

Figure 9.1: A graphical visualization of triple-based knowledge

The next layer of knowledge representation is when RDF kicks in, as it allows us to define some extra structure to the triples. The predicate called `rdf:type` allows us to declare that certain objects are of a certain type. On top of it, RDF Schema or RDFS (`https://en.wikipedia.org/wiki/RDF_Schema`) allows us to define classes and relationships between classes. A related technology, OWL, also allows us to express relationships between classes, but the information it provides about your data model is richer in terms of constraints and annotations.

RDF can be serialized (that is, exported) into a number of different formats. While XML is probably the most well-known approach, there are also other options such as N3 (`https://en.wikipedia.org/wiki/Notation3`). This is to clarify that RDF is a way to represent knowledge with triples, and not just a file format.

JSON-LD

We have already encountered the JSON format in almost all the previous chapters and appreciated its flexibility. The connection between JSON and Linked Data is materialized by the JSON-LD format (`http://json-ld.org`), a lightweight data format based on JSON, hence being easy to read and write for both humans and machines.

When linking data from different data sources, there is an ambiguity problem that we might face. Let's consider the following two JSON documents that represent a person:

```
/* Document 1 */
{
  "name": "Marco",
  "homepage": "http://marcobonzanini.com"
}
/* Document 2 */
{
  "name": "mb123",
  "homepage": "http://marcobonzanini.com"
}
```

We will notice that the schema is the same: both documents have the `name` and `homepage` attributes. The ambiguity spawns from the fact that the two data sources may use the same attribute names with different meanings. In fact, the first document seems to use `name` as the person's first name, while the second document uses `name` as a login name.

We have a feeling that these two documents refer to the same entity because the value of the `homepage` attribute is the same, but without further information, we are not able to resolve this ambiguity.

JSON-LD introduces a simple concept called *context*. When using the context, we are able to resolve ambiguous situations like this one by exploiting a notion we are already familiar with—the URL.

Let's consider the following snippet taken from the JSON-LD website:

```
{
  "@context": "http://json-ld.org/contexts/person.jsonld",
  "@id": "http://dbpedia.org/resource/John_Lennon",
  "name": "John Lennon",
  "born": "1940-10-09",
  "spouse": "http://dbpedia.org/resource/Cynthia_Lennon"
}
```

The document uses the `@context` attribute as a reference to its own list of valid attributes and their meaning. In this way, there is no ambiguity about what kind of attributes we expect to see in a document and their meaning.

The previous example also introduces another special attribute used in JSON-LD, `@id`. This attribute is used as a global identifier. Different applications can use the global identifier when referring to the same entity. In this way, data from multiple data sources can be disambiguated and linked together. For example, an application can take the standard schema defined for a person (`http://json-ld.org/contexts/person.jsonld`) and augment it with additional attributes.

The *context* (list and meaning of attributes) and a way to globally identify an entity are the foundations of Linked Data, and the JSON-LD format solves the problem in a simple and elegant way.

Schema.org

Launched in 2011 as a collaboration between some of the major search engine players (Google, Bing, and Yahoo!, who were later joined by Yandex), this initiative is a collaborative effort to create a shared set of schemas for structured markup data to be used on web pages.

The proposal is about using the `schema.org` (`http://schema.org/`) vocabulary along with microformats, RDF-based formats, or JSON-LD to augment the website content with the metadata about the site itself. Using the proposed schemas, content curators can label their websites with additional knowledge that helps search engines and other parsers to understand the content better.

Schemas about organizations and persons are used to influence systems such as Google's Knowledge Graph, a knowledge base that enhances Google's search engine results with semantic information whenever a particular entity is the subject of the search.

Mining relations from DBpedia

DBpedia is one of the best-known sources of Linked Data. Based on Wikipedia, it augments the content of the popular wiki-based encyclopedia with semantic connections between entities. The structured information from DBpedia can be accessed via the Web using a SQL-like language called SPARQL, a semantic query language for RDF.

In Python, while we have the option of querying the database with SPARQL, we can take advantage of the RDFLib package, a library used to work with RDF.

From our virtual environment, we can install it using `pip`:

```
$ pip install rdflib
```

Given the complexity of the Semantic Web topic, we prefer to dig into an example so that you can have the flavor of the capabilities of DBpedia, and at the same time, get an overview of how to use the RDFLib package.

The `rdf_summarize_entity.py` script looks up for a given entity and tries to output its summary to the user:

```
# Chap09/rdf_summarize_entity.py
from argparse import ArgumentParser
import rdflib

def get_parser():
  parser = ArgumentParser()
  parser.add_argument('--entity')
  return parser

if __name__ == '__main__':
  parser = get_parser()
  args = parser.parse_args()
  entity_url = 'http://dbpedia.org/resource/{}'.format(args.entity)

  g = rdflib.Graph()
  g.parse(entity_url)

  disambiguate_url = 'http://dbpedia.org/ontology/wikiPageDisambiguates'
  query = (rdflib.URIRef(entity_url),
```

```
                rdflib.URIRef(disambiguate_url),
                None)
    disambiguate = list(g.triples(query))
    if len(disambiguate) > 1:
      print("The resource {}:".format(entity_url))
      for subj, pred, obj in disambiguate:
        print('... may refer to: {}'.format(obj))
    else:
      query = (rdflib.URIRef(entity_url),
               rdflib.URIRef('http://dbpedia.org/ontology/abstract'),
               None)
      abstract = list(g.triples(query))
      for subj, pred, obj in abstract:
        if obj.language == 'en':
          print(obj)
```

The script uses `ArgumentParser` as usual. The `--entity` argument is used to pass the entity name to the script. The script builds up the entity URL on DBpedia, following the `dbpedia.org/resource/<entity-name>` pattern. This URL is initially used to build an RDF graph using the `rdflib.Graph` class.

The next step is to look for any disambiguation, or in other words, checking whether the given name might refer to multiple entities. This is done by querying the triples in the graph using the entity URL as subject, the `wikiPageDisambiguates` relationship as predicate, and an empty object. In order to build subject, predicate, and object, we need to employ the `rdflib.URIRef` class, which takes the URL of the entity/relationship as the only argument. The `None` object as one element of the triple is used by the `triples()` method as a placeholder for any possible value (essentially, it's a wild character).

If disambiguation is found, the list is printed out to the user. Otherwise, the entity is looked up, and in particular, its abstract is retrieved using the `triples()` method and leaving the `None` object. Multiple abstracts can be available for a given entity because the content could be available in different languages. As we iterate over the results, we will print only the English version (labeled with `en`).

For example, we can use the script to summarize the description of the Python language:

```
$ python rdf_summarize_entity.py \
  --entity "Python"
```

Using just the word `Python` to search on Wikipedia is not directly leading to the result we expect because the term itself is ambiguous. There are, in fact, several entities that can possibly match the query term, so the script will print out the complete list. The following is a short snippet of the output:

```
The resource http://dbpedia.org/resource/Python:
... may refer to: http://dbpedia.org/resource/Python_(film)
... may refer to: http://dbpedia.org/resource/
Python_(Coney_Island,_Cincinnati,_Ohio)
... may refer to: http://dbpedia.org/resource/Python_(genus)
... may refer to: http://dbpedia.org/resource/Python_(programming_language)
# (more disambiguations)
```

As we identify the precise entity as `Python_(programming_language)`, we can rerun the script with the correct entity name:

```
$ python rdf_summarize_entity.py \
  --entity "Python_(programming_language)"
```

This time, the output is exactly what we were looking for. A shortened snippet of the output is as follows:

```
Python is a widely used general-purpose, high-level programming language.
Its design philosophy emphasizes code readability, (snip)
```

This example shows how combining the high-level conceptual model of RDF based on triples with a Pythonic interface is a relatively straightforward task.

Mining geo coordinates

As previously described, `geo` and `h-geo` are microformats for publishing geographical information. While reading a book about social media, one may ask whether geographical metadata falls into the description of social data. When thinking about geodata, the core idea to keep in mind is that geographical information can be exploited in so many applications. For example, users may want to perform a location-specific search for businesses (as in Yelp) or find pictures taken from a particular location. More in general, everybody is physically located somewhere or is looking for something physically located somewhere. Geographical metadata enables applications to fulfill the need for location-specific customizations. In the age of social and mobile data, these customizations open many new horizons for application developers.

Back to our journey through semantically marked up data, this section describes how to extract geographical metadata from web pages using Wikipedia for our examples. As a reminder, the classic `geo` microformat markup looks as follows:

```
<p class="geo">
  <span class="latitude">51.50722</span>,
  <span class="longitude">-0.12750</span>
</p>
```

The newer `h-geo` format is also very similar, with some changes in the class names. Some Wikipedia templates use a slightly different format, as follows:

```
<span class="geo">51.50722; -0.12750</span>
```

In order to extract this information from a Wikipedia page, there are essentially two steps to perform, retrieving the page itself and parsing the HTML code, looking for the desired class names. The following section describes the process in detail.

Extracting geodata from Wikipedia

The process of extracting geodata from a web page is fairly easy to approach from scratch, for example, using libraries that we have already discussed, such as **requests** and **Beautiful Soup**. Despite this simplicity, there is a Python package dedicated to this particular problem, called **mf2py**, which offers a simple interface to quickly parse a web resource given its URL. Some helper functions to move the parsed data from Python dictionary to the JSON string are also provided by this library.

From our virtual environment, we can install `mf2py` using `pip` as usual:

```
$ pip install mf2py
```

The library offers three approaches to parse semantically marked up data as we can either pass a piece of content as a string, a file pointer, or a URL to the `parse()` function. The following example shows how to parse a string with semantic markup:

```
>>> import mf2py
>>> content = '<span class="geo">51.50722; -0.12750</span>'
>>> obj = mf2py.parse(doc=content)
```

The `obj` variable now contains a dictionary of the parsed content. We can inspect its content just by dumping it as a JSON string for pretty printing:

```
>>> import json
>>> print(json.dumps(obj, indent=2))
```

```json
{
  "items": [
    {
      "type": [
        "h-geo"
      ],
      "properties": {
        "name": [
          "51.50722; -0.12750"
        ]
      }
    }
  ],
  "rels": {},
  "rel-urls": {}
}
```

If we want to pass a file pointer to the parsing function, the procedure is fairly similar, as follows:

```
>>> with open('some_content.xml') as fp:
...     obj = mf2py.parse(doc=fp)
```

On the other hand, if we want to pass a URL to the parsing function, we need to use the `url` argument rather than the `doc` argument, as follows:

```
>>> obj = mf2py.parse(url='http://example.com/your-url')
```

The parsing functionality of the mf2py library is based on Beautiful Soup. When calling Beautiful Soup without explicitly specifying a parser, the library will try to guess the best option available. For example, if we have installed **lxml** (as we did in Chapter 6, *Questions and Answers on Stack Exchange*), this will be the chosen option. Calling the `parse()` function will anyway trigger a warning:

```
UserWarning: No parser was explicitly specified, so I'm using the best
available HTML parser for this system ("lxml"). This usually isn't a
problem, but if you run this code on another system, or in a different
virtual environment, it may use a different parser and behave differently.
To get rid of this warning, change this:

 BeautifulSoup([your markup])

to this:

 BeautifulSoup([your markup], "lxml")
```

This message is raised by Beautiful Soup, but we are not interacting with this library directly, so the suggestion on how to fix the problem might be confusing. The workaround to suppress the warning is to pass the desired parser name explicitly to the parse() function, as follows:

```
>>> obj = mf2py.parse(doc=content, html_parser='lxml')
```

After this long introduction of the mf2py library, we can put things in context and try to parse geographical information from the Wikipedia pages.

The micro_geo_wiki.py script takes a Wikipedia URL as input and shows a list of places with the associated coordinates, if any geo markup is found in the content:

```python
# Chap09/micro_geo_wiki.py
from argparse import ArgumentParser
import mf2py

def get_parser():
  parser = ArgumentParser()
  parser.add_argument('--url')
  return parser

def get_geo(doc):
  coords = []
  for d in doc['items']:
    try:
      data = {
        'name': d['properties']['name'][0],
        'geo': d['properties']['geo'][0]['value']
      }
      coords.append(data)
    except (IndexError, KeyError):
      pass
  return coords

if __name__ == '__main__':
  parser = get_parser()
  args = parser.parse_args()

  doc = mf2py.parse(url=args.url)
  coords = get_geo(doc)
  for item in coords:
    print(item)
```

The script uses `ArgumentParser` to get the input from the command line. The `--url` argument is used to pass the URL of the page we want to parse.

The script then calls the `mf2py.parse()` function, passing such URL as an argument, obtaining a dictionary with the microformat information.

The core of the logic to extract the geographical coordinates is handled by the `get_geo()` function, which takes the parsed dictionary as input and returns a list of dictionaries as output. Each of the dictionaries in the output have two keys: `name` (the place name) and `geo` (the coordinates).

We can observe the script in action, for example, with the following command:

```
$ python micro_geo_wiki.py \
  --url "https://en.wikipedia.org/wiki/London"
```

Running this command will produce the following output:

```
{'name': 'London', 'geo': '51.50722; -0.12750'}
```

Unsurprisingly, on the Wikipedia page about London, the only coordinates that we find are the ones centered on the city of London.

Wikipedia also offers many pages with lists of places, as follows:

```
$ python micro_geo_wiki.py --url \
"https://en.wikipedia.org/wiki/List_of_United_States_cities_by_population"
```

Running this command will yield a long output (more than 300 lines) with geographical information of several American cities. The following is a short snippet of the output:

```
{'geo': '40.6643; -73.9385', 'name': '1 New York City'}
{'geo': '34.0194; -118.4108', 'name': '2 Los Angeles'}
{'geo': '41.8376; -87.6818', 'name': '3 Chicago'}
# (snip)
```

The example has demonstrated that extracting geodata from a web page is nothing particularly difficult. The simplicity of the mf2py library allows us to perform the task with only a few lines of code.

The following section goes one step further: once we have some geographical information, what can we do with it? Drawing a map seems to be a straightforward answer, so we'll take advantage of Google Maps to visualize our geographical data.

Plotting geodata on Google Maps

Google Maps (`https://www.google.com/maps`) is a service so popular that it probably doesn't need much introduction. Among its many features, it offers the possibility of creating a custom map with a list of points of interests.

One way to automate the creation of maps, and guarantee interoperability between different applications, is to employ a common format to share coordinates. In this section, we will discuss the use of Keyhole Markup Language (**KML**) (`https://en.wikipedia.or g/wiki/Keyhole_Markup_Language`) as a way to export data in a format that is recognized by Google Maps. The KML format is an XML notation to express geographical data in two- and three-dimensional maps. Originally developed for Google Earth, another Google product, it's now used for a variety of applications.

The following snippet shows an example of the KML document to represent the position of London on a map:

```
<?xml version="1.0" encoding="UTF-8"?>
<kml xmlns="http://www.opengis.net/kml/2.2">
  <Document>
    <Placemark>
      <name>London</name>
      <description>London</description>
      <Point>
        <coordinates>-0.12750,51.50722</coordinates>
      </Point>
    </Placemark>
  </Document>
</kml>
```

We notice the value for the `coordinates` tag. While the geodata extracted from Wikipedia follows the `latitude; longitude` format, the KML markup uses `longitude`, `latitude`, `altitude`-with altitude being optional, and assumed to be zero if omitted as shown in the preceding example.

In order to visualize a list of geographic coordinates on Google Maps, our intermediate task is to produce such lists in the KML format. In Python, there's a library called **PyKML** that simplifies the process.

From our virtual environment, we can install the library using `pip` as usual:

```
$ pip install pykml
```

The following `micro_geo2kml.py` script expands on the previous extraction of geodata from Wikipedia in order to output a KML-formatted file.

The script tries to use the lxml library to handle the XML serialization to a string. If the library is not present, it will fall back to the ElementTree library, part of the Python standard library. For details on the lxml library, refer to `Chapter 6, Questions and Answers on Stack Exchange`.

```python
# Chap09/micro_geo2kml.py
from argparse import ArgumentParser
import mf2py
from pykml.factory import KML_ElementMaker as KML

try:
    from lxml import etree
except ImportError:
    import xml.etree.ElementTree as etree

def get_parser():
    parser = ArgumentParser()
    parser.add_argument('--url')
    parser.add_argument('--output')
    parser.add_argument('--n', default=20)
    return parser

def get_geo(doc):
    coords = []
    for d in doc['items']:
        try:
            data = {
                'name': d['properties']['name'][0],
                'geo': d['properties']['geo'][0]['value']
            }
            coords.append(data)
        except (IndexError, KeyError):
            pass
    return coords

if __name__ == '__main__':
    parser = get_parser()
    args = parser.parse_args()

    doc = mf2py.parse(url=args.url)
    coords = get_geo(doc)
    folder = KML.Folder()
    for item in coords[:args.n]:
        lat, lon = item['geo'].split('; ')
```

```
            place_coords = ','.join([lon, lat])
            place = KML.Placemark(
                            KML.name(item['name']),
                            KML.Point(KML.coordinates(place_coords))
                            )
            folder.append(place)

    with open(args.output, 'w') as fout:
      xml = etree.tostring(folder,
                        pretty_print=True).decode('utf8')
      fout.write(xml)
```

The script uses `ArgumentParser` to parse three arguments from the command line: `--url` is used to get the web page to parse, `--output` is used to specify the name of the KML file used to dump the geographic information, and the optional `--n` argument, defaulted to `20`, is used to specify how many places we want to include in our map.

In the main block, we will parse a given page and get the geographic coordinates using the `get_geo()` function as we did before. The return value of this function is a list of dictionaries, each of which has `name` and `geo` as its keys. In KML terminology, a single place is called a *placemark*, while a list of places is called a *folder*. In other words, the script has to translate the Python list of dictionaries into a folder of placemarks.

This task is performed by initiating the `folder` variable as an empty `KML.Folder` object. While we iterate through the list of dictionaries with geographical information, we will build a `KML.Placemark` object for each item in the list. The placemark is composed by a `KML.name` and `KML.Point`, which is the object holding the geographical coordinates.

In order to build the coordinates using the KML format, we need to split the coordinates string, initially in the `latitude; longitude` format, then swap the two values, and replace the semicolon with a comma so that the final string, stored in the `place_coords` variable, is in the `longitude,latitude` format.

Once the list of placemarks is built, the final step is to dump the object into its XML representation onto a file. This is performed using the `tostring()` method, which returns a `bytes` object, and hence needs to be decoded before writing on file.

We can run the script with the following example:

```
$ python micro_geo2kml.py \
  --url "https://en.wikipedia.org /wiki/
    List_of_United_States_cities_by_population" \
  --output us_cities.kml \
  --n 20
```

The geographical data is now saved in the `us_cities.kml` file that can be loaded in Google Maps to produce a customized map.

From the Google Maps menu, we can select **Your places** for a list of our favorite locations, and then **MAPS** for a list of custom maps. *Figure 9.2* shows the menu with the list of customized maps:

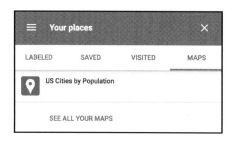

Figure 9.2: The list of customized maps in Google Maps

Once we click on the **CREATE MAP**, we have the opportunity to import the data from a file, which could be a spreadsheet, CSV, or KML file. When we select the `us_cities.kml` file produced with our script, the result is shown in *Figure 9.3*:

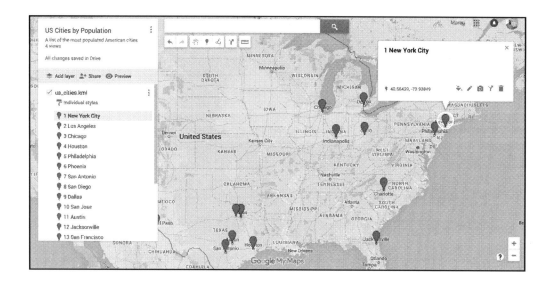

Figure 9.3: The list of US cities by population displayed on Google Maps

Each placemark is identified by a pin on the map, and clicking on a single pin will highlight its details, in this case, the name and coordinates.

Summary

At the beginning of this chapter, we referenced the vision of Tim Berners-Lee, the creator of the Web. Considering the Web as a social creation rather than a technical one is a point of view that softens the border between social and semantic data.

We also described the bigger picture of the Semantic Web and how the different technologies proposed throughout the years fit together and offer the opportunity to make this vision concrete. Even though the hype and hope about the Semantic Web have been quite high in the past 15-20 years, Tim Berners-Lee's vision is not ubiquitous yet.

Community efforts such as those promoted by the W3C, and by governments and other private companies, such as `schema.org`, attempt to make a strong push towards this direction. While the skeptics have plenty of material to discuss why the promises of the Semantic Web are not fully implemented yet, we prefer to focus on the opportunities that we have at the moment.

The current trends of the social media ecosystem show that social and semantic data share deep connections. This book has approached the topic of mining data from several social media platforms, using the opportunities offered by their APIs and employing some of the most popular Python tools for data mining and data analysis. While a single book can only scratch the surface of the topic, we hope that, at this point, you can have an appreciation for all the opportunities that are available in the context of social media for data mining practitioners and scholars.

Index

URL 120
followers' profiles
  downloading 93
followers/ids endpoint
  URL 88
followers/list endpoint
  URL 88
followers
  data mining 105, 108, 109, 110, 111, 112
  URL 88
friends' profiles
  downloading 93

G

Gensim 41
geo coordinates
  geo data, extracting from Wikipedia 309, 311, 312
  geo data, plotting on Google Maps 313, 315, 316, 317
  mining 308, 309
geo data
  extracting, from Wikipedia 309, 311, 312
  plotting, on Google Maps 313, 315, 317
GeoJSON
  about 117, 118, 120
  URL 117
geotagging 91
GitHub
  open source software, mining 274
  URL 274, 275
  URL, for data access 274
Google account
  URL 163
Google Developers Console
  URL 268
Google Maps
  geo data, plotting 313, 315, 316, 317
  URL 313
Google+ activities, fields
  actor 178
  etag 178
  id 178
  kind 178
  object 178

published 178
title 178
updated 178
url 178
verb 178
Google+ API
  about 163, 164
  activities 176, 178, 179
  notes 176, 178, 179
  searching 167, 168
  URL 168
  URL, for activities 178
Graph API Explorer
  URL 132
graph mining 21
graph theory
  URL 303
Greenwich Mean Time (GMT) 68

H

HTTP
  simplifying, for custom Python client 289
httpbin.org
  URL 289

I

identification of entities 262
influence
  measuring 100, 101, 104
influencer
  about 100
  URL 100
information extraction 259, 262, 263, 264, 265
Internet Archive
  URL 202
Intro to Text Mining 20
Inverse Document Frequency (IDF) 106, 180
iterables 58

J

jieba
  URL 250
Jinja2 library
  about 169

N

n-grams
  phrases, capturing 187
N3
  URL 304
Naive Bayes (NB)
  about 32, 214, 215
  URL 214
Named Entity Recognition (NER) 259
natural language processing (NLP)
  about 36, 37, 40, 41, 42, 190, 233, 248
  information extraction 259, 262, 263, 264,
    265
  text, preprocessing 248
Natural Language Toolkit (NLTK) 74, 160
  about 37, 249
  URL 38
network
  analyzing 95, 98
NetworkX 42, 113
Neural Networks (NN) 32
NLTK library 182
Numerical Python (NumPy)
  about 27
  characteristics 29

O

OAuth client ID 166
Oauth2 token
  URL 275
ontology 296
Open Authorization (OAuth) 18
open data 301, 302
open source software
  mining, on GitHub 274, 282
order attribute, values
  date 271
  rating 271
  relevance 271
  title 271
  videoCount 271
  viewCount 271

P

pandas
  about 27
  features 30
Pareto principle
  URL 80
Part-of-speech (POS) tagging 251, 252, 253
Penn Treebank Project
  URL 251
pickle package 226
Pillow 158
pip
  about 24, 25
  URL 24
Plotly
  URL 46
polysemy
  URL 258
Portable Document Format (PDF) 44
Portable Network Graphics (PNG) 44
posts endpoint
  URL 235
posts, attributes
  attachment_count 237
  attachments 237
  author 237
  categories 237
  content 237
  date 237
  discussion 237
  excerpt 237
  feature_image 237
  global_ID 237
  guid 237
  i_like 238
  ID 237
  is_following 238
  is_reblogged 238
  like_count 238
  meta 238
  modified 238
  short_url 238
  site_ID 238
  slug 238

77971189R00188

Made in the USA
San Bernardino, CA
31 May 2018